DO NOT REMOVE
CARDS FROM POCKET

Economic Inequality

Economic Inequality

CONFLICT WITHOUT CHANGE

Joel I. Nelson

COLUMBIA UNIVERSITY PRESS
NEW YORK   1982

Clothbound editions of Columbia University Press books are Smyth-sewn and printed on permanent and durable acid-free paper.

Columbia University Press
New York   Guildford, Surrey

Library of Congress Cataloging in Publication Data

Nelson, Joel I.
    Bibliography: p.
    Includes index.
    1. Income distribution—United States.
2. Comparative economics. I. title.
HC110.I5N44   339.2'2'0973   82-4164
IBN 0-231-05416-5   AACR2
ISBN 0-231-05417-3 (pbk.)

CONTENTS

2233478

P R E F A C E

ON THE BRINK of the eighties, liberals in America were in disarray. Many in the liberal camp were bearing witness to a curiosity of recent politics: an attempt by a Republican administration to dismantle critical components of the welfare state. These programs were the cornerstones of welfare, reflecting the peculiar chemistry of New Deal politics: humanitarian concerns coupled with economic expediency to increase aggregate economic demand. Importantly from the liberal perspective, these programs (in spite of their discrimination and bureaucratic stipulations) more or less worked, providing assistance to the aged, to the handicapped, to those without resources to care for themselves; providing through antipoverty programs broad aid to those below general government standards of adequate subsistence.

The liberal vision is a vision of welfare as progress against economic adversity. I think that idea is fundamentally incorrect. In fact, recent American politics has made few inroads into inequality, whether defined as the ratio of profits to wages, as the proportion of the well-to-do, or as the percentage of persons classified as poor in the population at large or in specific subgroups—among them, American blacks. The liberal perspective may be incorrect in another sense. It misses the broad consensus among most politicians, of both liberal and conservative bent, as to the vitality of American capitalism, and the commitment to the corporate structure and to the very rich. This bipartisan consensus runs counter to any systematic administration of equality values—and in fact helps shape the general stability in inequality extant in American society today.

If the liberal vision is without merit in coming to grips with inequality of recent American experience, I do not think radical or Marxist views are necessarily more fruitful. Though sensitive to the institutional arrangements of the American economy, Marxists are probably incorrect in reducing all manners of conflict to class conflict in phrases of revolutionary fervor. Conflict is indeed rampant in America today. But it is neither class based nor the radical agent of change many Marxists would like to believe.

The impetus for this book was twofold: to document some remarkable stabilities in economic inequality, and to resolve some of the frustrations in selecting among liberal and Marxist theories to clarify this stability. I have not tried to document the sociological variations and intricacies of these two positions, as they have been amply addressed in critiques and histories of social thought. My major purpose is to show how each position only partially accounts for the mechanisms underlying inequality in American society, in which conflict over the spoils of the economy takes place within a consensus defined by the prerogatives of capitalism. This curious mixture of consensus and conflict has, in my view, broad ramifications for some traditional perspectives in sociology, particularly those with a Marxist and liberal heritage. Integrating these perspectives into a coherent focus is in part what this book is about.

I thank several of my colleagues for their help. In particular, David Cooperman and Lionel Lewis offered thoughtful critiques of the manuscript several times. I also acknowledge the continued support of my work by the University of Minnesota's Agricultural Experiment Station. Finally, my debt to my daughters—Nicole and Jennifer—for bibliographical assistance and endless encouragement. I trust their efforts were not misguided.

CHAPTER ONE

Introduction:
The Image of Affluence

THE IMAGE OF affluence was the image of America in the years following World War II. America, for many, was the land of widespread consumption, split-level homes, expanding sub-urban development, two cars, a color TV, and the full consumption package of furniture and appliances budgeted over the life cycle of the family. In coming to grips with what America of the sixties would look like, the editors of *Fortune* magazine (1960:13) wrote more than two decades ago:

The [1960s] may complete the inversion of the traditional income pyramid in which a few were in clover at the top, most were barely subsisting at the bottom. There may come to pass nothing less extravagant than an annual after-tax income of over seven thousand five hundred dollars for forty-five percent of all U.S. families. True poverty will be hard to find. As the decade closes, more than half of all disposable personal income is likely to be "discretionary," that is, over and above the amount required for the indispensables of life. The decade will see the blue-collar worker naturalized in suburbia, ancient class lines more blurred than ever before, "status symbols" rising, becoming well-nigh universalized. . . . A college education will become nearly as routine as high-school education now is. And the growing American population with its rising discretionary income and its improved education is likely to be more discerning than ever as to "fitness, beauty, order, and congruity" when it goes to market. The "new masses" of America will demand better quality, greater variety, the uncommon, the striking, in the goods and services on which they lavish their vast resources.

The wave of rising wages and untold affluence was taken by many to be the destiny of the capitalist state. For behind the abundance stood the phenomenal success and world domination of the American corporate structure. Did it not stand to reason that the capitalist state was responsible for this abundance—and further, that capitalism (in the form of stable profits) and socialism (in the form of increased wage security) were indeed compatible? Could not the pursuit of profits take place in the context of the egalitarian goal of an adequate income for all? This was indeed the promise of capitalism: the confluence of rising profits and rising wages. To many persons—both inside and outside the academic world—the juncture of rising profits and wages represented a utopian dream of economic development bringing fulfillment to all. And with this fulfillment, attractions to radical, revolutionary economic movements—the finale of the class struggle—would come to a halt.

Yet only a decade later, in the sixties and early seventies, these ideas fell into widespread disrepute. While wages continued to rise, they did so less rapidly and evenly than in the past. Blue collar workers no longer continued to gain against more prestigious occupations (Miller 1971). In the grip of inflation, unskilled workers fell behind skilled workers in wage gains (*New York Times* 1977). And poverty, according to government statistics, continued to mount irregularly but discernibly over the last decade (*Minneapolis Tribune* 1976). Furthermore, the sixties witnessed an era of militant race riots, which ripped into the heart of the national conscience and sounded a cry that the blessings of affluence were not equally bestowed. Contrary to reports of the satisfied worker, labor strife continued and unionization rose among formerly contented white collar personnel.

What do these trends and countertrends suggest? Poverty

amid affluence? Discontinuous economic growth? A new era of inequality and a new twist to the ancient struggle between rich and poor? Not coincidentally, flirtations with radical Marxist perspectives gained in the social science disciplines. Many academics felt that former contentions linking economic development and progress were utterly naive and that a re-thinking of inequality and its roots was in order.

To make sense of such trends and countertrends in post-war American society is the purpose of this book. Although a study of one society is little more than a case analysis, the United States illustrates some peculiar lines of development requiring the expansion and re-evaluation of some traditional theoretical perspectives. In discussing these perspectives, I will focus on two indicators for evaluating the impact of cap-italism on stratification: inequality as an indicator of the dis-persion of life chances, and conflict as an indicator of the tensions created by inequality and the solutions sought.

Countless frames of reference have been brought to bear on these two indicators. In this volume I will consider two frameworks traditionally viewed as dominant theoretical per-spectives in sociology: conflict as discussed by Marxists, and consensus as discussed by functionalists. These views stand poles apart in their vision of society and the destiny of the capitalistic structure, consensus theory reflecting a Durk-heimian emphasis on interdependence and on mechanisms for adjudicating divergent interests and disputes, and Marxism, in its critique of capitalism, stressing exploitation among those controlling and those working the means of economic production. Durkheimian sociologists point to the erosion of class conflict and growing solidarity. Marxists point to the relentless pursuit of profits and to continuing and increasing conflict as a signal of the demise of the capitalist order.

In this book I will argue that neither view is entirely correct—or incorrect—for understanding contemporary America. More specifically, I will maintain that the difficulty in analyzing stratification developments in post–World War II America lies as much in the complexity of events as in the rigidity of analysis. Is it possible that the last few decades can be understood by either conflict or consensus? Are these concepts antiquated global concepts attempting to capture entire epochs, whereas greater attention ought be given to the complexity, to the differentiation, to the discontinuities and ambiguities of social and economic change? Are understandings of complex events precluded by having to choose from either conflict or consensus views? To place epochs in one or the other framework is the unfortunate legacy of nineteenth-century social thought (Giddens 1976a).

Recent literature has stressed the similarities and differences in conflict and consensus analysis (Van den Berghe 1963; Kemper 1976; Lenski 1966). My point of departure is to maintain the distinctiveness of each perspective, and evaluate their partial utility for understanding the American scene. In doing this, we maintain that the choice of one view *or* the other is a false choice. Conflict and consensus both exist. Equality and inequality both exist. They are parallel rather than mutually exclusive forms. The rival frames of reference contained in the positions are each incomplete, neither being wholly supported by the available evidence. The challenge is twofold: to show how the accuracy of one view complements the inaccuracy of the other; to show how parallel forms are intertwined rather than mutually exclusive events.

Briefly, my agenda for doing this is to argue as follows:

1. That conflict and consensus views speak to different images of inequality,
2. which are both correct,
3. are in fact related,
4. and result in a form of conflict unaccompanied by social change.

The last pharase is important. Considerable ink has been spent in debating the potential for various forms of conflict in industrialized societies. Whatever the merits of this debate, my assumption is that the key point in sociological analysis rests less heavily on the prevalence of conflict than on its potential for altering the social structure. Otherwise, conflict arguments devolve into a static view of society. Conflict may produce change—but not necessarily. It is this possibility which makes the American case interesting and inviting.

More broadly, I suggest a different twist to the traditional choice between conflict and consensus views, one less optimistic of the resolution of inequality. Put somewhat differently, both conflict and consensus perspectives are distinctly optimistic of society's capacity to broach and resolve problematic concerns: the consensus view in adjudicating differences and seeking new compromises satisfactory to all; the conflict view in bringing issues to a head, so that the current structure is ultimately altered. The alternative I suggest directs more attention to mechanisms supporting the status quo than has been given in recent literature. The following chapters will review the issues of inequality and conflict in contemporary America and show that they are not totally supportive of the consensus or conflict perspective. In this chapter I first review what has been much discussed elsewhere—the consensus and conflict views—and second, suggest the desirability of exploring broader alternatives than either position separately suggests.

Conflict and Consensus—I, Inequality

In spite of attempts to reconcile the divergent strands in consensus and conflict perspectives (Van den Berghe 1963; Kemper 1976; Dahrendorf 1959; Lenski 1966), the two are usually considered mutually exclusive (and sometimes exhaustive) perspectives. This polarization has proceeded to the point where each position speaks past the other, and focuses on an array of trends compatible with its own assumptions. Although the support in sociology today tilts more toward conflict than toward consensus (in contrast with the situation a decade or two ago), and although the consensus view is considered by many today to be utterly naive, the view contains some grains of truth which cannot readily be dismissed.

To facilitate review of these issues I have divided the argument into two sections—on inequality and on political conflict. My interest is neither in laying out the differences among the multitude of particular theorists nor in the nuances of any single writer. Scholarly treatments of Marxism (Robinson 1949; Sweezy 1964; Poulantzas 1973; Dahrendorf 1959) and consensus theory (Smith 1973; O'Brien 1972; Higgins 1977; Coser 1964) are readily available. The concern here is not in the history of social thought so much as in some central predictions flowing from the two views.

Consensus and Inequality. The consensus position gained popularity in the prosperity of the 1950s, with its intellectual roots in functionalism and in a Durkheimian (Durkheim 1960) perspective on social structure. Commonalities cut across traditional social science boundaries: on industrialization and equality in economics (Kuznets 1958, 1963), on value consensus in political science (Dahl 1967), on democracy and pluralism in sociology (Rose 1967; Lipset 1959a), on institutionalized mediation in industrial relations (Kerr et al. 1960). Although writings on the consensus view cannot be identified with any single theorist—or with an integrated school of thought similar to Marxism—several common themes create some unity in emphasis. Implicit in many consensus writers is a recognition of gradual economic development and its consequences in furthering social differentiation and economic affluence. Differentiation and affluence are both seen as instrumental in diminishing the likelihood that Marx's prophecy of a conflict-ridden, polarized society will come to pass. Differentiation proliferates diversity among interest groups; affluence extends the possibility of widespread economic benefits. But there is no false optimism in this view that differentiation and affluence necessarily create harmony in the social order; the dividends of each are not automatic.

Instead, they are problematic and dependent on the political structure. To the extent that interests can be channeled into democratic political processes, it may be possible to achieve a tentative consensus on the just distribution of rewards among highly diversified interests. On these anticipations, consensus theorists rest their case.

As it pertains to inequality, the consensus view was introduced as a counterpoint to orthodox Marxist critiques of mature capitalist societies. The position parallels earlier attempts to revise Marx so as to better account for contemporary events. Revisionists such as Eduard Bernstein (1965), for example, explicitly attacked the use of Hegelian dialectics in Marx's writings. The dialectic portrayed change as cataclysmic—a volatile break from past to future. In Bernstein's view, a more gradual transition to socialism was possible owing to growing economic prosperity and change through parliamentary government. Alliances with any progressive force were conceivable routes for ameliorating the plight of the working class.

Contemporary consensus theorists did not challenge the possibility that Marx may have been correct for his time. On the contrary, they only suggested that Marxism inadequately accounted for a new stage in the development of the industrial state. Rapid economic growth was at the core of this development. Growth brought agrarian and semi-industrialized nations into untold affluence—an affluence in which all parties, to varying degrees, would more equitably share.

The processes responsible for the more equitable division of income were two. The first was some variation of the "trickle-down theory" whereby capital investment for economic development had a wider payoff in expanding wages of ordinary workers. One variation of this argument considered the possibility of an "expanding economic pie," workers and corporations simultaneously profiting from simple growth in the gross national product. A related variant specified that with growth in national income, elites could acquire more absolute wealth than they assumed in the past and yet take a smaller slice of the surplus, hence leaving more wages for workers (Lenski 1966). Still others stressed the rising skill levels associated with the industrial process, in the form of technically trained blue collar workers and an increasing core of white collar specialists involved in administrative functions. The implied contrast was between the polarization of wealth in the hands of a minority elite in the nonindustrialized society and the swelling percentage of middle-income white and blue collar workers in the industrialized society. The presence of middle-income workers reduced the income disparities of a former age. Consensus theorists seized on a second process creating greater equality in industrial societies: the socialistic trend of an economy partially managed by governments. The trend, brought about by the democratization of politics—which itself rested on a necessary base of affluence—thrust national governments into the distribution of income. Through progressive taxation, minimum wage laws, social security programs, and related legislation, governments aided in the triumph of welfare over privilege. While by no means eliminating income differences, these legislative efforts allegedly affected income extremes and resulted in an attenuation of income differences.

The predictions, if correct, are of major consequence. They ascribe to the industrial order the fulfillment of the utopian dream of economic equality and prosperity for all. Furthermore, equalitarian developments, from the consensus view, represent a direct challenge to the position long propounded by Marxists: that the continued search for profits in the mature, industrial capitalist society would necessarily and inevitably bring about pauperization and political revolution.

Marx, of course, had been challenged previously by American social scientists, largely on the basis of some vague notion that America was "middle class" (Bernard 1956; Wilensky 1961; Mayer 1954, 1955; Tiryakian 1975). But the challenge here was more direct than a simple lack of fit between the manners and morals of Americans and the rigidity of class relations described by Marx. The challenge was an attempt to illustrate alterations in the very path of the industrial process, a path that Marx allegedly miscalculated. Hence the suggestion of some global variables—equality and democracy—that altered the history of the class struggle. And hence the addition of a stage other than intense class conflict and revolution to Marx's evolutionary scheme. Growth in equality simply made wholesale class conflict archaic.

This emphasis on the declining differences between rich and poor reflects, as I have previously mentioned, Durkheim's (1960) influence in the dominant school of sociology in the 1950s. Durkheim too was consumed with the idea of capitalism creating a polarized society. In *The Division of Labor* he discussed the "anomic division of labor," the "pathology," the "industrial or commercial crises," the "conflict between capital and labor," which were "so many partial breaks in the organic solidarity" (Durkheim 1960:353–73). These phrases reflected his concern with particularly vulnerable aspects of industrial society: disintegrative forces emanating from the competitiveness and vicissitudes of a complex economy and their consequences in undermining the moral sentiments of individuals. Yet it is the contribution of Durkheim to sociology to point out that even in advanced stages of the division of labor, solidarity was possible. And it is precisely this suggestion which consensus theorists seized. For if it was indeed the case that all parties benefited from economic growth, then it would become apparent to everyone that the aims of business and labor, of capitalism and socialism were not contradictory but complementary. As one author put it (Lipset 1963:271):

many of the political-economic issues that occasioned deep conflict between representatives of the left and of the right were resolved in ways compatible with social-democratic ideology. . . . The dominant strata, business and other, discovered that they could prosper through economic reforms that they regarded a decade earlier as the rankest socialist measures.

Hence the basis for an alliance or consensus between workers and capitalists.

To the Marxist, the vision of an alliance between business

and labor is pollyannistic in tone and utterly naive as well. Whatever the merits of the Marxist critique—and they are many, as I will shortly argue—the consensus view is not without support. For behind the contentions of consensus theory stands massive and persuasive evidence suggesting this as a central point of agreement: the more industrialized the nation, the higher the per capita income, and the more equal the distribution of income itself (see the review in Kravis 1973). Furthermore, consensus theorists are likely correct in arguing that industrialization, rather than polarizing societies into rich and poor, apparently homogenizes the stratification structure. As one writer put it (Mayer 1955:77):

shifts in the occupational structure and distribution of income which have occurred during the first half of the twentieth century reflect highly significant transformations of the class structure. If the same trends were to continue for another few decades, the lower classes, as currently defined, would gradually disappear and our society might in fact come to approximate the well-known cliche that "America is Middle Class."

To be sure, these may turn out to be overly sanguine speculations, the realization of which depends upon a long-continued further expansion of the economy. There is little doubt, however, that the shifts which have already occurred indicate a distinct leveling and equalizing process. The rising standard of living has made many elements of a middle-class way of life, such as home-ownership, paid vacations, and highly valued consumer goods, available to ever increasing numbers of wage earners. At the same time stiff taxes and the rapid disappearance of lowly paid domestic services have brought about a diminution of upper class extravagance. In short, the discrepancies between rich and poor have been reduced.

Though this is somewhat optimistically phrased, there is little question that industrialized societies indeed have more equalitarian distributions of income than less industrialized societies—the United States being no exception. While this is not critical validation of the consensus view, it is nonetheless consistent with the general line of argument consensus theorists maintain.

Conflict and Inequality. The conflict position sharply contrasts with the consensus position, in its link of inequality to elite decisions rather than to impersonal technological developments, in its emphasis on the incompatibility of interests, in its focus on abrupt revolutionary transitions.

While there are many brands of conflict analysis, Marxism is the most useful in understanding inequality. Marx's classic analysis and critique of capitalism is well known and need be reviewed only briefly here. The central concept of *Klasse an sich* is essentially an attempt to map the structural relations between classes of workers and owners in capitalist societies and their unequal relationship to the means of production. These relations, in Marx's view, involved economic ties based on private capital and wage labor. The owners of capital monopolized the means of production, the instruments of work itself. In turn, the worker had his labor, and that alone, to sell in order to survive. This particular arrangement created an asymmetry in economic relations. Capital and property were the bases for authority, which in turn was dependent on them.

Clearly, Marx focused on some of the very same dimensions as Durkheimian sociologists: the exchange relations and interdependence implicit in the economy. Yet, for him, exchange implied not mutual benefit but power over others. As noted in the *Grundrisse* (quoted in Nicolaus 1968:48–49):

The universal reciprocal dependence of individuals who are [otherwise] indifferent to one another forms their social bond. This social bond is expressed in *exchange value.* . . . An individual exercises power over the action of others, he lays claim to social wealth, insofar as he possesses *exchange value, money.* He carries his social power and his bond with society in his pocket. . . .

From Marx's vantage point, economic exchange and interdependence under capitalism do not reap mutual advantage; on the contrary, they engender dominance, wealth, and exploitation.

Previous eras, of course, also had elites who used ownership to their advantage. But the hallmark of capitalism, from Marx's view, was to "extract the greatest possible amount of surplus-value, and consequently to exploit labor-power to the greatest possible extent" (Marx 1936:363). The issue of surplus value is a central chord in Marxist writings. Workers, from this perspective, put in double time: the time necessary for self-maintenance; the time necessary for profit. This latter activity, the surplus value of production, was a chief variable cost in the economic equation. In the form of hours worked or wages paid, it was a continually available and easily manipulable source of surplus value—especially when economies were plagued with depression or market outlets were otherwise unavailable. The long-range prognosis for wages and unemployment was decidedly pessimistic: as the capitalist system continued to develop and expand, unemployment would increase, and wages would ultimately be driven to a level barely capable of supporting the working class.

Marx focused the brunt of his critique on the mechanisms within capitalism which brought about its own destruction. In Marx's view, profits would decline as a consequence of overproduction. Each periodic wave of overproduction was intertwined with mechanisms to further impoverish workers: cutthroat competition, which resulted in pressure to lower costs (and wages as well); the extensive use of labor-saving devices, which created unemployment; the cycle of wage and consumer demand, which fed on each other like the proverbial snake biting its tail, lower wages reducing economic demand and in turn providing the catalyst for further wage reduction. Each wave of these events worsened depressions and played havoc with the financial structure to a point where the capitalist bubble would simply break—as Marx indeed predicted it would.

Of course, much has transpired since Marx's time. Neo-Marxists, however, have not been oblivious to recent trends, among them the indications of more equalitarian income dispersions considered by consensus theorists. The response by many Marxists has been to label these trends conceptually rather than deal with them as such. Specifically, by drawing on the distinction between classes and status groups (Ossowski 1963; Rose 1958)—the one referring to common relationships to production, the other to hierarchical arrangements of status indicators—neo-Marxists merely assert differences in relevance: that statistics pertaining to residence, occupation, education, income, or other status indicators are relevant to the hierarchical arrangements of the stratification structure rather than to the class structure as such (Dahrendorf 1959:76):

Wherever classes are defined by factors which permit the construction of a hierarchical continuum, they are wrongly defined; i.e., the term has been applied wrongly. Status, ranking by others, self-ranking, style of life, similar economic conditions, and income level are all factors which define social strata but not social classes. However one may interpret, extend, or improve Marx, classes in his sense are clearly not layers in a hierarchical system of strata differentiated by gradual distinctions.

Class is always a category for purposes of the analysis of the dynamics of social conflict and its structural roots, and as such it has to be separated strictly from *stratum* as a category for purposes of describing hierarchical systems at a given point in time.

The implication is clear. Potentials for classes exist regardless of dispersions (or concentrations) of income, occupation, or similar criteria. Hence data pertaining to trends in income equality are simply misplaced, and in any event, do not deny—from the neo-Marxist's view—the persistent reality of profiteering and worker exploitation in industrialized, capitalist societies (Birnbaum 1969).

Inequality: Multiple Meanings. The foregoing highlights the contrasting senses of inequality fashioned by consensus and conflict theorists and the vastly different visions of inequality each attempts to grasp: one vision speaks to income dispersions and the rising income of workers, and the other speaks, in structural terms, of differential power and exploitation–as evidenced, for example, in economic surplus or wage-profit ratios.

Clearly, any attempt at dealing with conflict and consensus views cannot rest content with mere awareness of these differences, leaving the issue of their validity to diverse preferences or allowing different observers to pick and choose between them as they may. There have been a variety of attempts to connect these two senses of inequality. The particular one I will deal with in this book is a variation on the "trickle-down theory"—but a variation with a darker side. For it stresses the way corporate profits trickle not to all but only to a select few, and that only under highly specific conditions. This particular point of departure is illustrated in the literature which has attempted to fill in Marx's relative neglect of monopoly capitalism (Baran and Sweezy 1977). The chief idea here relates to the dual labor market (Doeringer and Piore 1971). Dual labor markets contain different rates of pay for similar work. The upper echelons of a dual labor market reflect the possibility of high wages afforded under conditions of economic monopoly. Where few firms dominate a market, high wage bills can be passed on to consumers— without jeopardizing corporate profits or a company's competitive position.

I will discuss the details of the dual labor market in the following chapter. For the moment, however, I grant the following possibility: that higher wages in monopolistic industries may indeed create greater income equality in industrialized societies. In so doing I reject the conventional Marxist contention that industrial capitalism inevitably spells declining opportunities for all wage workers. Implicit here is the idea that income equality in part reflects a narrowing gap between the wages of ordinary workers and other, wealthier elements in the population. But in rejecting the Marxist contention on declining opportunities I accept the Marxist idea that added income does little to alter the dependence and limited power of the working class (Birnbaum 1969:24).

Clearly, the dual labor market notion shares with other

trickle-down hypotheses the capacity to link income equality to corporate growth and the capitalist quest for profits. In this sense the idea affords a bridge for the divergent views on inequality fashioned by Marxist and consensus theories, pointing to the possibility of greater income equality for workers within the context of persistent inequality in the allocation of profits and wages to business and labor. Workers' incomes may rise—if and only if such rises are compatible with stability in profits guaranteed under monopoly capitalism. Thus Marxists and consensus theorists may each be right in their respective domains.

The dual market idea has some other advantages, specifically with reference to the causes and consequences of inequality. By simultaneously emphasizing income opportunities and the framework of corporate profits, the dual labor market conception underlines consensus theory's insensitivity to power and conflict, and Marxist theory's insensitivity to equality and partial opportunity. These respective voids in the two theoretical positions lead to some predictions unanticipated in either school of thought: specifically the prediction of conflict, but conflict without major structural changes. This, in my view, is the form conflict probably assumes whenever it is carried out in the context of opportunities for worker income mobility.

The relevance of the dual labor market notion for existing voids within the consensus position is most evident. By seeing wage gains as contingent on corporate power to control markets and deflect labor costs to consumers, the dual labor market conception links increasing wages to profits in problematic rather than automatic form. Implicit is a caution against any loose inference from trends in income equality to either a reduced interest in profits among capitalists, or a permanent business-labor consensus, or a benevolent elite. Income mobility provided by the dual labor market may merely mask stability in profits. By providing higher wages, capitalists do not necessarily sacrifice their own interests. Labor may always be a cost. In fact, if monopolistic conditions are threatened, the consensus seen by Durkheimian sociologists may very well fragment. For the dual labor market concept assumes no permanent wedding of business interests to the goals of labor. Indeed, wage gains granted to workers—with costs passed to consumers—may be only another form of social control: to keep militance in check and maintain an available labor force at minimal cost to the industry in question.

Yet there is no assumption within the dual labor market conception that conflict will not prevail. Indeed, the reverse may occur. By emphasizing the priority given to profits, the concept reinforces the Marxian precept of the insatiability of economic expansion and growth into new markets and new products. Unlike individual elites, corporate appetites for profits may never be satiated. Each market is a hedge against profit uncertainty. Now if it is indeed the case that corporate wealth is (1) highly valued, (2) scarce, and (3) continually uncertain, then the institutions which guard this wealth may do everything to keep it and increase it. Funds for capital investment (and ultimately profits) will not be readily relinquished to higher wages for workers.

Hence even within the upper echelons of the dual labor market, the industries which border on monopolistic control, income gains in the form of high blue collar wages are not automatic but continually problematic. That is, elites may not readily adjust their economic designs except when forced to do so. If this is true, then it is likely that the consensus theorists' suggestion of peaceful adjustment by business to labor is distinctly optimistic. To gain higher income and to preserve such income from the inroads of inflation or similar threats, conflict may prevail. With the pursuit of profits and tight business control, high income for workers is quite compatible with (and, as we shall see, contingent on) widespread labor strife and conflict.

The prophecy of sustained conflict in industrialized societies is in one sense consistent with neo-Marxist writings; but the form such conflict assumes is different, I believe, from the form Marxists traditionally envision. The fact is that however manipulated by monopoly capital, greater income equal-

ity in industrialized society exists. It cannot be simply ignored, as sometimes has been suggested in treatises on the
capitalist exploitation of creative labor (see, for example,
Stolzman and Gamberg 1973).

Class action, in Marx's view, is prompted primarily by
worker inability to enhance life chances through mechanisms
other than revolution. Polarization prevents mobility within
the capitalist structure. Yet the dual labor market is one
mechanism providing latitude for worker mobility, and may
be viewed as an opportunity for expanding life chances. The
issue is this: if such opportunities exist, then it is highly likely
that the labor conflict prevalent in industrial America will
not follow the radical change Marxists envisioned. To put the
matter somewhat differently: Marx's outline of the unequal
access of workers and owners to the means of production
(*Klasse an sich*) may be reasonably accurate, but his estimate
of workers' reaction to this access (*Klasse für sich*) may not.

It is in this sense that I suggest the prevalence of conflict—but conflict without structural changes in the allocation
of wealth and profit. From this view, worker conflict to gain
income is carried out against a backdrop of stability on the
larger issue of the percentage of the nation's income allocated
to profits and wages. The broader idea here of individual
change against structural stability parallels Parsons' (1964)
conception of dynamic equilibrium—which may be seen as
points of temporary individual maneuvering against a status
quo characteristic of the larger social structure. The idea of
a dynamic equilibrium suggests the capacity of capitalism to
partially adapt to worker demands but at the same time leave
unquestioned and unresolved the larger issue posed by Marxists—the allocation of income to institutional groups.

Conflict and Consensus—II, Politics

Conflict and Conciliation. As consensus theorists take issue
with the exploitative relationships described by Marx, they
likewise take issue with the inevitability of violent, intense

conflict. This challenge touches the heart of the Marxian perspective. It speaks directly to the processes of social change, where dialectic forces are embodied in clashing interests which give birth to a new epoch.

This aspect of the Marxian perspective has also been amply discussed in the literature and need only be touched on here. The position stresses the inevitable incompatibility of economic interests whenever one group controls and dominates another. Emphasis is placed on pauperization and the initial futile efforts—of sabotage or union militance—on the part of the working class to demand just rewards. From Marx's view, the futility of these efforts flows from the essence of the capitalist structure: a bastion of privilege with ruling elites unwilling to relinquish their prerogatives.

The obstacles posed by elites give rise to the frequently cited process by which workers are transformed from a simple category to a distinct class, conscious of its destiny. The process points to the ironies of the capitalist system. Labor worked the productive process but received less and less reward for its work. Capitalists, alternatively, continued to try to wrench profits from this enterprise, although little work and risk were involved. The spark of revolution emerged out of this discrepancy between what the workers gave and what the capitalists took. Classes of workers gradually would come to be conscious of this discrepancy and organize to defend their economic interests. Small independent businesses would go bankrupt. Societies would polarize into distinct groups of workers and capitalists. The tremors of continual conflict would set the stage for the final confrontation in the Marxian scenario: the eruption of revolution, pitting class against class.

Importantly, the Marxian perspective provides a full-blown view of social change. That is, the perspective is more than a description of objective categories—workers and owners, for example. The theory provides processes of change in class consciousness and revolution as well as agents of change in the form of the working class. Furthermore, it also provides a theoretical view of change through the prism of the dialectic, in which opposing societal forms give birth to new societal forms. In Marx, the dialectic is contained in classes embodying diverse and conflicting interests. Change occurs as suppressed classes advance their claims. In the demise of capitalism, this assumes a very specific form: the socialist state turns property relations aside, thus heralding a new epoch.

Consensus theorists reject this fatalistic view of capitalism. In their view, industrial societies expand opportunities and alternatives for reversing deprivation. Growing economic equality tends to be associated with industrialization and economic development; this is effected through rising education, a diminution of workers employed in low-paying agricultural jobs, an upgraded occupational skill structure made necessary by an expanding service economy. These developments increase the potential for upward mobility and provide alternatives to class movements as a basis for altering life chances (Wilensky and Edwards 1959; Chinoy 1955; Mizruchi 1964).

There is also in the consensus view recognition of the fact that in spite of these trends some economic inequality persists. This residue of inequality is the base on which conflict pivots in industrial states. The mechanisms for this conflict are not, however, class conflict and revolution. Rather they revolve on the political manipulation of interest groups in a democratic forum. And, as the Marxian model reflects a future state of revolution, so too this alternate model reflects developing pressures toward homogeneity and consensus on values in industrial states.

The consensus is made possible by the political system implied in the universal voting privileges of democratically based governments and through the mediation process of organized labor (Bendix 1961; Marshall 1965; Lipset 1959a). When the vote is extended to workers and labor has the right to organize, differences between labor and business can be negotiated. The goal of these negotiations is in further reducing income disparities and arriving at a compromise which allows greater profits for business and higher wages for labor.

In this sense, the disparities between affluence and poverty are a basis for negotiation. And, the more general channels of mobility and democracy afford possibilities for effecting change beyond the confrontations implied by Marx.

Conflict: Its Persistence. There is unquestionable merit in the consensus examination of democracy and organized labor as new institutional mechanisms for the adjudication of conflict. Yet in spite of this emphasis, one other fact looms from the analysis of the consensus view: the inadequacy of handling conflict, particularly of a parapolitical nature. There is some agreement today in the literature that conflict is a normal, rather than an extraordinary, extension of everyday political activities (Tilly 1973; Gamson 1975; Oberschall 1973). This suggests that in spite of the obstacles cited by consensus theorists, Marxists are probably correct in pointing to the persistence of conflict in industrialized societies.

Besides the opportunities for mobility provided under capitalism, consensus theorists point to two other mechanisms which reduce the potential for overt class conflict: the development of methods for adjudicating interests; the fragmentation of these interests themselves. The first is expressed in frequent allusion to the institutionalization of the democratic class struggle (Lipset 1959a). In the consensus view, democracy and labor negotiation provide an agenda, a slate of representatives, and a set of rules for adjudicating conflict. Representation conveys the sense of equal weight in decisions, that power is diffused rather than centralized. The agenda and rules convey the "rules of the game" for proceeding in the adjudication process. Implicit here is the understanding that democratic rules and procedures are to be preserved at all costs—which means that parties abide by decisions reached. This emphasis reflects the distinctively Durkheimian touch to the consensus notion: the search for mechanisms of interdependence, and the hope that secondary groups will modify conflicting desires and conciliate their demands.

Consensus theorists are also of the opinion that interests have fragmented, hence further lowering the possibilities of bipolar confrontations. In the consensus view, the rich and poor are neither distinctive nor are they classes as such. Rather their influence is felt through economic interest groups which color the political spectrum: voting blocs, labor unions, poverty coalitions, professional associations, business lobbies, and so forth. These groups reflect the growing complexity and differentiation of industrial societies. They also contrast with the politics and allegiances of traditional class structures. Differentiation and complexity rule out a simple division of societies into classes of workers and capitalists.

There is unquestionable merit to the emphasis within the consensus position on the institutionalization of mediation procedures as well as the fragmentation of interests. Yet on closer examination, weaknesses in this generally pluralistic view of social structure are evident, and with respect to adjudication mechanisms have been effectively countered by conflict theorists. It is necessary to note only that democracies are procedures for determining majority decisions of representative bodies. There is no guarantee within democracies that right will win out—or that numerically superior groups will be protected against small but well-organized (and well-financed) minorities. While consensus theory expresses the hope that corporate power will be relegated to one of many in the array of pluralistic interests, this may be naive in light of the organization, centralization, and interdependence of the corporate structure (Mills 1956; Domhoff 1967; Zeitlin 1974).

Nor have Marxists been oblivious to the possibilities of fragmentation among workers—by race, industry, region, and so forth (Harrington 1972; Ben-David 1963–64; Mills 1962). Yet, in their view these points of differentiation are neither challenges to basic Marxist principles nor difficult to handle within the confines of Marxist perspective. That is, in terms of whether there is a "real working class" or just interest groups, it would be comparatively easy to follow the leads provided by Birnbaum (1969), Dahrendorf (1959), and others in linking the activities of specific occupational groups to class interests—if these interests can be shown to exist. Likewise, it is less important to portray whether or not exploitation is carried out in the bipolar manner Marx suggested than whether exploitation is indeed a dominant force generating reactions in contemporary American society.

These issues have led to a recognition of the possibility that conflict in industrial societies may not be carried on by classes as such, that is, by well developed liaisons across entire segments of workers. Rather the class battle may be carried out by agents of the working class, who nevertheless reflect class exploitation and the continuing efforts of the class struggle. As Birnbaum (1969:5), for example, has noted:

It is in these more profane forms of antagonism, after all, that most of the stuff of modern class conflict can be found. The fact that conflict is often obscured, that it takes partial and particular forms (not involving whole sectors of society pitted consciously against each other but groupings struggling in limited areas), is evidence for a change in the structure of these conflicts and not, as is vulgarly supposed, evidence for their historical elimination.

Marxists have extended such arguments to other arenas of conflict, as for example race riots, where the argument has likewise considered such eruptions to be activated by underlying capitalistic exploitation (Leggett 1968).

The implications of these views parallel studies suggesting changes in labor strife rather than its demise: changes from conflicts infrequent, small in number, and long in duration to a modern profile of conflicts which are frequent, large in number, and short in duration (Hibbs 1976; Shorter and Tilly 1971). Such trends are consistent with another current in the literature: that the interest groups looked upon by consensus theorists as binding individuals to negotiation may have the opposite effect of readying them for conflict by mobilizing their sentiments (Pinard 1967, 1968). Hence the possibility that labor strife may be more frequent and more substantial in number as well as more effective in the industrial state.

All this is to suggest that consensus theory has simply been unable to deal with the array of theoretical and empirical materials on the persistence of conflict in highly industrialized societies. Where they have attempted to do so—a point detailed in a later chapter—they have relegated the origins of conflict to discontented elements, bypassed by the sweep of industrialization. Yet even in this attempt, consensus theory reflects the weaknesses of the Durkheimian view of society, specificially in the failure to see that conflict—intense and violent—may reflect diverse and persistent strands in contemporary society itself (Coser 1964). That is, the consensus view skirts the real possibility that conflict may be more than a vestige of the past and may indeed be an outgrowth of the organization of society around contemporary but diverse interests. The incapacity of a position to explain adequately a phenomenon—in this case the persistence of conflict—signals the necessity of entertaining fresh perspectives or incorporating older ones into it. Does Marxism, in classical or revisionist views, qualify as a wholly adequate understanding of such conflict? I think not.

Conflict: Radical and Militant. I have suggested (with slight modifications in regard to income differentiation) that workers have unequal access to the means of production, and that Marx's *Klasse an sich* may indeed be a reality in American society. My second contention is that the *Klasse für sich* is inapplicable to the American condition—and this in spite of the persistence of economic conflict. I depart here from the usual reasoning attributed to Weber (1958), that the probability relations between *Klasse an sich* and *Klasse für sich* are contingent on adequate organization or on blocked perceptions of the structural roots of economic problems. The argument pursued here is somewhat different.

Recall that the *Klasse für sich* in Marxian theory is not a photograph of capitalist society. Rather the concept is an integral part of a theory of social change. In this theory, classes contain divergent pressures or strains in society. As these pressures clash, change is brought about. Consistent, then, with contemporary ideas, conflict in Marxian theory provides a clue as to the direction and form change will assume. Classes are the major mechanism for effecting change.

In labeling labor strife as reflective of the class struggle, it is necessary to show also that such strife is indicative of and directed toward social change. The fact that it erupts primarily because of exploitation or domination does not qualify it as part of the class struggle as such, unless a struggle toward some revolutionary end or other structural change is involved. While there are some important differences among kinds of labor strife, it does appear for the majority of such strife in the United States that the direction of conflict is toward gaining the spoils of the system rather than altering the system itself. No recent major conflict, for example, has challenged the profit-wage balance, or questioned the justice of profits. Profits are the keystone of capitalism, but they have not been rallying cries in recent domestic strife. If anything, such strife appears to be used primarily as an instrument of income mobility and status maintenance. While it is possible to refer to such strife as class conflict, doing so would be only terminologically convenient. The fact is that such conflict is different from class conflict in the dialectic perspective, where class conflict embodies challenges to the existing structure and seeks to alter the structure in significant ways.

Many Marxists, in my view, have been misled in linking contemporary labor strife to class conflict because of its persistence, duration, and the aggressive strategies employed. They see within labor's activities the seeds of revolutionary change (Birnbaum 1969; Westergaard and Resler 1977; Goldman and Van Houten 1977). Yet, as Marx and others were quick to point out, the link between trade union activity and class conflict is tenuous. In the *Critique of the Gotha Programme*, Marx (1938) lambasted the limited aims of the German Workers' Party. Lenin (1929) likewise spoke of trade union activity as the "sops of economic politics." In a slightly

different vein, I distinguish between two dimensions of conflict: in terms of whether the means used are militant—that
is, whether they employ aggressive, hardline tactics; in terms
of whether the ends pursued are radical—that is, whether
they seek extreme or drastic alterations of the social structure.
Clearly, militant conflict may prevail without radical intent,
and it is my contention that this is what occurs in American
society.

This distinction suggests the need in stratification analysis for widening the meaning of conflict to a rubric of economic conflict, which would include the radical class conflict
described by Marx and other sorts of conflict as well. And this
also suggests the dimensions of the stalemate in theoretical
views alluded to in the beginning of this chapter. Exploitation
exists, conflict exists, but the conflict is confined to the parameters set by the capitalist structure. Hence the dilemma:
conflict without much change. And hence the theoretical inconsistency in traditional views: conflict contrary to the consensus posture and stability contrary to the Marxian posture.
In this sense I am partially in accord with the consensus
position that revolutionary conflict is absent in American society, although other kinds of conflict may be much in evidence.

Mobility and Conflict. The distinction between militant and
radical conflict is meant to suggest a slightly different framework for viewing class conflict. At the base of this framework
is the understanding that societies are structures of differential (and conflicting) access for altering life chances. From
this perspective most collective, economic activity, class conflict included, is motivated by a desire to improve life chances
(Dahrendorf 1967).

Other things being equal—particularly the capacity for
mobilization—I suggest, following Dahrendorf (1967), that
the potential for radical class action is heightened when opportunities for altering life chances are minimal, that is, when
advantaged positions are monopolized by some particular

group or when elites otherwise manipulate the chances of workers. Under such conditions, the probability increases that worker differences in background and in minor economic interests will be dropped and class action will emerge. To reiterate: class action arises when the opportunity for altering workers' life chances is small; under such circumstances radical demands for altering the elite monopolization of resources is the only route by which life chances can be improved.

What occurs when the opportunities are somewhat more plentiful? This is the classical question raised by Sombart (1906) in his consideration of the impact of mobility on class activity. The contemporary answer usually follows some variant of the position outlined by Nisbet (1959)—namely, that individuals will forsake class activities and rely on individual initiative to gain income or other desired evidence of status (Trieman 1970). In fact, this has given rise to a genre of research—spurred by Weber's (1958) concept of status—that has emphasized both the means and consequences of individual status attainment. Although individual status attainment exists and is followed unquestionably by countless individuals, other instruments are simultaneously sought. Many of these instruments may be collective—unions, consumer groups, coalitions of minority members, or poverty groups clamoring for a larger slice of the economic pie. At times these groups may pursue simple pressure tactics—such as those encompassed by democratic procedures envisioned by consensus theorists—but as often as not they will engage in outright conflict. By conflict here I refer to the use of sanctions to attain desired ends, as would be true, for example, in a labor strike. A broader definition of conflict will be introduced in the next chapter.

There are several reasons why conflict emerges in regard to the pursuit of these ends. First, tight control over the economy by the dominant corporate structure means that attempts to infringe on corporate profits are resisted—until mechanisms can be sought and tried to grant wage increases and at the same time maintain profits. In that the use of such mechanisms requires some risk, it is usually resisted. Given the power of the corporate structure, outright conflict is a most effective means of attaining any shift on the part of corporations. Also important is the fact that continual shifts in the economic scene ranging from inflation to threats of foreign competitors invading domestic markets are such that worker advantages are continually offset by economic contingencies. Since wage adjustments are usually not automatic (and even where they are, they might not be sufficient), continued pressure is put on all parties in economic relationships to review the position of each. This contributes to the probability that conflict will be longstanding. Against these trends individual action is limited. As a consequence, collective activity revolving around conflict becomes a stable feature of contemporary stratified societies, even when opportunity for mobility exists.

Marx, of course, recognized labor strife as an indicator of class emergence, in the initial development of a *Klasse für sich*. Given, however, motivation for profits, capitalists would never, in his view, give up their prerogatives of power and privilege. Hence in the long run labor militance would be futile. Yet, as was previously suggested, it may be possible to maintain through monopoly capital both high wages and high profits. The high wages create a ladder of income differentiation, giving workers some prospects for income mobility as well as alternatives to class conflict. Since prospects for mobility are typically advanced by collectivities which use explicit sanctions as an organizational tactic, these confrontations qualify as conflict. But they most frequently devolve into conflict over the spoils of the system rather than over the legitimacy of the system itself. Hence such conflict does not qualify as class conflict.

In one sense, pressures for conflict may be pressures for individual rather than structural change. This suggests a type of "dynamic equilibrium" whereby the stability of the profit system is preserved behind the facade of superficial change at the individual level. It is not necessary to treat such change as a required step toward either greater equality or inequality. Conflict need not inevitably herald change. Nor is it necessary that conflict be based on fundamental issues regarding some social structure. Conflict over rewards in this context indicates a stratification structure that is continually problematic, where goals are accomplished primarily through the use of rationalized conflict and where the problem of who gets what is only partially and incompletely resolved.

The possibility that superficial change may mask stability has long been recongized by sociologists. In using Parsons' (1964) concept of dynamic equilibrium, I emphasize the possibility that conflict may be seen as temporary maneuvers that maintain a system within a steady state (Boudling 1963). I give no credence to the idea that this conception is inherently conservative; on the contrary, the idea may depict a situation in which the power of certain parties is so great that change is resisted. Nor is it necessarily true that the concept of "dynamic equilibrium" is antithetical to the growth of conflict. In fact, events such as inflation, for example, may keep the rates of exchange unfavorable to certain parties and require conflict, overt and violent, merely to keep the distribution of rewards consistent with past rates. Furthermore, the concept of "dynamic equilibrium" contains a direct challenge to traditional conflict analysis—to wit, that conflict necessarily and inevitably points to the form and direction social change will assume.

It is important to note that because conflict refers not to the basic issue of the relationship between wages and profits but to a subsidiary issue of wages after profits, it is no less important to the individuals involved. The militance of the tactics accompanying conflict is geared to the intensity of feelings brought to an issue rather than to whether sociologists or other observers feel that such conflict involves core issues. Suffice it to say, the issue of wage hikes for workers or deprived minorities, for example, brings with it considerable hostility and resentment. And this is true even though the conflict in question does not portend structural change but only a new mixture of individuals in a stratified income hierarchy.

In admitting the possibility of conflict within consensus, then, I am giving more importance to an individual's position in the stratification order than Marxists ordinarily do. This, however, is not to dispute Marx's attempt to develop a theory of class relations and social change rather than of stratification and mobility. It is merely to point out that opportunities for mobility in the stratification structure and attempts to radically alter the class structure are probably related.

Phrasing the matter in these terms offers several advantages. It puts both militant and radical conflict under the same rubric of a general set of attempts to alter the life chances of individuals—in the one case by militance within the confines of the capitalist structure, in the other by radicalism through changes in the capitalist structure. Also, both behaviors are partially explicable by the same variable: whether or not opportunities for mobility are effectively monopolized by elite groupings.

These generalizations suggest the possibility of explaining behaviors of individuals with no clear-cut base in the bipolar class structure of Marxian analysis. Considerable ink has been spent on various kinds of people—status groups, minority groups, petty entrepreneurs—who are neither capitalists nor agents of the working class in Marx's sense. Yet they share with others the same goals of expanding life chances. Mobility through conflict should be a way to enhance life chances both for groups Marxists felt were working class and for groups they felt were not.

What I am calling for here is a broader understanding of economic activity. The possibility of stressing economic rather than class dimensions has previously been suggested by Marxist revisionists (Bernstein 1965). From this view, class conflict is seen as only one instance of a broader set of activities pertaining to economic conflict. And the very considerations applicable to the working class (or its agents) may likewise apply to some of the divergent interest groups which highlight consensus theory's vision of pluralism. Given the heightened differentiation in American society, and its relative affluence, it seems reasonable to retain an economic perspective but dispense with frameworks requiring that economic malaise be expressed only by broadly based class groupings.

This alternative and the others previously discussed outline an agenda for connecting divergent strands in conflict and consensus views: (1) linking trends in partial income equality to persistent inequalities in the allocation of wages and profits; (2) tracing this opportunity structure to the uses of conflict to solidify mobility claims—but without the intent of structural change, radical or otherwise; (3) applying these considerations to working classes, their agents, and others with interests only remotely related to traditional class concerns. In Part I I will consider the first two themes, and in Part II, the third.

Inequality and Conflict

THE OVERALL THEME outlined in the introduction was that Marxists may be correct in emphasizing the relentless pursuit of profits, but are likely incorrect in estimating worker reactions. From this view, economic elites are not benevolent, do not relinquish any share of profits to labor, and are primarily motivated by the growth and stability of profits. At the same time, limited opportunities for income mobility direct worker attention to the pursuit of higher wages rather than to revolutionary mechanisms for altering the capitalist structure.

The upshot of this process may be an implicit consensus among dominant institutions, labor and government included, as to the legitimacy of the quest for profits. This latter issue, however, is neither broached nor resolved by the parties involved. The only point of contention is how wage demands can be reconciled within the profit ledger. I have argued in this regard that conflict may be persistent and violent. But the agents of conflict are at the same time agents of status maintenance and mobility within the context of the capitalist structure. The granting of wage demands is subject to their compatibility with stable profits. The equilibrium maintained is just that then: a point of stability, turning neither to the consensus dream of a happy liaison of capitalism and socialism nor to the Marxian prophecy of conflict and strife shaking and ultimately transforming the foundations of the capitalist structure.

I will now review the evidence which bears on these claims. Chapter 2 considers the interrelationships of the varying dimensions of inequality, arguing essentially that the partial trends toward income differentiation reflected in American experience have all occurred within the context of a remarkably stable profit ledger. Chapter 3 considers the institutional framework in which these trends are based: labor unions pursuing policies of conflict without stepping into the area of radical demands; governments likewise attempting to meet demands for equality, but only if they are consistent with the growth and viability of the corporate structure.

C H A P T E R   T W O

Stability and Change in Economic Inequality

IN THE PRECEDING chapter I speculated on a society in stalemate: with problematic issues left unresolved, with adjudication and conflict offering little more than faint hope of change. This chapter considers the considerable stability of American society through the prism of the economic structure.

In discussing the evidence on stability I focus almost wholly on economic inequality. Inequality indicates dispersion of the economic resources needed to command goods and services. While income equality has partially increased in the past century of American experience, this trend must be viewed in the context of (1) stability in individual wealth, (2) stability in corporate profits, and (3) meager efforts in the public sector to effect more dramatic shifts. Furthermore, mechanisms for increasing economic equality are not apparent in America today.

Equality is relevant to the compatibility of capitalist and socialist demands. It is a key indication of the just distribution of life chances. It reflects also social dedication to provide welfare for many rather than privilege for the few. In the view of consensus theorists, trends toward equality are already well advanced in highly industrialized societies. As one set of au-

thors noted (Janowitz and Segal 1967:601), highly industrialized societies

produce greater equality in the social structure. . . . The number of
persons in the upper working class and the lower middle class exceed
those in the end groups, the upper middle class and the lower working class. It is a society in which the line between working and
middle class is not very distinct, and there is a fusion into the life
style of the middle stratum.

This contention is significant, in light of the evidence (to
be reviewed shortly) suggesting few exceptions to the following generalization: the more economically advanced the society, the greater the income equality within it. The critical
issue is what such equality reflects. There is little agreement
on this point, even within the consensus framework. Some
have advanced functional arguments concerning advanced
occupational needs of industrial societies and the associated
increase of highly skilled middle-income workers; others have
spoken of elite benevolence or the possibility of an "expanded
economic pie" providing sufficient income for workers and
sufficient profit for business. In many of these arguments
there is an implication of advanced industrialized economies
containing a motor driving toward ever more equalitarian
distributions.

In discussing explanations of equality and industrialization I will pursue two directions in this chapter. The first
follows the functional processes suggested by consensus theorists: industrialization pressing certain technical requisites on
a labor force, upgrading its skill level, and moving workers
out of agriculture into higher paying jobs in manufacturing.
I will point out that whatever merit the argument may have
in accounting for past changes, it is highly dubious ground
for forecasting future trends. Simply put: economic development contains no hidden mechanisms for automatically and
inevitably furthering equality. In fact, if just "technical requisites" are considered, the future probably promises greater
inequality.

An alternative direction I will pursue is to abandon altogether the functionalist assumptions. Doing this reflects the

contention that industrialization imposes no requisites or imperatives which are necessary, automatic, inevitable (Smith 1973). In the place of functionalist assumptions, I substitute alternate assumptions and facts pertaining to contemporary, industrialized societies: economic resources are considered (1) highly valued, (2) scarce, and (3) uncertain, by both individuals and corporations. And the facts pertain to the increased concentration and consolidation of corporate power in the economic sector. Two points follow from these assertions. First, those in positions of power ordinarily pursue activities to maintain control over scarce and highly valued resources. Second, the capacity of corporations and wealthy individuals to exert control over their resources is vast. Both suggest further inroads into inequality to be highly problematic.

More generally, the evidence on increased income equality—while real and accurate—represents no essential structural changes in the willingness of elites to share their wealth or corporations to relinquish their share of profits. In this sense the inequality changes suggested by existing evidence point to limited income mobility and differentiation rather than structural alterations in the distribution of profits and wealth. If anything, income equality has proceeded only under the stipulation that profits be guarded from erosion.

In many respects, therefore (but not in all), I believe that Marx's discussion of a *Klasse an sich* is appropriate for the American situation, with reference to the unequal access and control over the corporate structure by high administrative officials and wealthy individuals. I will illustrate in this chapter some relative stabilities in wealth and profit in the United States; these stabilities strongly suggest that in the past and today, elites are able to manipulate the system to their advantage.

Equality and Industrialization: The Economic Motor

Capitalism, from the consensus view, is the triumph of business and labor to reconcile prior differences and share the fruits of affluence. In this particular sense consensus theory departs from the hypothesis of polarization in the capitalist state. My initial discussion of this view in the present section is divided into two parts. In the first part I consider the evidence on equality integral to the consensus position; particular attention will be given to equality as an outgrowth of the technical requisites of industrialization. In the second part, I temporarily accept the broader outline of this argument but question whether its underlying assumptions can account for recent economic trends. The overall gist of my position is this: crescive or unplanned change has no logical or necessary outcome for equality.

Affluence and Equality. In the analysis of affluence and equality, the United States has special meaning. For it represents a pinnacle of wealth and abundance under capitalism. John Galbraith's position, expressed more than twenty years ago, is typical (1958:1):

The experience of nations with well-being is exceedingly brief. Nearly all throughout all history have been very poor. The exception, almost insignificant in the whole span of human existence, has been the last few generations in the comparatively small corner of the world populated by Europeans. Here, and especially in the United States, there has been great and quite unprecedented affluence.

This is the context of affluence in which consensus theorists wrote. To them affluence had a special promise: to lighten the burdens of poverty and abbreviate the economic differences between rich and poor. There are two implications here: industrial capitalism raises the average level of living; at the same time, it reduces disparities in income. But does industrialization indeed have these effects—and if so, why?

The view that industrialization has equalizing effects rests on a functional interpretation of economic structure. Industrialization is seen as imposing certain demands on the economy connected to the use of highly mechanized technology. These demands in turn are fulfilled by a rising middle stratum whose very presence reduces the polarity between rich and poor. Two important changes are recognized, one with reference to the economic sector of production, the other with reference to characteristics of the labor force.

Industrialization involves the sectorial relocation of workers out of agriculture and into manufacturing (Moore 1963:61–72). This transition upgrades worker productivity: manufacturing is capital intensive, creating products beyond what was possible with less advanced technology; goods are drastically transformed, hence increasing their market value. Furthermore, industrialization entails complex technology, with the resulting demand for a more sophisticated labor force. Productivity as a result of skill and technology is the basis on which claims for higher wages ultimately rest.

The link to equality is easily drawn. Nonindustrialized societies are unequal because of the enormous disparity between rich and poor. As industrialization proceeds, ordinary workers gain—moving median income to a point where it attenuates disparities between the rich and the average worker. Hence overall equality increases as the economic pie expands. In comparison with nonmechanized agriculture, capital-intensive manufacturing increases productivity, hence stimulating sales and profits. Higher wage demands can be simply applied against greater profits, allowing all parties to benefit simultaneously from the growth spurred by industrialization.

This is a highly idealized version of the relationship of industrialization to equality—which I will modify later in a number of important respects. For the moment, however, I must note that a central implication of the view is probably correct: disparities between median income and the income of the very wealthy are likely to be reduced under industrialization. Consider as a case in point some statistics for the selected group of countries reported in table 1 (Lydall 1968). The statistics are shown in proportion to median income. Compare, for example, the wealthiest 5 percent (P95/P50) in the

TABLE 1.   INCOME RATIOS FOR TWENTY-FOUR COUNTRIES
(NONFARM INCOME OF MALES)

Country and Year	Income Ratios (in percent)	
	P95/P50 (× 100)	P25/P50 (× 100)
Czechoslovakia, 1954	165	85
New Zealand, 1960–61	178	83
Hungary, 1964	180	83
Australia, 1959–60	185	84
Denmark, 1956	200	82
United Kingdom, 1960–61	200	80
Sweden, 1959	200	78
Yugoslavia, 1963	200	80
Poland, 1960	200	76
West Germany, 1957	205	77
Canada, 1960–61	205	79
Belgium, 1964	206	82
United States, 1959	206	75
Austria, 1957	210	80
Argentina, 1961	215	75
Spain, 1964	220	75
Finland, 1960	250	73
France, 1963	280	73
Japan, 1955	270	64
Brazil, 1963	380	—
India, 1958–59	400	65
Ceylon, 1963	400	—
Chile, 1964	400	—
Mexico, 1960	450	65

SOURCE: Lydall (1968:153)

less industrialized countries—Mexico, Chile, Brazil, for example—who earn at least 400 percent more than the median, with the more industrialized countries, where the wealthy average approximately 200 percent more than the median. Likewise with the poorest 25 percent (P25/P50), although here the differences are less dramatic: the poorest 25 percent earn 65 percent of the median in India and Mexico, as compared with a similar percentage for Japan, 75 percent for the United States, 80 percent for the United Kingdom, Austria, and Yugoslavia and approximately 84 and 85 percent for Australia and Czechoslovakia, respectively. There is no implication here that industrialization reduces wealth or eliminates poverty but only that through opportunities for some segments of workers, inequality declines.

These statistics do not stand alone. Although exceptions exist (Adelman and Morris 1973), the evidence suggests broad support for the contention that inequality is more abbreviated in industrialized than less industrialized nations (Lenski 1966; Paukert 1973; Rubinson 1976; Kuznets 1963; Cutright 1967; Ward 1978). This appears to be true, furthermore, not only between nations but between more and less industrialized regions within nations (Aigner and Heins 1967; Kuznets 1958; Dye 1969; Young and Moreno 1965; Al-Samarrie and Miller 1967). A comprehensive and authoritative survey of inequality (Kravis 1973:66–67) concluded that:

Despite all [the] comments about the imperfections of the data, it seems fairly clear that incomes tend to be distributed less equally in poor countries than rich countries. . . . [Likewise] among the socialist countries of the world, inequality tends to be higher in poor countries.

Can the same conclusions be extended to industrial development and inequality shifts in the United States? The implication is that they can. For the United States has evidenced the very changes pointed to by consensus theorists: a dramatic shift from agriculture to manufacturing, an increasingly skilled labor force, and real growth in the gross national product.

In light of these trends, it would be surprising indeed if American experience proved to be an exception to the generalization linking income equality to industrialization. Unfortunately, reliable income statistics are usually not available before the 1930s. But where they have been unearthed, they do show support for this generalization. Soltow's (1971) detailed economic history of income disparities over a 100-year period in the state of Wisconsin is a case in point. For his analysis, Soltow pieced together a variety of data sources,

among them income figures from 1863 to 1868 published by
a leading newspaper in Milwaukee county, income tax records
for the 1860s, other tax figures from the 1920s. Each of these
income estimates was incomplete; but biases were corrected
by testing various assumptions about missing data and checking them with known statistics on average annual growth
rates in income. Soltow's (1971:318–39) conclusions on income
inequality are consistent with the generalizations advanced:

> The materials . . . on income indicate that income of men in Wis-
> consin is distributed less unequally now than it was a century ago.
> The highest income subset does not have so large a portion of the
> income aggregate as it did fifty or one hundred years ago. Middle-
> income groups have fared much better, at least since World War I;
> we are uncertain about low-income groups. . . . Urban groups prob-
> ably have experienced greater leveling of income than rural groups.
> The strongly urban area of Milwaukee County had an inequality
> coefficient of income somewhere between 0.55 and 0.75 in 1864. The
> coefficient was 0.35 in 1959.

Wisconsin is only one state—a fact which suggests caution in generalizing from Soltow's conclusions to highly industrialized nations. Yet the conclusions are consistent with
the cross-sectional data on industrialization and income
equality already cited. The data are also consistent with other
data on change from countries with parallel industrial experiences—Norway, Great Britain, and Sweden (Soltow 1965,
1968; Peters 1973).

The Assumption of Economic Growth. It is probable that income equality has accompanied industrialization in the past.
That it will continue to do so is less certain. But future developments are equally important for the consensus view, in
that the peace between business and labor rests on each group
simultaneously pursuing and gratifying its respective interests. If this is not possible, then presumably consensual alliances break.

The consensus view ties some implicit processes in industrialization to growth and then to equality. For the mo-

ment I grant the legitimacy of this view. That is, I will not discuss as yet whether gains made by workers are ever automatic—or whether, as is more likely the case, gains rest on pressure and conflict in one form or another. But aside from this, are the other assumptions reasonable?

Some assumptions are simply unclear—as is the case, for example, with economic growth. If growth does not continue, then profits from an expanding economic pie cannot possibly "trickle down" to labor, and the alleged consensus will simply shatter. As Heilbroner (1976:86) has noted in regard to potential antagonism between business and labor under conditions of economic inertia:

This antagonism must be intensified when it becomes impossible to satisfy the claims of the working majority by granting it ever-larger absolute amounts of real income. The constraints on growth thus exert their most severe effect on the distribution of income. When output ceases to grow, the claims of the poor cannot be appeased by increments of income that do not come out of the pockets of the rich but out of total larger output. In a growthless economic system, the contest over incomes becomes a conflict over rights, and in this impending struggle I find it difficult to believe that the rights of property will not be ever more deeply invaded or ignored.

Is future growth anticipated? It is pointless to speculate in detail here on something largely unknown. No one understands with certainty where the nation is on a long-term growth curve covering past and future, or of course, what the curve looks like. I only note here that the signs of sustained economic growth in the United States are not nearly so optimistic as they were decades ago: growth rates—in comparison with both industrialized and nonindustrialized nations— are down (Kravis 1973; U. S. Bureau of the Census 1975b:845); leadership in affluence (*International Herald Tribune* 1978e:3) and productivity in manufacturing (U. S. Bureau of the Census 1975b:851) are no longer assured. Furthermore, the gigantic rises in human capital skills which typified American experience over the last century may have little to do with productivity as such (Jencks et al. 1972; Collins 1971).

The persistence of economic growth is a central issue in

evaluating the consensus position. The limited treatment I give it here is not to deny its importance, so much as to admit scientific ignorance. In spite of recent efforts to consider the costs of growth—ecologically and otherwise (Heilbroner 1976; Mishan 1967)—consensus theorists may be as correct as others in their implicit forecast of continued growth trends. Far less speculative, however, is the question whether growth trends, if they continue, will sustain further equality in the future. That is, aside from planned intervention, are there any assurances that increases in equality necessarily accompany economic growth? The answer is simply no.

In contrast with nineteenth-century notions of progress in social evolution, few today subscribe to a logic inherent in change processes (Moore 1963). As Goldthorpe has aptly noted with respect to industrialization and equality (Goldthorpe 1969:652):

a broad trend towards greater economic equality *does* seem to be discernible in the case of all those societies which have so far progressed from a traditional to an industrial form. . . . But there are no grounds at all, in my view, for regarding the regularity in question as manifesting the operation of some process inherent in industrialism—of some general economic law—which will necessarily persist in the future and ensure a continuing egalitarian trend. Rather, the possibility must be left quite open that where such a trend exists, it may at some point be checked—and at a point, moreover, at which considerable economic inequality remains. In fact, in my assessment, the relevant data suggest that such a check may already be occurring in some of the more advanced societies of the West; or, at any rate, I would say that on present evidence *this* conclusion is indicated as much as any other.

Unfortunately, Goldthorpe does not further specify either how or why trends in equality may be brought to a halt.

A possible starting point for understanding both the how and why can be found in a reexamination of the consensus position. To summarize again: as societies industrialize, workers gain in skills and enter more productive economic sectors—in this case, manufacturing rather than agriculture. The confluence of sectorial relocation out of agriculture into manufacturing with the greater skill and training of the labor force provides, for some workers in the industrialized state, an income far greater than the income received by less skilled workers in an agricultural economy. As a consequence, median incomes are brought closer to the incomes of the very wealthy, and income inequality is reduced.

The brunt of the consensus view is rightfully on the rising incomes of blue collar workers in manufacturing enterprises. But if inequality is conceived of as a disparity in income between occupational groups, between white and blue collar workers, how long do trends toward attenuation of income differences continue? On this the consensus view is unclear. Income inequality may well decline as blue collar workers gain in skill, in training, in access to more productive, high-paying jobs. But do the trends persist indefinitely? Will blue collars one day receive, on the average, the same pay as white collar workers? Or is there a point at which disparities in income between occupational groups are arrested—or reversed?

The question takes on significance in light of the growing numerical importance of white collar workers in the future of the American economy. The numerical ascedance of white collar workers points to a central defect in the consensus view: it pertains to gains of blue collar workers in only a limited phase in the process of economic growth, the transition from agriculture to manufacturing. The view fails to consider fully the resources available to members of the labor force other than manual or blue collar workers. The transition from agriculture to manufacturing is now virtually at an end. A generation ago, Colin Clark (1940) argued that economic development involved shifts from primary (agricultural, extractive) activities to secondary (manufacturing) activities and ultimately into tertiary (service) activities. Although societies are always an admixture of the three, highly affluent societies do frequently focus on service functions. Bell (1973:130–31) estimates that in 1870 some 23 percent of the labor force was engaged in service functions; in 1968 this expanded to 64 percent, with the projection for 1980 at 68 percent. The implication of this shift for a mushrooming white collar labor force is profound: 17.6 percent in 1900, 36.6 percent in 1950 and a projection to 50.8 percent of the labor force in 1980 (Bell 1973:134; Browning and Singleman 1978). In 1979, 51 percent of the labor force was already employed in white collar occupations and 66 percent in service activities (U. S. Bureau of the Census 1980a:406, 418).

Unfortunately, less is known about the determinants and varying levels of white collar income than blue collar income. Yet what is known suggests it to be of potential importance in introducing new dimensions of inequality to the economy. Lenski (1966), for example, speculates that white collar incomes, particularly among sales and managerial personnel, skyrocket in industrial societies. Likewise, Lydall (1959) notes the widespread evidence in support of the so-called Pareto effect—the excessively elongated tail in the frequency distribution describing income in higher-income categories. Lydall cites evidence suggesting that these higher incomes are in part a function of the narrow-shaped pinnacles of bureaucracy reserved for white collar workers (Simon 1955). Higher average incomes may thus reflect income generated by a select percentage of high-paying white collar jobs in given sectors of the economy. Were bureaucratization to continue, disparities in income between occupational groups might increase, as might a general estimate of inequality, in spite of economic growth and higher overall median incomes.

One view of the proliferation of white collar workers is that greater supply will outweight demand and hence keep white collar salaries down. But this view is not consistent with the hypothesized pattern of soaring white collar wages. An alternate position is that demand increases, particularly with reference to specialized skills. That is, concomitant with the expansion of white collar jobs may be a redefinition of jobs for some segment of the labor force, covering new responsibilities, new and more highly specialized skills, higher prestige, and extremely high salaries to match. The comparison here is between the banker at the local bank and the specialist in foreign commodities at Chase Manhattan. Or Arrowsmith in Lewis' vision of 1920 medicine and researchers at Sloan-Kettering Institute. Can specialization create high salaries, income dispersion, and consequently income inequality as well?

It is now firmly established that white collar workers generally have substantially higher dispersions in income than blue collar workers (Mincer 1958; Long, Rasmussen, and Haworth 1977). This reflects more extended training and opportunities. As white collar personnel increase in the labor force, income inequality should increase as well. Lydall (1968:250–51), for example, has observed a general trend in this direction in the post–World War II experience of highly industrialized countries. He attributes this (ibid.:251) to "an unusual growth in the demand for highly educated and specialized managerial, scientific and technical personnel . . . a world-wide trend, but . . . especially marked in the richer countries."

It is indeed the case that with recent growth of white collar workers in the labor force, trends toward income equality have pretty much come to a halt in the United States over the last few decades. One set of data, based on census statistics (U. S. Bureau of the Census, 1970:301), showed a marked trend toward equalization up to approximately 1950 and general stability after that. Other studies have likewise noted either an abrupt halt in trends toward income equality or a slight decline indicating more inequality in recent years (Budd 1970; Schultz 1971; Henle 1972; Henle and Ryscavage 1980).

Importantly, the most recent data on blue collar–white collar income differentials also show abrupt shifts with respect to the recent past. In the period 1939 through 1960 substantial gains were registered in the comparative wage levels of blue collar workers; nearly every category—but most notably workers classified as craftsmen and operatives—showed an increase in wage levels when compared to white collar workers. In the years, however, from 1960 through 1978, these increases were more ambiguous and less apparent. With the exception of the blue collar "laborer" category, white collar workers registered gains equal to or higher than blue collar workers, with individuals classified in clerical activities showing the greatest gains of all (Miller 1966:82; U. S. Bureau of the Census 1980b:244–45). Stein and Hedges (1971) suggest that the income of male heads of household rose during the sixties at 2.2 percent a year if workers were blue collar and 2.8 percent if white collar (see also Sackley and Gavett 1971).

Income inequality indeed may be linked to white collar service expansion as Lydall broadly suggests. One study, for example, of the American states showed a curvilinear relationship between state median income and income inequality (Nelson 1978). As state median income increased, income inequality declined to a point after which for the most affluent states further gains in income were no longer associated with declines in inequality. A detailed examination of the upper income states suggested that white collar incomes diverged sharply from blue collar incomes. Such divergence, in the form of skyrocketing salaries for white collar workers, was associated not only with specialization in certain service activities (banking, real estate, insurance) but also with the proportion of salaried to self-employed managers—a straightforward index of bureaucratization (Frisbie 1975). The finding thus supports Lydall's (1959) and Simon's (1955) suggestion that white collar salaries increase geometrically as responsibility and position increase in the bureaucratic hierarchy.

Hence increases in affluence may, when accompanied by an expanding white collar labor force in service occupations, either arrest or reverse trends toward inequality. Economic growth does not, then, have any simple payoff in decreased inequality. An additional and more pointed illustration of this possibility is given in a study by Henle (1972). Henle cites data suggesting a decline in equality for the male labor force from 1958 through 1970. While a variety of factors appear to be influential, two are important from our perspective: (1)

earnings gains among higher paid white collar personnel; (2) the changing occupational structure, which has increased the number of workers in well paid occupations. In the 1958–72 period, for example, large pay raises were given to professional service employees, to public administrators, and to those employed in finances and real estate as well as to professional workers generally and managers and officials (Henle 1972:23):

Shifts in the composition of employment among occupations or industries mirror the economy's technological advances. These can also affect the earnings distribution. For the 1958–1970 period, occupational and industrial groups with higher earnings (professional and technical, managerial, professional services, finance and insurance) grew most rapidly, thus contributing to earnings inequality. . . . While advances in technology have eliminated routine lower paid work in many parts of the economy, they simultaneously have created similar jobs in other sectors, such as services. All in all, the net effect of the shifting occupational and industrial composition of the economy seems clearly in the direction of a more elongated earnings distribution, helping to produce the trend towards inequality.

Henle (1972:25) concludes with the comment that:

This suggests a continuing trend toward inequality in earnings, perhaps almost inevitable in an advanced economy, as technological organizational changes open the way for a higher proportion of the working population to attain earnings levels towards the top of the economic ladder.

These data imply a turning point in economic affluence beyond which increased affluence may no longer be associated with overall declines in economic inequality. This is not to argue that such trends necessarily will continue. But it is to say that income gains need not be uniformly reflected throughout a population. The notion propounded by consensus theorists—that slowly and incrementally economic development benefits all—is naive and reflective of older visions of evolutionary progress. Industrialized societies are more equalitarian than less industrialized societies. But this is not part of any persistent long-term trend.

At the same time, I do not deny the importance of greater income equality in the industrial state. We will return to this point in chapter 3. For the moment, however, I only wish to place the trend toward equality in the context of the consensus theorist's contention of growth, affluence, profits, and equality. The linkage between these factors is weak and in any event not automatic.

But if observed equality is not a simple consequence of economic growth, then what is it a result of? Does it arise from elite benevolence, the willingness of elites to take proportionately less of the economic pie so as to profit from an expansion of the absolute amount of funds involved? This is another dubious proposition. I will argue in the following two sections that wealthy elites and corporate bodies maintain their corner on economic resources, hence giving credence to Marx's vision of economies administered for the rich, of elite recalcitrance to forgo their privileges. In both sections I maintain that income equality, defined in terms of salaries and wages, does not offset remarkable stabilities in wealth and profit.

Inequality: Trends in Wealth

In discussing trends in wealth, Lenski (1966:314) put the matter this way:

A . . . factor which seems to have contributed to the reversal in the historic trend towards greater inequality is the rapidity and magnitude of the increases in productivity. In societies in which gross national product and per capita income are rapidly rising, and promise to continue rising, elities find themselves in the paradoxical situation in which they can maximize their net input of rewards by responding to pressures from below and making certain concessions. . . . In an expanding economy, an elite can make economic concessions in relative terms without necessarily suffering any loss in absolute terms.

Lenski's thesis refers to long-range trends in social development, from simple agrarian societies to the industrial state. Does this idea have any utility in the short-term experience of the American economy? Specifically, do elites indeed forgo a relatively smaller proportion of economic surplus with a view to garnering an absolutely larger share from an expanding pie?

At the risk of repetition, I reiterate my basic premises: that economic resources are considered (1) scarce, (2) valuable, and (3) uncertain. These assumptions suggest, crudely put, that no one gives up anything. Corporations are not benevolent institutions caring for the welfare of their workers. Nor are wealthy elites interested in dissipating their fortunes to the masses. If resources are valued, scarce, and uncertain, and if wealth is the primary goal in American society, then all efforts are made to retain it.

Wealth: Scope and Privilege. Statistics on income inequality are generally given in terms of wages or earnings. These statistics fail to reveal the access to wealth the very rich possess. By wealth, I refer to the total economic worth of families or individuals.

The statistics on wealth in American society are well known by students of stratification; only brief mention of them need be made here. Tax reports from 1977 suggest, for example, that at least 16 percent of reported income is derived not from wages and salaries but from investments, royalties, and rent. This sum is almost exclusively the province of the rich—which means that inequality in wages and salaries underestimates true inequality. The 1977 figures show, for example, that almost one-half of tax returns in the over $50,000 bracket derive earnings from sources other than wages and salaries; in the over $100,000 bracket this number increases to 58 percent; for the very wealthy (with annual earnings of more than $1 million) the number jumps to 88 percent. Compare this with returns in the more moderate $10,000–$11,000 bracket: only 13 percent of earnings are derived from sources other than wages or salaries, some of which unquestionably comes from welfare-related payments (U. S. Department of the Treasury 1979).

Considerable economic and accounting complexities prevent an easy link between elite access to wealth and trends in economic inequality. Where these complexities have been studied, however, the conclusions drawn are frequently the same: estimates failing to account for wealth substantially underestimate inequality. For example, one influential school of economists has suggested that *greater* inequality in income distributions might be apparent were it not for recent shifts in regard to undistributed corporate profits (Goldsmith 1957). Predepression policy in corporate profits involved distributing nearly all such profits to shareholders; with somewhat sterner income tax laws, dividends paid to shareholders were cut, with the remainder retained for further capital investment. As a result, the percentage of family income in this country attributable to dividends and interest decreased from 15.3 percent in 1929 to between 7 and 9 percent during the fifties, sixties, and seventies (Goldsmith 1957; U. S. Bureau of the Census 1980a:269). Legally, profits from corporate investment are, of course, the property of shareholders, although they do not show up as shareholder income. This suggests that income inequality (at the upper end of the distribution) may have been kept in check by what is tantamount to an accounting practice adopted by corporations within the last generation. Cartter (1955) estimated that if undistributed corporate profits were considered the property of shareholders, the wealth attributed to the upper income strata would increase substantially.

More exact estimates of this increase are given in a study by Herriott and Miller (1971). The authors compare two income distributions: unadjusted money income as shown in periodic reports of the census; adjusted money income, including such items as free fringe benefits, capital gains, re-

TABLE 2. SHARE OF INCOME RECEIVED FOR VARIOUS INCOME GROUPS
UNADJUSTED AND ADJUSTED FOR ALTERNATE INCOME SOURCES, 1968
(IN PERCENT)

	Unadjusted Income		Adjusted Income	
Income Categories	Families and individuals	Income controlled	Families and individuals	Income controlled
Under $3,000	19.3	3.6	16.3	2.0
$3,000–$7,000	27.5	16.1	17.9	6.9
$7,000–$10,000	20.5	20.4	14.8	10.4
$10,000–$15,000	20.7	29.5	23.1	20.9
$15,000–$25,000	9.8	21.2	19.9	31.1
$25,000–$50,000	1.9	7.4	6.6	17.7
$50,000 +	0.3	1.8	1.4	11.0

ADAPTED FROM: Herriott and Miller (1971:32)

tained corporate earnings, and other figures not usually reported in traditional income distributions. The difference in
these distributions is shown in table 2. As indicated, the un-
derreporting of "true income" largely benefits the rich: the
unadjusted distribution shows (in 1968) 2.2 percent of all families and individuals having incomes of $25,000 or more,
whereas the adjusted distribution indicates 8.0 percent in this
bracket. In dollar estimates, Herriott and Miller show that
personal income attributable to families and individuals is
inflated from $562 billion to $805 billion—an increase of 43
percent.

Although legal and accounting complexities abound in
guarding wealth from erosion, the devices for accomplishing
this are well known: tax shelters, deferred compensation contracts, pension funds, stock options, trusts, and income split-
ting. One commentator, for example, has observed the increasing number of older women among the top wealthholders
and the increasing amount of wealth they control (Lampman
1962). Another observer, commenting on similar developments in Great Britain, pointed to the growing number of
children with substantial incomes. In concluding his essay,
the British commentator brought attention to an underlying

suspicion of how income is handled by the rich: "Ancient inequalities have assumed new and more subtle forms; conventional categories are no longer adequate for the task of measuring them" (Titmuss 1969:199).

Wealth: Persistence Over Time. Ever-changing arrays of these
mechanisms permit the very rich to sustain their advantaged
position in spite of tax laws or other devices to trespass on
privilege. To be sure, these mechanisms may not withstand
dramatic long-term social changes, as Lenski (1966) and other
theorists imply. Yet in the shorter run, over the span of a
century or more, power and knowledge are used by the
wealthy to protect what from their view is a scarce and valued
commodity.

   Some insight into wealth stability is given in a study
previously discussed, Soltow's (1971) work on economic inequality in the state of Wisconsin. The data Soltow analyzes
are so rich in detail that it is worth recounting the sources
used. The baseline materials were drawn from an 1860 census.
Census instructions directed federal marshalls to obtain information on a broad array of possessions related to wealth—
a directive, incidentally, which was never repeated again
(ibid.:144):

12. *Value of Real Estate.* Under heading 8, insert the value of real
estate owned by each individual enumerated. You are to obtain this
information by personal inquiry of each head of a family, and are
to insert the amount in dollars, be the estate located where it may.
You are not to consider any question of lien or encumbrance; it is
simply your duty to enter the value as given by the respondent.
13. *Value of Personal Estate.* Under heading 9, insert (in dollars)
the value of personal property or estate. Here you are to include the
value of all the property, possessions, or wealth of each individual
which is not embraced in the column previous, consist of what it
may; the value of bonds, mortgages, notes, slaves, livestock, plate,
jewels, or furniture; in fine, the value of whatever constitutes the
personal wealth of individuals. Exact accuracy may not be arrived
at, but all persons should be encouraged to give a near and prompt

estimate for your information. Should any respondent manifest hesitation or unwillingness to make a free reply on this or any other subject, you will direct attention to Nos. 6 and 13 of your general instructions and the 15th section of the law.

These directives search for a broader definition of what it means to be rich—a definition beyond wages or salary, extending to property, possessions, bonds, and so forth.

Two important studies used these data to estimate wealth inequality as they appeared over a century ago. Soltow's sample consisted of every twentieth person in Wisconsin during the 1860s, with detailed analysis restricted to males, twenty years and older. A second study of the 1860 data, published by Gallman (1969), provides wider coverage in populations analyzed: (1) three large cities—New Orleans, St. Louis, and Baltimore; (2) two states in their entirety—Maryland and Louisiana; (3) and "cotton counties" in selected areas of the South. To this Gallman added an additional estimate, derived from data other than those presented in census material, of wealth concentration in New York City.

In spite of marked differences with respect to the samples analyzed, the 1860 wealth estimates were similar: the Wisconsin estimate showed that the top 35 percent of the families controlled 91 percent of the wealth; Gallman's estimate showed the top 30 percent controlled 95 percent of the wealth. A statistic designed to standardize these comparisons, the Gini coefficient, indicated an estimate of wealth inequality of 0.75 for Soltow's data and 0.82 for Gallman's (the higher the coefficient, the greater the inequality). The differences between the estimates are minor. Furthermore, Gallman (1969) reports his own estimate of concentration in wealth to be consistent with other materials examined for Boston and Richmond.

The statistics on wealth were collected over a century ago in a largely agrarian context, with negligible industrialization. More recent materials on inequality in wealth suggest remarkable similarities to the past. Consider the following three estimates as illustrations: (1) Soltow's (1971) Wisconsin study continued to chart out wealth estimates in the century following the 1860 census. By using estate data—statistics drawn from the estates filed at death for wealthy individuals—and by correcting for some of the biases implied in these materials, he estimated wealth inequality (with a coefficient different from the Gini) to stand at 0.67 in 1860, 0.68 in 1927–28 and 0.66 in 1963. (2) A study by Lampman (1962) likewise made use of estate data on some 36,000 individuals. Although the precise definition of wealth differed from Soltow's, there was a broad band of comparability. Soltow found that the top 2 percent of the population in 1860 controlled approximately 30 percent of the wealth; Lampman (1962) reported that for 1953, the top 2 percent of the population controlled 29 percent of the wealth. (3) Projector and Weiss (1966) sampled approximately 2,500 consumer units with dense sampling rates from those with appreciable wealth. Again direct comparability with past data is a problem: the wealth estimate used by Projector and Weiss involved liquid assets— cash, savings, and checking accounts—as well as investments including stocks and real estate. The Gini coefficient reported was 0.76 for 1962, compared with Soltow's 0.75 given for Wisconsin in 1860 and Gallman's (1969) 0.82 given for a more diverse range of the 1860 American population.

Problems abound in comparing contemporary wealth estimates over a hundred-year time span. Stock values may dramatically rise or fall, making estimates from limited time periods highly unreliable (Smith and Franklin 1974). And the quality of data on a topic guarded with secrecy is itself open to question. Furthermore, the mechanisms for retaining wealth may shift. As Lampman (1962), for example, has argued, substantial declines in wealth (from 1922 to 1953) are evident only if the individual rather than the family is the unit of analysis. In spite of these problems, the studies cited indicate that inequality in wealth, broadly defined, today and a century ago, may be nearly the same—and this in spite of enormous industrial development: a growing manufacturing sector, a shrinking labor force in subsistence agricultural pursuits, a society with minimum wage laws and extensive transfer payments. Although each such factor may upgrade the low income strata, the convergent estimates of wealth inequality suggest that the rich do not stand still. New ways may be uncovered to maintain investments that are not revealed in income and that preserve wealth from one generation of the rich to the next. In this way it is conceivable that the entire minimum level of economic rewards in the society is upgraded, but the distance or scale implied in the stratification system is preserved. To put the matter somewhat differently, in spite of greater equality in annual earnings, the data on wealth suggest the rich to be quite able to maintain their access to privilege. For them there is no trade-off. They give up nothing, in spite of a limited bulge in the middle of the income distribution.

Factor Shares:
Labor and Business

The brunt of Marxism is aimed at the institutional level. It is designed primarily to illustrate how classes rather than individuals or families, as examined in preceding sections, manipulate the economy for their advantage. In his 1847 lectures to the German workers' society, the embryonic statement of *Capital*, Marx alluded to the distinction between the incomes of workers and the wage-profit ratio characterizing the institutional arrangement of capitalism (1972:184):

> To say that the worker has an interest in the rapid growth of capital is only to say that the more rapidly the worker increases the wealth of others, the richer will be the crumbs that fall to him. . . .
> Even the most favourable situation for the working class, the most rapid possible growth of capital, however much it may improve the material existence of the worker, does not remove the antogonism between his interests and the interests of the bourgeoisie, the interests of the capitalists. Profit and wages remain as before in inverse proportion.

If capital is growing rapidly, wages may rise; the profit of capital rises incomparably more rapidly. The material position of the worker has improved, but at the cost of his social position. The social gulf that divided him from the capitalist has widened.

The focus, therefore, is on the ratio of wages to profits as an indicator of the plight of the working class under capitalism. It makes sense, therefore, to examine in addition what economists call factor shares, that is, shares attributed to business and labor in national income. This is an alternate measure of inequality, perhaps more closely attuned to understanding how classes relate structurally and exchange services and resources with one another.

I repeat here what I have said previously: in spite of some bulge in middle income categories in industrialized societies like the United States, there should be little indication that business shares more surplus income with labor than in the past. That is, greater income homogeneity does not likely reflect altered structural relations between business and labor.

There are several reasons for this stability. For business (as for individuals) economic resources are scarce, valued, and uncertain. But unlike individuals, businesses in corporate form are rarely satiated in their quest for such resources. Growth and development of the corporate enterprise is its raison d'être. This entails not merely a search for profits but also a persistent search for funds needed in capital investment. Investment, growth, diversification all minimize uncertainty and assure profit stability. In all of this labor is an economic cost. Like any other cost it must be minimized.

A second reason for the potential stability of the business-labor income ratio is that big business has maintained its power to resist erosions into profits. This power derives from the growth and concentration of the business enterprise itself: domination of assets and profits by only 100 or so corporations (U. S. Bureau of the Census 1975b:502–3); the erratic but discernible persistence of concentration in banking and industry (ibid.:469, 502); interlocking directorates tapping common resources and evoking common policies in nearly all large corporate enterprises (Allen 1974).

Through multi-million-dollar transactions, large commercial banks dominate the pool of investors in any particular corporation. They own leverage control stock—that portion of the stock in a business which gives them more bloc votes than any other investor. Given the great diversity of investors, many of whom hold only one or only a few shares in a corporation, owning 5 to 10 percent of total shares is generally sufficient to assure control. The implications of this are staggering, perhaps even to the most cynical observers. To illustrate, the House of Morgan (Morgan Guaranty Trust Company) probably has both leverage control stock and interlocking directorates with the following major corporations: United Aircraft, Burlington Northern, Union Carbide, Ford Motors, Avon Products, Southern Railway, Exxon, Merck and Company, Eastman Kodak, IBM, Atlantic Richfield, Continental Can, Coca-Cola, AT&T, General Motors, American Airlines, and General Electric (Roberts 1975). Morgan is also the principal voter of stock in 5 of the nation's 10 largest banks (*International Herald Tribune* 1978a). In total assets, Morgan is by no means the largest commercial banking institution; Bank of America and Chase Manhattan, for example, precede it in total assets.

Given this concentration of power, it is naive to believe that the business enterprise willingly or under duress relinquishes profits to labor. And this, in my view, is what the factor share literature suggests—in spite of complications and ambiguities. The complications stem from the changes that have occurred in the American economy over the last half-century or so, changes which obscure the business-labor ratio.

Overall, research generally indicates a rising share attributable to labor. In one typical study, for example, statistics are cited to indicate a general rise in labor's share from about 55 percent in 1909 to 61.2 percent in 1925; a more reliable data series shows labor's share again increasing from 58.2 percent in 1929 to almost 70 percent in 1957 (Phillips 1960). Another study likewise reports increases in labor's share from 58 percent in 1929 to 66 percent in 1952 (Dension 1954). But the general increase in labor's share of national income must be corrected by several contaminating trends—trends which have little to do with business allocating anything at all to workers.

The most important of these trends reflects simple growth in the labor force. Not only are increased numbers involved but also an increased percentage of persons classified as employees. This, in turn, is related first, to the decline of small proprietors as employers, and second, to the transition from an agricultural to an industrial economy. The transition raises labor's share primarily because of the large number of unpaid family workers in agricultural settings; these persons work but are without formal status in the labor force.

These trends are understandably important in considering labor's share. It is possible, for example, that the number of workers could rise faster than the number of business enterprises and proprietors. Under these circumstances labor might even increase its share of national income at the same time that the actual lot of the average worker is declining. Suffice it to say that when corrections are made for the increased number of employees and the transition from agriculture to industry, the temporal trend toward higher shares for labor is blurred. For example, for the years 1929–52—years, incidentally, which show a gradual decline in income inequality—Denison (1954) reports no alteration in labor's share of income among nonfarm workers. Likewise, Phillips' (1960) data suggest a negative correlation between temporal year and labor's share for the private, nonagricultural sector (-0.19). A negative correlation is also indicated between temporal year and a ratio of labor's share divided by the percentage of employees in the labor force (-0.40). The negative correlations suggest a slight to a moderate decline in labor's share from 1929 to 1957. Some of this decline is due to erratic influences on the statistics brought about by the depression. No sharp differences are found, however, if interest is focused only on the post-World War II era. Because of the unreliability of temporal data, not too much store can be placed in the exacting accuracy of the statistics cited in these studies—or in the negative correlations calculated. At a minimum they suggest only this: there has been no discernible long-term increase in labor's share of national income.

One other factor widely discussed in the literature is the expanding role of the government as employer. Clearly, governments do not work for profit as such. Their increased role as employers consequently inflates labor's share without increasing business profits. Just in the years 1950–75, employment in government increased by nearly 50 percent (U. S. Bureau of the Census 1975b:353). Kravis (1959) reports that when the government sector is excluded, nearly all of the increase in labor's share from 1900 to 1939 is eradicated. Grant (1963) and Weintraub (1958) come to similar conclusions with data from the turn of the century to the 1950s.

To digress for a moment: the data on government employment may have appeal in some quarters as a means of increasing labor's share in national income. That is, by nationalizing industry, labor's share could be increased without a concomitant increase in business profits. I will discuss government policy on this more fully in the following chapter. For the moment, I point to the possibility that surplus capital may more frequently wind up in a fund for technological and systemic development than in the pockets of workers. That is, nationalization has a superficial effect on increasing labor's share. The critical issue is how much capital is defined as surplus and, in turn, how much surplus is paid to workers. Conceivably, behind the facade of nationalization, public and private sectors are similarly committed to growth and expansion, and this at the cost of advancing the condition of the ordinary worker.

In any event, the assumption behind the stability in labor's share of national income is that similar stability is shown in shares devoted to business profits. And generally, this is in fact the case. Atkinson (1975:163), using data from a variety of sources, puts profits and interest between 12 and 15 percent from 1900 to 1965—with the 15 percent figure applying to the later year. Dension (1954) likewise finds stability in corporate profits over a lesser time span, from 1929 to 1952. Curiously, Dension reports other data to indicate that such profits are stable only if taxes on profits are ignored. If taxes are taken into account, profits drop between 1½ and 2½ percentage points during this same time period. While introducing taxes seems reasonable in this context, corresponding corrections should be made for individual income in calculating labor's share. For example, data from 1960 through 1979 suggest that while corporate profits increased at about the same rate as individual income, individual income tax increased dramatically more than corporate taxes (U. S. Bureau of the Census 1980a:260, 443).

These data do not—indeed cannot—reveal the intricacies of corporate accounting, the varying definitions of costs, depreciation, or profit, or the capacities of corporations to pass costs on to consumers. Nor do they account for the entire range of assets which represent benefits to business. Indeed, as Nicolaus (1968:53) notes in his review of the *Grundrisse*, Marx himself expressed doubts on the simplistic use of wage-profit ratios:

An index of exploitation and impoverishment which accurately captures the variables to which Marx was referring . . . would have to array on the one side the net property holdings of the working class, and on the other side the value of the entire capital stock of all the factories, utilities, infrastructural investments, institutions, and military establishments, which are under control of the capitalist class and serve its policy aims. Not only the economic value, but also the political power and social influence of these established assets would have to be included in the equation.

As Nicolaus suggests, this latter definition in Marx's later work represents a more critical test of exploitation under capitalism. In spite of the limitations in a simple wage-profit ratio, I have used it here as a first step to gauge inequality at a more institutional level than is contained in coefficients measuring annual earnings or employees' getting more from business or business giving up more to labor. In spite of added income in the middle ranks, then, there is considerable stability in business and labor's share of national income.

Sectorial Development

This position can be taken further: added income in the middle ranks is contingent on considerable stability in business' share of national income. It is my understanding that the substantial inroads into individual inequality relate to increasing the income of formerly poorly paid workers—that is, to higher wages for a segment of blue collar workers. In this section, I discuss the evolution of such wages in the context of profit stability.

Dual Labor Markets. Marx's prognosis for capitalism rested on the prophecy of a long-run decline in profits. Owing to what he believed to be relative stability in surplus value, the highly competitive race for more advanced technology to increase production would simply drive profits into a downward spiral. Small business would gradually be eliminated. Likewise, the attempt to grasp for declining profits would result in massive overproduction—sending tremors through the credit and financial structure of the capitalist economy.

Few today—even those sympathetic to Marxist analysis (Sweezy 1964; Robinson 1949)—subscribe to Marx's vision of declining profits under capitalism. Large corporations, through increased productivity, can raise surplus value and profits as well. At least, as Sweezy (1964) has suggested, there is no good reason to believe that profits must inevitably decline. What has emerged instead, at least in the United States, is a curious admixture of the competitive economy Marx discussed side by side with a system of monopoly capitalism. And along with it has emerged several ironies that radical critics of capitalism frequently allude to: vibrant business, brisk employment, high wages along with exploitation and unemployment. These ironies have been partially formalized around the concept of a dual labor market—markets of different wages for similar work. The concept is an important link in the argument concerning wage-profit stability.

Theorists discussing the dual labor market distinguish

between "core" and "peripheral" industries with certain clusters of traits (Gordon 1972; Doeringer and Piore 1971). Core industries, for example, are characterized by strong unions, high wages, employment stability, and well-developed systems of internal promotion. Peripheral industries are low-paying industries. Little training is involved, employment is highly unstable, unions are weak or nonexistent.

Substantial variation in wage rates exists across industries, even among comparably skilled jobs (Stolzenberg 1975). Craftsmen and operatives, for example, earn $13,500 if they are employed in durable goods manufacturing, $13,000 if in nondurable goods, $11,900 if in wholesale trade, $8,500 if in retail trade, and $8,000 in personal services (U. S. Bureau of the Census 1980b:259). While some of these differences are unquestionably explained by variation in region or educational level of the work force, not all such differences can be dismissed in this way. One study (Wachtel and Betsey 1972) shows male earnings to vary considerably by industry when both individual characteristics (such as education, race, and age) and structural characteristics (such as union affiliation, skill levels, region, and city size) are held constant. Bibb and Form (1977) report that core and peripheral industries explain more variation in wage levels than seven other structural and individual characteristics—superseded only by job tenure for men and firm size for women. A similar analysis showed the costs and benefits of being in core industries for white males to be between $3,000 and $4,000 in annual earnings; these estimates accounted for differences in such things as training and skill (Beck, Horan, and Tolbert 1978).

Core and Peripheral Industries. Variation in unionized labor is the traditional explanation of wage variation across industries. There are two contentions here. The first is that unionization is consequential in altering wages—and this is generally true. Although wage differences between unionized and nonunionized workers are not great, they do exist, amounting on the average to 10–12 percent (Lewis 1963; Freeman 1980; Parsley 1980). And, among the very poor, probably more workers are nonunionized than are unionized (Sternlieb and Bauman 1972). The second contention is that oligopolistic industries are more heavily unionized than competitive industries. This is likewise generally the case. Compare, for example, the highly unionized steel workers or auto workers with low-paying industries in textiles or in agriculture, where fewer than one in five are unionized (U. S. Bureau of the Census 1975b:371), and obstacles to further unionization are compounded by open shop polices prevalent throughout the South. More systematically, Bibb and Form (1977) report a discernible tendency for workers in core industries to be more frequently unionized than those in peripheral industries. Beck, Horan, and Tolbert (1978) indicate that 30 percent of the workers in core industries are unionized in comparison with 14 percent in peripheral industries.

The implication is that organization and militance are required to wrench higher wages from industry. In the following chapter I will show that unions in core industries engage in quite distinctive types of conflict. For the moment I suggest that the aggressiveness of these unions in pursuing high wage policies is a useful antidote to the consensus theorists' notion that business and labor form alliances or partnerships to facilitate the pursuit of mutual interests. Labor is a cost to business. Wage hikes are not willingly granted. And, as I will argue elsewhere, wage hikes are contingent on lengthy and costly strikes.

At the same time, a simple view of unions wrenching wages from industry is incomplete. To attribute core-peripheral wage differences to unionization alone fails to take into account the substantial power of industry in determining wage scales. A number of things stand out about core industries which suggest that wage hikes can be rendered as incidental costs. These are: capital intensivity and monopoly control. Neither of these characteristics, in my view, reflects business-labor alliances or dominant labor power. And both allow wages to be raised without unduly eroding corporate profits.

The first refers to the automation of work: core industries tend to be capital intensive; peripheral industries tend to be labor intensive. Investments, for example, in plants and equipment tend to run higher in core than in peripheral industries on an annual basis. Illustrations abound: in 1976, $55,000 was invested per worker in the chemical industry, $150,000 in petroleum, $102,000 in transportation $39,000 in electrical machinery. Compare this with illustrative peripheral industries: $20,000 per worker in lumber, $18,000 in textiles, $10,000 in furniture, $6,000 in apparels (U. S. Bureau of the Census 1980a:561). Similar differences are suggested by contrasts in the value added to products as a function of the work-hours used to produce the product. Generally, core industries have higher ratios of value added than peripheral industries. The ratio in chemicals, for example, is 52 to 1, in motor vehicles 24 to 1, compared with 10 to 1 in textiles or 11 to 1 in apparels (U. S. Bureau of the Census 1980a:4–21). More detailed analyses generally bear out this contention of more intensive capital investment in core industries (Averitt 1968).

The highly sophisticated technologies prevalent in core industries are labor-saving devices. Per unit of production, therefore, wage bills in core industries are generally smaller than in peripheral industries. Since wage bills are a smaller proportion of costs, core industries can more easily raise wages in a manner incidental to total expenses. For peripheral industries this is clearly not the case, since wages form a larger share of the total operating budget.

A second factor contributing to core-peripheral differences is market domination. Capital-intensive industries limit the entry of new firms into the marketplace. Initial investment in technology is higher, as is the cost of updating this technology. Hence core industries are typified by oligopoly and limited firm turnover. Contrariwise, peripheral industries have multiple firms in competition and higher turnover. Compare, for example, the four largest firms in motor vehicle manufacturing controlling 93 percent of domestic production, in steel mills 45 percent of domestic production, in primary metal cans 59 percent of domestic production, with the situation in apparels: the four largest firms in women's dresses dominate 8 percent of domestic production and in hosiery 20 percent of domestic production (U. S. Bureau of the Census 1981b:12–61).

This suggests that core industries can more easily pass costs on to consumers. Since the relative number of firms is small and fixed, informal arrangements between firms are more easily arrived at. Also, the lack of competition allows the industry to present a unified front with respect to pricing and price hikes. By this mechanism, wage raises can be handled simply by raising the price of the product without jeopardizing the stability of any one firm. The situation in peripheral industries is presumably quite different. Since many firms are in direct competition, wage pressures on any one firm represent either an infringement on profits or a basis for pricing a company's product out of competition—if an attempt is made by a single firm to raise prices. Hence pressure to raise wages is more threatening to industries with many small firms in competition than to those with few firms in an oligopolistic arrangement.

Three factors, then, probably contribute to wage differentials in core and peripheral industries: unionization, capital intensivity, and an oligopolistic market. Unionization is a pressure on wages. The smaller wage bill and oligopoly allow such pressures to be responded to without infringing on corporate profits or firm stability. It is also probably the case that core industries are high-profit industries (Galbraith 1967). This factor interacts with the others already noted to provide a "permissive economic environment" in which wage gains are sought and realized (Bluestone 1972:297):

These factors do not act independently, but rather bear systematic relation to each other. High product market concentration and high profits provide the footing for a "permissive economic environment" in which strong unions can reap economic and social rewards for their members. Where an industry is inhabited by a few massive price-setting, highly mechanized, non-competitive, publicly visible, and highly profitable firms, entry of new firms is highly improbable and, indeed, quite rare. The needed initial resources are too vast to be accumulated by a newcomer. Consequently, unions, once they have become established, are relatively secure and free from the competition forced on them by an unorganized sector in the industry. Free to press for higher wages without fear of eliminating jobs by pricing their firms product above unorganized competition, the union can demand their share of productivity and productivity gains. . . .

Because of this environment higher wages in core industries represent no loss in profit. The costs of a small labor force per unit of production and the near-monopolistic control of the market allow corporations to pass on added costs to the consumer. Hence from a class perspective, shares to business and labor in this particular segment of the market remain constant, and an equilibrium is maintained between business and labor. Wage inequality declines somewhat, but the indicators more appropriate to class shares remain constant.

In emphasizing this equilibrium I am not suggesting that it is eternal but only that it adequately describes America's industrial past. Future trends may not mirror the past. Recent data on imports show partial breakdown of monopoly control—with dramatic implications for the stability of core business-labor liaisons. I will discuss these possibilities in greater detail in the concluding chapter.

Ambiguities in the Dual Labor Market Concept. While studies generally support the impact of core-peripheral industries on wages, not all have done so. This failure in support is particularly evident in research designed to unravel what it is precisely about core industries that affects wages—unionization, monopoly control, productivity, and so forth.

An excellent example of these efforts is given in Leonard Weiss's pioneering (1966) research on industrial concentration and labor earnings. Weiss found that industries which are highly unionized and approximate monopolistic control do in fact have higher wage rates. However, once differences in the "quality of labor" are taken into account—differences related to region, skill, schooling, race—monopolistic effects on wages evaporate (ibid.:115): "Once personal characterit-stics are introduced, the relationship between concentration and earnings is no longer significant and is negative about as often as it is positive." The effects of unionization in Weiss's research are more equivocal; and the author correctly attributes these ambiguities to the failure to measure adequately this variable at the level of the firm.

There are various difficulties in interpreting Weiss's results, of which two are most important for our present discussion. The first relates to some technical issues in research design. Weiss's findings support the finding of high wage rates in monopoly industries marked by high unionization—except when the personal characteristics of workers are taken into account. Yet there is some question as to whether wage differentials should be examined independently of these characteristics. Consider the example of race. Should wage rates be considered independently of race or as integral to the employment policies of peripheral industries? That is, peripheral industries may seek to employ powerless minorities so as to facilitate low wage scales. Likewise with respect to region or urbanization: do peripheral industries purposely locate in the rural South so as to avail themselves to cheap labor supplies?

Adequate answers to these questions lie in distinguishing between wage rates for occupational positions and wage rates for individuals. If the dual labor market concept is to explain industry wage differences for comparable positions, then only positional variables should be taken into account. Occupational skill levels in an industry would be one such variable, educational resources perhaps another—although even this is open to question (Collins 1971). But to consider race as a positional variable is to think of blacks as less productive workers. This is highly questionable. It is likewise questionable to consider women, southerners, rural residents as less productive—or merely as powerless workers unable to demand more. If interest is in individuals, then such considerations as sex, race, and so forth must be introduced and controlled in the analysis. Yet the dual labor market concept implies a structural perspective. There is no reason why race or sex, for example, must be considered individual indicators of labor quality or productivity. If anything, such variables might best be considered processes by which peripheral industries effect low wages. For this reason, Weiss's conclusions must be qualified.

There is a second and more general concern with regard to the ambiguous support for core-peripheral effects on industry-wage differentials. This concern relates to whether such differentials are apparent at all times and in all circumstances. More specifically, the link of low wages to peripheral industries involves some assumptions about elasticity in the demand for their products. Presumably, consumer decisions about apparel, for example, are elastic and hence sensitive to price increases. This presumably is not the case with respect to machinery or plastics, which are seen to be vital to individual and economic well-being. The more elastic the demand, the greater the obstacles in passing costs on to consumers.

Regardless of the merit of the specific examples given, there is some question as to whether elasticity has temporal dimensions. For example, in times of economic growth, full employment, and brisk consumer demand, it is conceivable that the presumed elasticity of peripheral industry products is lost. Were this the case, peripheral industries might in these contexts successfully raise prices and wages. The pressure for raising wages in peripheral industries is likewise evident in periods of prosperity: full employment entails greater competition for available labor.

These possibilities suggest that core-peripheral wage differentials should be more apparent in periods of economic slack and less so in periods of economic prosperity. Consistent with this view, a recent study by Haworth and Reuther (1978) found the effects of concentration and unionization on wages to be substantially less in the prosperity of the late sixties than in the recession economy of the late fifties.

The long-term meaning of temporal swings in consumer demand for trends in the American economy is unclear. Recent indicators of economic well-being are ambiguous. Wages are high, but inflation is rampant. Furthermore, industrial productivity and economic growth are low—leading to the "stagflation" of popular conception. A recent argument suggests the development of trends with disastrous consequences for workers in peripheral industries (Hong 1978; see also, Wachtel and Adelsheim 1977). The author provides evidence to illustrate that management in high monopoly-profit industries is increasingly passing costs on to consumers. In former eras, profits and labor costs may have been taken from soaring productivity, but there is some real question as to whether these patterns persist with flagging rates of production.

If these patterns continue, wage workers in peripheral industries will suffer. There is some indication that these disastrous consequences may already be in effect. In an article on a Bureau of Labor Statistics study, labor analyst A. H. Raskin (*New York Times* 1977:D1, D5) wrote:

> Inflation has sharpened the line between haves and have nots in the American labor force.
> There has been a distinct widening of the earnings gap that separates employees in steel, autos, oil refining and other technologically advanced industries with concentrated ownership and a high degree of unionization from those holding jobs in such fields as laundries, hotels, apparel shops and textiles, where skill requirements are low and the proportion of women workers is high.

In the core industries Raskin reviewed, increases (from 1973 to 1976) were of the order of 30 to 45 percent—bringing wages up to an average of approximately $300 per week. These figures did not account for a variety of other premiums. At the lower end, relative increases were lower—from 20 to 30 percent—and absolute increases still lower. Workers in hotels and motels, for example, had increases of approximately 22 percent, bringing their base weekly wage just shy of $100; workers in women's apparel had increases of 18 percent, bringing their income up to about $85; laundry workers had increases of approximately 26 percent, bringing their weekly income to $116.

The long-range effect of inflation on inequality is as yet unclear, although government action in raising minimum wages is the most usual alternative pursued. Unfortunately, wage workers at the lowest pay scale—in agriculture, in private household work, in retail trade, and in sundry service activities—are only partially covered by minimum wage rates. Also, it is conceivable that higher minimum wages may shrink overall demand for employment. But the data are insufficient to definitively state this to be the case (Doeringer and Piore 1971; Feldstein 1973).

Other responses to increased wages likewise underline the plight of peripheral industries. If unionization is partial, drives for higher wages can price products out of the market (if costs are passed on to consumers) or threaten a firm's stability (if costs are absorbed). If unionization is industry wide, higher wages may merely lead employers to step up the drive to reduce labor costs, either by using cheaper labor pools in lesser developed countries or by searching for labor-saving means of automation. Escalating labor costs have been reported to accelerate automation in the meat packing industry (Fogel 1970). More recently, similar experiences confronted Chavez' United Farm Workers (*International Herald Tribune* 1977b:4): "The improved wages won only recently by farm workers after almost a decade of strife have created a backlash, accelerating the development of machines that will put more and more farm workers out of jobs." The news article goes on to discuss the impact of automatic harvesting machines which could displace upwards of 10,000 workers over the next year. The union estimated technological unemployment at between 100,000 and 250,000 workers over the next decade—if the search for the use of such equipment continued. Unfortunately, it is not known how general such backlash responses may be. Nor is the magnitude of other responses to wage hikes in peripheral industries clearly understood—as, for example, exporting production to lower-cost labor markets in the underdeveloped world.

In spite of blind spots in our understanding of the dual labor market, the distinction between core and peripheral industries is important. The distinction clarifies: how added income accrues to certain workers without infringing on profits; how wage hikes rely on both union militance and corporate power; how inflationary wages in core industries put pressure on wages in peripheral industries—all to maintain at best a steady state of inequality. Although consensus theorists may be correct in estimating lower income inequality in the industrial state, there is no overall evidence of partnership between business and labor that simultaneously benefits all sectors of the economy.

Political Intervention: The Effects of Welfare and Taxation on Inequality

Industrial Trends. Economic development, from the consensus perspective, is one way in which industrialization influences inequality. Government intervention is another. In the view of Lipset (1959a) and other theorists (Lenski 1966; Marshall 1965), political development—through a recognition of citizenship, through the universal extension of voting privileges to the working class—upsets a balance of power traditionally tipped in favor of a business elite. And with this, the legislation of the welfare state materializes, granting aid to the poor with taxes levied on the rich. This is the sense in which consensus theorists consider government intervention in the allocation of scarce resources to be relevant; with such intervention, inequality is further attenuated in the industrial state.

On one score this position has merit. The available evidence indicates that industrialization is indeed linked to government intervention in the manner suggested. For example, Cutright (1965) has shown that highly industrialized countries, as indexed by the mean level of energy consumed, are likely to have longer experience with social security programs. Likewise, Paukert (1968), in a cross-societal analysis of welfare expenditures, found a small but positive association between industrialization and the absolute sums allocated for expenditures. In more industrialized nations, the percentage of the gross national product devoted to social security measures was lower but the absolute sum allocated was higher. Security coverage was generally spotty and fragmentary in the less industrialized nations.

The American experience parallels those in other industrialized nations. Funds for welfare in the past few decades have skyrocketed—as has the reliance by the poor on these payments. In the 1920s and 1930s transfer payments accounted for between 2 and 4 percent of family personal income; in 1979 more than 13 percent of personal income was accounted for by such payments (Goldsmith 1957; U. S. Bureau of the Census 1980a:445). Counting all welfare programs— social insurance as well as health, education, and housing— expenditures at the state, federal, and local levels jumped from $48 billion in 1960 to $377 billion in 1978 (Skolnick and Dales 1972; U. S. Bureau of the Census 1980a:288). These increases, furthermore, are not simple responses to inflation. In 1960 these payments were 9.5 percent of the GNP; in 1978 they were 17 percent. Likewise, many such payments have truly kept pace with increases in the general wage scale, as illustrated by periodic increases in old age survivor payments (Pechman, Aaron, and Taussig 1968).

Few would deny the greater monetary investment of industrialized nations in welfare expenditures. Consensus theorists see this as a step toward the welfare state. Marxists are more cynical in their view of welfare. While Marx himself had a limited conception of income opportunities in advanced capitalist societies, recent theorists working in the Marxist tradition have filled this void. O'Connor (1973), for example, interprets welfare as the government's role in supporting the underpinnings of monopoly capital. In a competitive economy, decreased sales are accompanied by lower prices and lower wages. Not so under monopoly capitalism; declining sales may be accompanied by stable (or advancing) wages and prices. To reduce costs, the monopoly capitalist's response is to partially shut down productive capacity, thereby increasing unemployment. In turn, governments literally underwrite these vicissitudes in the economy. Through mechanisms such as unemployment compensation, government assumes the costs of recessive economies under monopoly capitalism—thus exacerbating, in O'Connor's perspective, the fiscal crisis of the state.

But does welfare do anything else, either with respect to making lighter the burden of individuals, or more broadly, attenuating disparities in income? That is, is there any indication that welfare reduces inequality in the manner both popular ideology and consensus theorists suggest? The affluence of a nation indicates that substantial expenditures can (and perhaps will) be directed toward targeted poverty areas— but do these sums alter the targets? Do they attenuate the range of inequality? Our previous discussion does not encourage optimism. At least in recent years America has shown few signs of a decline in inequality, although welfare expenditures continue to soar. The stability in inequality suggests that welfare expenditures may be dedicated to something other than equalitarian concerns—and this in spite of the continual fascination of consensus theorists with welfare as a redistributive mechanism.

Poverty Trends. My overall contention is that the increasingly massive welfare budget has negligible effects on inequality or poverty. In fact, the reverse question should be raised: why should inequality be affected? I have already argued that the major inroads into inequality are derived primarily from a system of monopoly capital. There is no implication that everyone benefits—merely the highly unionized in certain segments of the economy.

I will review general government policies on economic issues in the next chapter. Suffice it to say here that government is a willing partner in the growth and development of big business interests. Only partial support is given to reducing inequality as such—and this more in the form of band-aid measures than anything else. Where poverty is dealt with, consequences rather than structural causes are considered. The welfare system is little more than a floor to subsistence. Programs to reduce unemployment are directed toward the supply side, attempting to raise labor's skill levels rather than effectively guaranteeing jobs. Drastic inroads in unemployment are made primarily in the boom periods of a wartime economy (Ackerman et al. 1971; Solow 1960). There is little question, in fact, that high levels of unemployment are a standard part of government policy—to "cool off" the economy and brake soaring inflationary wages.

This state of affairs has prompted critics to prick the bubble of affluence (Myrdal 1963:48–49):

> It is perfectly possible for the majority of Americans to live together with practically everybody they have primary contact with, in a situation of full and even overfull employment, where there is brisk demand and competition for their labor, while they read in the newspapers that there is large and growing unemployment beneath them. That this can be so is the result of the nature of unemployment being to a large extent structural in character.
>
> While this is happening at the bottom of American society it is perfectly possible that there is ever greater social mobility, liberty, and equality of opportunity and a generally rising economic and cultural level in majority America. More and more individuals and families may move further away from the neighborhood of the dividing line. Social welfare polcies have . . . been framed to give greater security especially for that middle group in the nation. And there might even be some successful passing of the poverty line by individuals coming from beneath it, which then gives a false assurance that America is still the free and open society of its cherished image and well established ideals.

But as less and less work is required of the type the people in the urban and rural slums can offer, they will be increasingly isolated and exposed to unemployment, to underemployment and to plain exploitation.

As Myrdal implies, the illusion of the government's role in reducing poverty persists. A more recent newspaper article commented as follows (*Minneapolis Tribune* 1976:2a):

The number of poor people in the United States increased by 2.5 million in 1975, the largest increase in a single year since the government began keeping poverty statistics in 1959.

The percentage of people living in poverty declined steadily from 1959, when it was 22.4 percent through 1963, when it had fallen to 12.1 percent. The figures have zig-zagged since then, rising in 1970 because of a recession, falling again from 1971 through 1973 when they hit a low of 11.1 percent, rising again in 1974 and sharply rising in 1975 to 12.3 percent.

The implication is that long-term trends in the eradication of poverty have been suddenly though ever so slightly reversed. Government statistics indeed suggest this to be the case. For example, in 1959 22 percent of the population were reported to be below the poverty level; in 1978 that number was effectively cut in half—to approximately 11 percent (U. S. Bureau of the Census 1980a:464).

Yet, these reported trends are contingent on a particular interpretation of poverty. The government definition is based on a Social Security Administration estimate of individual and family budgets. This budget provides the costs necessary for an economy food plan and additional costs for fuel, clothing, shelter, and sundries. Persons with income below these costs are cast in the poverty category. Each year, furthermore, these costs are revised to keep up with rising prices. As of late, they are simply gauged to reflect rises in the general consumer price index. In 1959, for example, the poverty level for a family of four was pegged to an income of $2,973; in 1978, the consumer price index rose 124 percent—and so did the poverty cut-off, to $6,662.

The averages of the Social Security Administration are

one way to define poverty: through an annually revised budget reflecting needs specified more than a decade ago. An alternate definition is in terms of current affluence. There is, after all, no good reason to require the poverty-stricken to live in conditions reflecting another era—be it the early sixties or any time before. Although this is entirely judgmental, a case can be made for defining poverty relatively in terms of contemporary standards of adequate income (Townsend 1974; Miller and Roby 1970).

If such an approach is taken, the Social Security Administration's definition looks worse, as do the numbers living in poverty. For example, the poverty line (according to the government's definition) for a family of four in 1959 was 55 percent of the median income for all families. Today the poverty line, in spite of inflation adjustments, is only 38 percent of the median for all family income (U. S. Bureau of the Census 1980a:464). Using median family income as a guideline for poverty, we see that current definitions are approximately 45 percent less than they were in 1959. Given the large numbers of families and persons who would be caught within the poverty net were it readjusted to reflect current family income, it is hard to believe that the substantial drop in poverty reported by the government is anything more than the failure of administrative definitions to keep up with contemporary standards.

Indeed, this is exactly what the data show. Defining poverty as one-half of median income—which was approximately the case according to government standards in the early sixties—were this same definition applied today, the proportion in poverty is virtually identical over the last two decades. There is no mathematical reason why this should be the case. The identity in the figures merely points to the stability of poverty, which the government has done little to alter (Fuchs 1969).

Welfare Trends. In underscoring the stability of poverty, there is no implication that welfare funds are wasted—or that they fail to reach the impoverished. One study (Lampman 1970) shows that the poor—defined on the average as those with less than $3,750 in income—receive 3 percent of all family income prior to welfare transfer payments and 9 percent after transfer payments. These payments, furthermore, account for: 4 percent of the income of the nonpoor; 55 percent of the income of the poor; 42 percent of the income of those moved into the nonpoor category by welfare transfer payments (Lampman 1966).

Welfare expenditures reach their targets. While the funds expended unquestionably provide some relief from the hardships of poverty, the question here is whether they do anything else; specifically, are soaring expenditures sufficient to alter the bands of economic inequality? Certainly the monumental budgets allocated to welfare suggest that they are more than window dressing. Theorists such as Lipset (1968) and Lenski (1966) have argued that such expenditures provide a major basis for reversing long-time trends toward inequality. Yet a review of the evidence on welfare and inequality suggests—at least for the American case—scant support for this position. Although the materials to be presented here are well known, this elementary review is necessary in light of the continued fascination of various theorists with welfare as a central mechanism in governmental efforts to reduce inequality.

It is necessary first to underscore that these budgets are only partially gauged to benefit the poor. Much of the allocations are in the form of education and health improvements targeted to the general population rather than the poor as such. Even programs such as social security or Medicare involve only loose income tests. Their benefits are more generally extended to all who qualify by virtue of age or dependency. One estimate notes that only 13 percent of the welfare budget has a specific income test designed to target funds to individuals in poverty (Lampman 1974). The poor, of course, receive more than 12–13 percent of the welfare budget—in fact, they probably receive around one-third. But this point must be borne in mind: the astronomical figures related to welfare have major ramifications throughout the society, not only for those at the lower reaches of the income distribution.

The proportion of the budget targeted to the poor is confounded by its source. The idea of welfare attenuating inequality assumes that welfare funds are taxed from the rich and directed to the poor. But this is not necessarily or inevitably true. Many welfare programs function as insurance programs: persons pay in at one point in time with a view to recovering these payments at some distant point in time. This is the case with respect to social security payments to the elderly, which represent close to 75 percent of the funds allocated to income maintenance programs. The elderly are among the poorest groups in the population. But the income they receive is not necessarily income redistributed from rich to poor; it is income redistributed over the span of a lifetime. This point was summarized by Joseph Califano, the Secretary of Health, Education, and Welfare in the Carter administration (*International Herald Tribune* 1978b:3):

> Mr. Califano said that most people think of his Department, which handles much of the programs for the elderly, as an agency that transfers money from the well-to-do to the poor. But another way to view it, he said, is as a giant mechanism for "distributing money generationally"—from young and middle-aged taxpayers to the elderly and retired.

Two other points are important in this connection. First, social security income is taxed at a fairly regressive rate, which means that contributions to social security take a larger percentage of the income of the poor than of the rich. Second, and this has yet to be shown, is the possibility that the poor who contribute to social security programs are less likely to reap its benefits as a result of ill health and shortened life expectancy.

Furthermore, while the poor receive some amounts allocated by the government, the rich are not without their own resources in this respect. The well-to-do receive institutional coverage, guarantees of security by the private corporate sector. For example, a study some years ago by Morgan and his colleagues (1962) showed family transfer payments to be related curvilinearly to gross income: high in the lower income categories, dipping in the middle, and high again in the upper income brackets. The transfer incomes at the lower end are largely government transfer payments; those at the upper end are drawn from the private sector, principally in the form of pensions. Clearly, upper income individuals are not without their own means of receiving income—income not attributable to wages, salaries, or dividends as such. Yet the effect of transfer payments on inequality can most dramatically be felt in a zero-sum account, when the poor receive all transfer funds and the rich receive little or none. Private transfers, however, offset government payments as an influence on inequality.

Another factor deterring the influence of welfare on inequality is the direction welfare programs have taken—more in the form of extending welfare privileges than in concentrating such payments on hardcore poverty. The liberalization of criteria for assistance has permitted persons to receive part or full assistance who otherwise may be forced to work. Since such assistance is used in lieu of earned income, the transfer did not reduce inequality; it merely substituted transfer payments for what otherwise would have been income in the form of salaries or wages. In regard to aid for dependent children, for example, the welfare rolls swelled from 4.4 million in 1965 to 8 million in 1970 and to 11 million in 1973 (Steiner 1974). Some of this explosion is likely due to the growing divorce rate. But there is little question that the bulk of this growth is an effect of a liberalized interpretation of the program itself; an interpretation initially reaching only a fraction of poor families without male heads, to one covering most needy single-parent families as well as families with unemployed or incapacitated fathers. Similar situations occurred with respect to other programs. Every few years, for example, social security benefits are extended to additional occupational categories. Further liberalization has taken the form of reducing the waiting period for benefits—permitting retirement as early as age 62. Hence persons otherwise in the labor force were permitted welfare payments. The result is clear: budgets increase but the effect on reducing income inequality is minimal. With the liberalization of criteria for assistance, persons otherwise forced to work receive welfare. Such liberalization is unquestionably in keeping with the spirit of a welfare state. Yet the money—from welfare in one case, from earned income in another—is constant, as is the effect on inequality itself. Needless to add, attempts to curb or reverse liberalization make even more remote any equalitarian effects of welfare funding.

In part, also, the failure to affect inequality is attributable to overall inadequacies in the welfare program. Most programs require the poor to initiate participation rather than receive automatic transfers on the basis of annual income earned. This results in substantial attrition. In addition, the criteria for wages earned are in many cases so restrictive that the poor are actually discouraged from working—hence detracting from any dramatic impact welfare might make.

The major reason, however, for a failure of welfare to offset inequality simply involves lack of funds (and commitment) for anything other than a meager impact. The benefits of social security for the aged, for example, are so meager that anyone receiving that and that alone falls below government poverty cut-offs. Were equalitarian aims the goal of welfare, the actual expenditures would have to be massive—many times the amount now allocated for assistance. For this reason, few persons are willing to support the taxes required and few politicians have rallied to champion its cause. It is far easier to gain consensus on the minimal task of combating poverty than on the monumental task of managing the redistribution of income. As one economist phrased the issue (Lampman 1974:73):

Although economists are wont to look to an index of inequality of income shares in comparing the fairness of result of one political economy with that of another, this particular measure has never had any standing among political leaders. None has rallied political troops with a plan to change the shares of the several fifths [of income] in a stated way. Concern with income inequality has been more indirect; the focus has been on "fairness" in taxation, relief for those "unable" to work, replacement of income lost without fault, sharing the cost of extraordinary expense, and helping people get a minimum provision of "essentials" in order to assure "equality of opportunity." It is interesting to note that advocates of such schemes as progressive income taxes and social security often deny that they are concerned with income redistribution. These have been more acceptable political approaches to equity questions than have wide sweeps to "correct" the distribution of income as such. The goal of eliminating poverty is a modest addition to the array of apparently politically useful rationales for redistribution.

Taxation. Welfare is one face to the coin of redistribution. Taxation is the other. If inequality is to be affected, funds traditionally the province of the rich are taxed and redistributed to the poor. Yet, as with welfare, taxation is largely ineffectual as a basis for furthering equalitarian aims. Taxation is simply proportional rather than progressive in effect.

The inadequacies of the tax structure are now widely understood by the American public: the presence of special loopholes, of regressive taxes, of options permitting the transfer of income to nontaxable categories. What is less well understood is the magnitude of the sums involved. A government report gave the following estimate (*International Herald Tribune* 1978c:3): "A small minority of wealthiest U. S taxpayers is getting the lion's share of the benefits from $84 billion in special tax preferences, credits and other tax breaks now in the tax code. . . ." An earlier tax report prepared by the Ways and Means Committee (U. S. Congress 1972) specified how this was allocated among income groups. Approximately 45 percent of the tax breaks are given to a little more than 5 percent of the wealthiest taxpayers. Contrariwise, only 7 percent of the tax breaks are given to the lowest income category—accounting for approximately 38 percent of the taxpayers. The more recent government report, also by the Ways and Means Committee, put the total cost of these tax breaks at $84 billion. The earlier report put the figure at approximately $42 billion.

These breaks offset progressivity in the federal tax structure. One estimate of the "true" federal tax rate paid on income illustrated the dramatic reductions in progressivity involved (Herriott and Miller 1971). Taxes included not only direct taxes—such as federal and state taxes, sales taxes, and so on—but also hidden or indirect taxes such as those corporations pass on to consumers. The results indicated some general progressivity, with a number of important exceptions. First, the tax burden is greatest in the highest and lowest income categories. Second, there is no progressivity whatsoever in the entire range of middle-income groups ($20,000 to $50,000). Overall the progressive effects of the total tax structure are modest.

These conclusions are not unique. Other studies containing different assumptions with respect to hidden taxes (as, for example, those passed on to consumers by corporations) have shown similar results. A study by Pechman and Okner (1974) investigated tax liabilities by income under a variety of such assumptions. The details of their conclusions differ somewhat from those noted above. But the broad generalization reached is the same—the tax structure is not significantly progressive (ibid.: 10):

> The U. S. tax system is essentially proportional for the vast majority of families and therefore has little effect on the distribution of income. The very rich pay higher average effective tax rates than does the average family, but the difference is large only if the corporation income and property taxes are assumed to be borne by capital. If they are assumed to be shifted to consumers to a considerable degree, the very rich pay tax rates that are only moderately higher than average.

Estimates in fact suggest that at best taxes reduce inequality by only approximately 4 percent (Okner 1974). The conclusion is inescapable: taxes function to generate government revenue and affect economic demand. They do not seriously alter inequality.

What, then, is the net effect of redistribution in the United States? One typical estimate is given by Herriott and Miller (1971:40). Their statistics show that the tax-transfer system as a whole benefits the very poor. Persons with less than $2,000 in income, for example, receive approximately 100 percent of their income from government transfers and pay in only one-half of their income to taxes—resulting in a net gain of 56 percent. In contrast, the wealthiest income category, with persons earning incomes in excess of $50,000, pays out 45 percent of income in taxes and receives, on a percentage basis, almost nothing back in public transfer payments. For most other categories, the tax-transfer system shows few differences. In a similar vein, Reynolds and Smolensky (1977:67–83) show that for the years 1950, 1960, and 1970, welfare and taxation (omitting general government expenditures) reduce the Gini inequality coefficient by approximately 10 to 15 percent. These various estimates, as Reynolds and Smolensky acknowledge, are marred by several methodological difficulties. One difficulty is that pre- and post-transfer income distributions are not independent of one another. More liberal welfare legislation may prompt an AFDC mother not to work or an elderly man to retire at 62. Their pretransfer income may drop to nothing, hence exaggerating the effects of government transfers. An additional difficulty is that annual estimates of government transfers omit lifetime economic patterns. Social security, for example, which accounts for the greatest share of welfare, is made up of contributions over a lifetime of work. What, if anything, is paid in during retirement years is not indicative of contributions to this fund. As noted previously, this insurance characteristic of social security likely exaggerates the effects of government transfers.

What then can be said about soaring government transfers and their impact on inequality? Ignoring some of the difficulties alluded to above, the conclusions from Reynolds and Smolensky's (1977) study are instructive. From 1950 to 1970, government taxes from all sources increased from $51 billion to $232 billion; welfare expenditure rose during the same time period from $23 billion to $145 billion—representing an increase of 33 to 44 percent of all government expenditures (U. S. Bureau of the Census 1977:278, 317). Reynolds and Smolensky show that in spite of relative stability in pretransfer income inequality over these two decades—and in spite of soaring revenues and expenditures—post-transfer income inequality is virtually unchanged over these years. I concur with their conclusions (Reynolds and Smolensky 1977:96):

Average income rose remarkably between 1950 and 1970, the government share has grown relative to the private sector, the composition of expenditures and taxes has changed, and yet on balance there is no detectable shift in the relative size of after-government income differences. . . . It appears to be a common view that, even in a predominantly market economy, the distribution of income, however defined, is subject to governmental manipulation. We are not convinced that the conventional wisdom is correct.

From this view, it is doubtful whether redistributive mechanisms continually affect inequality, at least in the American experience. Other attempts to estimate the equalitarian effects of alternate government programs—the minimum wage, for example—have likewise found them ambiguous (Doeringer and Piore 1971; Feldstein 1973). What the system has done, and this is not to be ignored, is liberalize criteria for welfare, thus allowing some of the needy to receive aid without the necessity of work.

In brief, the post-World War II period has had enormous upsurges in welfare spending; but income inequality has remained almost constant and poverty has not been noticeably reduced. Even this stability in inequality may be jarred by the impact of politically conservative interpretations of inequality—to rationalize welfare cuts and enlarge tax advantages for the wealthy. Though long-term trends are difficult to foresee, there are at this time some indications that increases in inequality may be in the cards in the coming decade (Thurow 1981).

Summary

The data cited in the present chapter are in partial agreement with the consensus view on greater equality among individuals and families. But there is little indication of support for other essential aspects of the consensus position: (1) that growth in equality is a necessary outcome of economic development: (2) that growth in equality reflects an alliance between business and labor. My position is that, given the enormity of influence in the business sector—as well as the dominating priority given to profits and growth—wage gains probably reflect only collective action on the part of workers, coupled with effective sanctions. And even these pressures are not yielded to unless they can be reconciled with profit stability.

It is not my intention to deny the opportunities highlighted by consensus theorists, limited and partial as they may be. For these opportunities call into question Marxist assumptions pertaining to the monopolization of resources by classes other than production workers. If such resources are indeed monopolized, then conflict with a view toward altering the existing structure becomes a most viable alternative for securing wage gains. Yet if opportunities exist (in attempts to capitalize on or approximate dual labor market conditions), then existing conflict will be directed toward wage gains without at the same time attempting to alter the existing structure. Since the system of profits does not emerge as problematic in conflict, stability in the capitalist system is partially assured. How precisely this is accomplished is the topic of the next chapter.

CHAPTER THREE

Inequality and the Institutional Order

TRENDS IN AMERICAN society defy any simple forecast of greater equality or inequality. If anything, such trends suggest ambiguity: greater equality in income distributions but little alteration in the distribution of wealth; stability in the ratio of profits to wages but increases in welfare receipts. Any simple notion prophesizing major trends toward inequality or equality is insufficiently sensitive to the complexity of American society.

In the present chapter I will trace the complex trends in inequality to ambiguities in institutional goals. Specifically, I will examine labor and government policies with respect to the corporate structure. My intention is to elaborate on the persistence of conflict without change—and to illustrate how ambiguities in institutional goals devolve into government and labor support for the status quo.

In pursuing this theme, I reject conflict and consensus perspectives as adequate explanations of institutional complexity and ambiguity. To reiterate: these respective notions suffer from generality and abstraction. They push towards a monolithic view of the social order without allowing for the simultaneous occurrence of conflict *and* consensus—of agreement on some issues and disagreement on others. Although this failure has previously been noted, particularly by Dahrendorf (1959), its implications have yet to be analyzed fully (Weingart 1969).

What is most notable about the activities of unions and governments is an absence of any clear overriding policy, internally consistent and continually pursued. Labor pecks away at corporate surpluses but does so in a way as to leave profits untouched. Conflict is the weapon but it is not used to dismantle the capitalist structure, which suggests implicit agreement with it. For its part, government also equivocates: here pushing welfare reform, there providing an optimum environment for corporate growth and development for the pursuit of profit. Again, no straightjacket view is useful.

In dealing with ambiguity, we must admit two points about social institutions. First, they are complex and have multiple goals. These goals may be ambiguous, divergent, inconsistent. The strain for consistency in institutions without strong ideologies is simply lacking. Second, decisions and policies are situational. They are framed in temporally limited economic contexts. Prosperity dictates one set of decisions, austerity another. The decisions may seem contradictory but are not necessarily seen as such by the participants. They appear to be reasonable responses to the prevailing economic climate. They are outcomes of situational factors rather than thorough planning in the context of overarching commitments—which is noticeably absent in many American institutions.

To reconcile the conflict and consensus views, it is necessary to come to grips with these institutional ambiguities. How is this to be handled? As pragmatic politics, and that alone? The concept of pragmatism (or more appropriately, expediency) tells little, however, about institutional activities. It may be necessary to go beyond pragmatism to specify competing institutional goals, and the contexts in which they are variously pursued. One interesting illustration of this possibility is given in a recent volume by the economist Arthur Okun (1975) entitled *Equality and Efficiency: The Big Trade-off*. As implied in the title, Okun sees welfare measures as a trade-off between efficiency and equality. Efficiency refers to industrial efficiency and requires, in his view, greater play for the market enterprise: free movement of prices as well as profit incentives and tax breaks for capital investments. Equality refers to welfare, to fringe benefits for health and retirement, to minimum wages, to guaranteed employment and other mechanisms to decrease disparities between rich and poor. Okun's position is that equality detracts from efficiency: by switching capital from productive into consumptive capacities (welfare); by raising tax rates and lowering the incentive for investment; by keeping market mechanisms in check—through wage policies and price regulation—so as to offset erratic swings in economic cycles.

Equality, from Okun's view, is not totally outside the domain of policy concern. Rather it is a variable institutional interest which at times may be ignored to stimulate efficient business operation. The result of efficiency, of course, highlights (Okun 1975:1)

the double standard of a capitalist democracy, professing and pursuing an egalitarian political and social system and simultaneously generating gaping disparities in economic well-being. This mixture of equality and inequality sometimes smacks of inconsistency and even insincerity. Yet I believe that, in many cases, the institutional arrangements represent an easy compromise rather than fundamental inconsistencies. The contrasts among American families in living standards and in material wealth reflect a system of rewards and penalties that is intended to encourage effort and channel it into socially productive activity. To the extent that the system succeeds, it generates an efficient economy. But the pursuit of efficiency necessarily creates inequalities. And hence society faces a trade-off between equality and efficiency.

In a different guise, Okun is recounting the functional theory of stratification, not as a principle of organization but as criteria for decisions from an institutional vantage point (Davis and Moore 1945). All the functional ingredients are here: differential pay and financial incentives making for efficiency in task completion; greater equality reducing the capacity to work effectively. Okun's subject, however, is not the individual as such but the economic organization. Nonetheless, the specter advanced in the functionalist perspective is present in his formulation. Inequality is necessary to effective functioning. This is the vital trade-off.

In using Okun's formulation to address institutional goal ambiguity, I by no means concur with the functionalist position. In my view, the theory is logically deficient (Hempel 1959) and probably overplayed in the literature. Without getting into a lengthy debate surrounding the position's merit (Demerath and Peterson 1967), I may note that it provides few answers to the questions it broaches: whether efficiency and equality are mutually exclusive, or exhaustive alternatives; whether incentives are necessary for making all work "effective" or "efficient"; how differential incentives must be.

What Okun's position does, however, is offer a framework for understanding the equivocation (and ambiguities) in institutional policies—and the reasons given for why different goals are variously pursued. For it may be true that in times of financial pressure on national currency, in times of galloping inflation, in light of competitiveness in national industries, a frequent government response is to: (a) cut back funds from welfare expenditures, and (b) increase the profit margin of industries through various subsidies and credit allowances for production and capital investment. Likewise, prosperous times may encourage welfare measures from legislative bodies, wars on poverty, funds for restoring the viability of inner cities. The very same reasoning can also be applied to labor: to explain, for example, why union conflict is keyed to times of prosperity when employment is high, rather than to periods of recession when deprivation is substantial.

In fact, it is conceivable to see decisions relating to equality and efficiency in somewhat cyclical form. The success of one set of decisions and priorities acts dialectically to stimulate the other. Were this the case, two plausible outcomes should follow. First, labor conflict ought to be persistent, in that workers are always reacting against cycles of "efficiency" and therefore constantly in a league of playing "catch-up ball." Second, swings from equality policies to efficiency policies (and back) should effectively guarantee that nothing happens, that the status quo is preserved.

In discussing Okun's distinction, I reiterate my disagreement with his contention: that bolstering efficiency in times of economic crisis—at the cost of equality—is how societies should function. Furthermore, it is also possible that the importance assigned to efficiency and equality does not carry equal weight in all quarters. If American society is indeed ordered on the basis of capitalistic principles giving priority to profits and economic growth, then it is efficiency first and foremost which receives consideration. This means that in government (and in unions alike) attention is directed primarily to the well-being of the business enterprise. The viability of business then becomes the fountainhead for high employment, for wages, for brisk competition in national and international markets. This, of course, is implicit in Marx's meaning of *Klasse an sich*: societies structured to further the interests of a particular sector. Equality or the demands of unions need not be ignored, but they may only be given secondary consideration in the hierarchy of economic priorities, making inroads into poverty and inequality problematic.

Unions: Instruments
of Status Maintenance

Labor unions play a pivotal role in conflict and consensus perspectives. In one view, they are opportunities for working class militance, vehicles for confrontation. In the other, they are bases for mediation and integration, providing a formal liaison between labor and business interests. The two perspectives share an optimistic view that through these mechanisms, the economic problems of workers can somehow be ameliorated or resolved.

I argue in this section that such optimism is unfounded. In fact, neither the consensus nor the conflict view is totally appropriate for understanding business-labor relations. In pursuing this theme I will elaborate on the dual commitment notion implicit in the equality-efficiency perspective: of union organizations at once committed to bolstering the economic advantage of their rank and file and at the same time forming sectorial alliances with industry to increase stability in profits. In effect I raise this as a possibility: that an outcome of the highly unionized dual labor market is an understanding on labor's part of a link between its welfare and the viability of business. Were this the case, business might be harrassed, cajoled, embarrassed, even subject to strike—but all within the parameters for protecting industry's long-range interests.

Is this in another guise the vision of industrial harmony and business-labor alliance argued by consensus theorists? For a variety of reasons, I will argue in this section that it is not? In the first place, the dominant view underlying the consensus perspective, of the integration of the working class, is simply false. The consensus view places labor in the nexus of two integrative forces: economic integration defined in terms of affluence; and social integration defined in terms of labor-management mediation and communication. Both forces presumably strip labor's potential for militance. Yet this essentially Durkheimian position is tantamount to viewing labor as an alien element, whose militance rests on the absence of commitment and links to the wider society. If the questionable use of the term "integration" is dropped, an alternate argument is probably more consistent with the facts: that affluence is contingent on militance, and that the evolution of organizational forms, such as unions, provides mechanisms for the expression of militant stands. This alternative view presupposes no automatic dividends for workers from the industrial process; any new affluence workers enjoy is a likely consequence of conflict—and even to sustain such affluence, conflict mechanisms may likewise have to be employed. Conflict, in this view, is integral to worker opportunities.

Even if affluence and mediation mechanisms vitiated labor militance, is there any evidence to indicate business' willingness to form an alliance with labor? Consensus theorists assume such evidence exists. This is a second questionable assumption in their argument. At the risk of repetition, I note again that economic growth and profit stability are the raisons d'être of the corporation, and that corporate wealth is viewed as valuable, scarce, and uncertain. What this means is that labor claims for higher wages are honored by business only insofar as these can be accounted for in increased productivity, increased prices, or other mechanisms to offset labor costs. And even so there is no guarantee that business willingly, of its own free will, shares profits in an air of benevolence.

Labor, as a consequence, may be in a state of continual jeopardy. With each wave of inflationary prices reflecting costs passed on to consumers, labor is always in process of catching up. And, if I am correct in my estimate of recalcitrance on business' part to willingly grant wage hikes, then strikes in one form or another are integral to labor's chances for mobility, or at least status maintenance. Hence the vision of business-labor harmony is likely nothing more than an illusion.

But if this vision is an illusion, I am not prepared to argue that conflict stimulated by visions of radical change is necessarily the order of the day. Conflict is used, but my estimate is that it is only a mechanism of persuasion rather than a weapon of change. As pointed out in Tannenbaum and Kahn's (1958) concept of the dual loyalties of the union member, one face of loyalty points toward labor, the other toward industry. Both are seen as key factors in labor's long-range well-being. There is no intent on labor's part to alter what from its view is the goose with the golden egg. That is, in spite of union rhetoric, organized labor may indeed accept the principle of efficiency and thereby business perogatives with respect to profits. Were this the case, labor strife would be less a sign of change and more a linchpin in maintaining the status quo.

In arguing the case of conflict without change, my first order of business is in examining the evidence of industrial harmony propounded by consensus theorists. I will further argue that while conflict is persistent, the strategy behind such conflict is keyed to keeping business interests intact— and indeed has precisely this effect.

Industrial Harmony: The Illusion of Worker Integration. By conflict I refer not merely or necessarily to procedural differences but to situations (1) involving groups with incompatible goals, (2) where the goals of one can be advanced only at the cost of the other (3) and where advancing group goals requires threats, violence, or other sanctions (Fink 1968; Mack and Snyder 1957; Dahrendorf 1958). Conflict in this form presupposes distinct groups, with firm lines between them. It also assumes a clear adversary relationship. The fewer the links between groups, the less these groups share in common, the greater the probability is that antagonistic rather than cooperative efforts will evolve. Against this backdrop, consensus theorists have elaborated two principle cases for the integration of the working class, one with respect to mediation mechanisms, the other with respect to affluence. Their argument is that integration vitiates militance. My argument reverses this sequence and shows how militance is related to integration. I turn to mediation mechanisms first.

The mediation mechanisms are seen as an evolution of formal links between business and labor, prompted primarily by unionization and collective bargaining. Presumably as these forms evolve, conflict gradually changes from violent outbreaks to a simple search for mechanisms of adjudication. Kerr and his colleagues (1960:208), for example, outline four major forms of protest—with each stage characteristic of a particular form of industrialization:

(1) absenteeism and sabotage
(2) spontaneous work stoppages
(3) industry strikes and political protests
(4) labor-business bargaining through formal machinery and binding arbitration.

As societies industrialize, spontaneous outbreaks and militant strikes or work stoppages will be rare and institutional mechanisms will prevail (Kerr et al. 1960:209):

> As time passes, formal organizations of workers emerge, and . . . the forms of overt protest become more disciplined and less spontaneous. The organizations gradually become centralized, formalized, legitimized, and viable. The industrializing elite develops its strategies and means of controlling, limiting, or directing worker protest. Protest expressions are stripped of the inchoate and volatile character of the early stages. Sporadic riots, violence and explosive outbursts are replaced by an industrial relations system for establishing and administering the rules of the workplace.

The consensus view is rooted in some factual but anachronistic situations associated with labor strife. In this view, militance and radicalism are nurtured in the isolation of the working class from a larger and more conservative public (Lipset 1968:285). And it is in fact the case that many studies attribute labor militance to extreme working class isolation—to residence in occupational communities. Consistent with this view, Kerr and Siegel (1954) found labor strikes to be highest in industrial settings characterized by homogeneous occupations, either in isolated rural settings or in distinctive enclaves in urban areas: among miners, maritime workers or longshoremen, for example, rather than in the dispersed work settings typical of railroad or agricultural employees. Additional supporting evidence on strike behavior is suggested in the comment that community cohesion is critical if strikes are to proliferate: "unrest finds expression only if workers have some social cohesion and tradition of common action" (Knowles 1954:215; Petras and Zeitlin 1967). Two factors related to isolation are generally singled out in these studies as precipitating worker revolt: internal cohesion and external segregation. Each serves to create a "proletarian environment" stressing a distinction between "them" (the bosses) and "us" (the workers) (Lockwood 1968:101)—a symbolic schism serving to polarize communities and facilitate the eruption of labor-management conflict.

The assumptions underlying this view of worker militance are probably correct. Countless studies, for example, on social interaction have shown that social relations confined to a particular class heightens class consciousness and class awareness (Laumann 1966; Cotgrove and Vamplen 1972; Cole 1969; Berelson, Lazarsfeld, and McPhee 1954; Almy 1973; Segal and Wildstrom 1970; Linz 1969). It is also likely that segregation from larger publics may indeed strengthen militance, although not all studies have been equally supportive of this view. Recent years in American experience have seen public support for workers in the form of food and apparel boycotts. Jenkins and Perrow (1977), for example, point out that the relative success of the United Farm Workers (and the failure of the National Farm Labor Union) to secure union contracts was due in some part to public support. Similar community support was apparently effective in increasing the solidarity of the New York teachers strike in 1966 (Goldberg 1974).

But the central issue in the consensus position is whether the expansion of working class interaction to other strata indeed "integrates" this class in a way to strip its potential for labor militance. The facts on interaction are themselves clear enough: urbanization and industrialization probably have broadened the bands of social interaction beyond that normally found in segregated occupational communities (Blauner 1966). In this sense, the working class is indeed "integrated" as consensus theorists suggest. Although it may be true that at any particular point in time, class-related interaction may more likely be found in large industrial plants (Linz 1959; Lipset 1963; Nordlinger 1967; but see also Ingham 1970) and in urban areas (Ennis 1962; Cox 1970;

Hamilton 1967; Schuech 1969), the broad effects of industrialization, in part through the spread of mass culture (Wilensky
1964), has probably been to widen the bands of working class
interaction.

But does the fact of cross-strata interaction preclude the
eruption of conflict? To see conflict as erupting solely from
deprived occupational communities in backwash industries
is to identify conflict as emanating from marginal persons in
marginal economic areas. This, of course, may be the case.
But it is equally true that routes to conflict other than the
alternatives described above exist. Conflict is not marginal
to a system; it is probably part of it whenever disparities in
rewards exist.

More specifically, the error in the consensus view lies in
its preoccupation with primary-group worker interaction as
the major motivating force behind labor militance. Militance
and the call to strike are, however, in contemporary industrial
societies, more frequently framed as policy in the boardrooms
of labor executives than in spontaneous meetings among
workers. It is the access to union organizations, rather than
primary worker ties as such, which underlies militance. One
study, for example, illustrated that the association of worker
concentration in particular industries with strike behavior is
almost wholly accounted for by unionization (Lincoln 1978).
Another study suggested that the degree of unionization in
an industry is the best predictor of the number of days idle
from work stoppages as well as the number of persons involved
(Britt and Galle 1972). And still another study likewise concluded that organizational capacity is the most effective explanation of strike activity (Shorter and Tilly 1974).

What unionization likely does is alter conflict so as to
reflect greater organizational rationality rather than decrease
it altogether. In nonindustrialized societies, when organizational capacities are weak, strikes tend to be frequent and
long, and involve few workers. In industrialized societies,
strikes are fewer and shorter but large in the number of workers involved (Shorter and Tilly 1971). The distinctive indus-

trial profile of conflict is probably a tribute to the effectiveness of unions in gaining their demands, and to the consolidation of industries as well. Importantly, however, the overall "volume" of conflict (frequency times duration times number of participants) is similar in industrial and less industrial states.

Even within industrial societies, variation in organizational resources, such as strike insurance, predicts the duration of strife. As Hibbs (1976:1035) observes:

The strike profiles of the United States . . . more nearly [resemble a] trench warfare pattern. . . . Unions . . . have large dues paying memberships and as a result command the substantial strike funds necessary to engage in comparatively long trials of strength against management.

The evidence, then, does not favor the idea that unions alter labor-management relations from industry strikes to continuous bargaining procedures. To be sure, the presence of unions may alter the form of conflict; but unions do not inevitably forecast conflict's demise. Furthermore, such alterations are not even clearly foreseen in the select wealthy nations where the long duration of conflict may resemble those of less industrialized states. In such societies, the working class is very much integrated into the society, both in terms of its interaction patterns and in the general acceptance of unionization itself. Yet conflict fails to evaporate. The evidence, then, suggests a conclusion at odds with the anticipation of consensus theorists: that conflict will attain a level consistent with the resources available for its expression.

To the formal mechanisms for binding business-labor differences, consensus theorists introduce an additional factor mitigating conflict: newfound affluence for the working class. This idea is likewise ill-founded, misunderstood, and again fails to examine seriously the alternative roles labor unions may play. The reasoning supplied is simple: rather than having nothing to lose from conflict, the modern working class has everything to gain from restraint. Ross and Hartman (1960), for example, interpret the lessened use of strikes in economically advanced societies as a partial response to changes in class relations. These changes reflect fuller employment, declining class bitterness, and widespread affluence—all of which act as conservative influences on the working class. In Lipset's (1968) work, these same developments are seen as evidence of a newfound alliance between business and labor. The two are partners in economic development, with each offering the other needed services—and with each providing the other goals otherwise unobtainable.

Unfortunately, much of the literature on worker affluence has examined the social-psychological issues pertaining to worker attitudes rather than the structural issues pertaining to labor conflict. But even here the evidence favors the view of affluence as consistent with a militant labor force. The central social-psychological interpretation plays on the concept of *embourgeoisement,* that is, the gradual transition by which blue collar workers begin to earn additional income, take on the trappings of a middle class life-style, and ultimately support conservative politics. Consensus theorists have used this concept to suggest a push for labor-management tranquillity in the industrial state. As Kerr and his colleagues (1960:194–95) put it:

The significance of protest has declined primarily on account of the greater positive attractions of industrialization . . . . : clothing, transport, movies, education, health, and so on. . . . The level of protest has declined, since programs to escape, to avoid, or to overthrow the industrial order have lost any appeal. The choices for workers are seen to be more limited: how to accommodate, to participate in the industrial order, and to share in the gains. Experience has tempered visionary aspirations, sobered expectations, and thereby constrained worker protest.

The implication is clear: improved life-styles among workers strip the potential for militance.

Increased income among manual workers indeed has the effect of generating greater satisfaction (Runciman 1966:193, 207). But the concept of embourgeoisement raises the question of what such satisfaction implies: wholesale acceptance of conservative politics and a newfound trust for the economic order?

Or merely contentment from having a margin of safety against a continually threatening economic order?

The evidence on these questions is far from conclusive. Most indications, however, suggest that added income does not necessarily catapult workers into the ranks of a middle class life-style with highly conservative political orientations. The classic piece of evidence for this assertion is taken from the extensive studies of Goldthorpe and his colleagues (1968) on highly unionized, higher income blue collar workers. The research covered various skill levels of workers employed primarily in three heavy manufacturing plants in Great Britain. Workers were categorized as more or less affluent according to income, home ownership, and perceived standards of living. When workers in the more and less affluent categories were compared, voting intentions were nearly identical. In no case were the more and less affluent separated by more than five percentage points in their intentions to vote for the Labour Party. Goldthorpe and colleagues note in conclusion (1968:47):

our sample as a whole, while clearly affluent by comparison with lower white-collar and other manual workers, is strong and stable in its allegiance to Labour, as indicated both by voting history and by voting intention at the time of our interviews. So far as politics is concerned, this is the most important conclusion of our study and it provides no backing at all for those who claim that affluence is incompatible with a continuing high level of support for Labour among the industrial labour force.

Similar evidence has been cited for the United States (Hamilton 1972:207–9).

How precisely these attitudes translate into decisions to strike is a complex and more relevant question. Strike decisions are frequently made by labor executives in the central offices of the union. Furthermore, unions differ widely in their democratic procedures and hence in their capacity to reflect the attitudes of the rank and file (Edelstein and Warner 1977). Nonetheless, the available data suggest that the wealthier the workers, the more militant the union. The relationship here is probably complicated: with large strike insurance funds at their disposal, wealthy unions can afford to strike, and those who strike are likely to receive a large share of their demands. As I suggested in the preceding chapter, wealthier workers in the core industries are also the workers who are highly unionized (Bibb and Form 1977), and unionization is the best predictor of strike frequencies (Britt and Galle 1972).

These inferences are supported by a direct examination of strike propensity statistics available from the Bureau of Labor. The variation of hourly earnings among production workers in nonagricultural industries is, of course, enormous—ranging from a low in 1979 of $4.24 for workers in apparel to $9.26 for those in construction (U. S. Bureau of the Census 1980a:413–14). Perusal of labor statistics strongly suggests that the workers in the wealthier part of the income range are the more militant. For example, of the two industries just mentioned there were, in 1973, 40 work stoppages among apparel workers and 385 among construction workers. These statistics are not at odds with those reported in previous years. More specifically, the hourly wage of production workers in manufacturing correlates positively with two well-established indicators of labor conflict: $+0.35$ for work stoppages and $+0.50$ for workdays idle during the year per 1,000 workers (U. S. Bureau of the Census 1980a:413, 432). These statistics are for the 20 industries reported by the Bureau of Labor statistics for which information is available.

The relationships implied here are unquestionably more complex than is suggested in a simple equation of wealth influencing strikes (and vice versa). We do not know whether and what type of relationships might be obtained if industry unionization, for example, were taken into account. Nonetheless, these data do not square with the expectations of consensus theorists. Wealth does not detract from the potential for labor conflict. In fact, one feeds on the other. Furthermore, these conflicts appear to be more than ritual displays of strength for, as noted, they are frequent and of long duration.

There is little merit, then, to the consensus vision of declining militance among a working class integrated into the larger society. Affluence is contingent on militance rather than a consideration in its reduction. Unions, furthermore, are formal mechanisms for mobilizing worker sentiment, for providing the leadership and resources necessary for conflict. If these mechanisms are available, then it requires no great leap of imagination to predict that they will be used—in long, open, and perhaps violent conflict.

The Persistence of Conflict. The conclusions suggest that labor strife has not dramatically altered in the last decades. Where evidence to the contrary has been offered by consensus theorists, they have frequently been based on deficient interpretation or faulty data. A glaring example is in Ross and Hartman's (1960) statistics indicating a downward secular trend in workdays lost through strikes per union member from 1900 to 1956 (see also Ross 1961; Dubin 1965; Stern 1964). Clearly, if union membership increased at a quicker rate than increases in the total labor force, the following anomaly could result: workdays lost per union member could decline while workdays lost per worker could increase. As Hibbs (1976:1036) has observed, this may indeed have been the case in the era of intensive union mobilization from the beginning of the twentieth century to the mid-1950s.

Certainly, in the last quarter of a century or so in the United States, there are few indications that the use of the strike has subsided. For example, with respect to workdays idle per striker involved, no consistent declining trend is exhibited: from 16.1 days in 1950, down to 10.7 in 1955, up again to 20.1 in 1970, down to 12.4 in 1973 and up again to 22.8 in 1978. Likewise with respect to the percentage of workers involved in strikes as a function of the total labor force: erratic trends varying from 5.1 percent in 1950 to 2.5 percent in 1965, up to 4.7 in 1970 and down to 1.9 in 1978. In fact, the only time series data suggestive of a trend at all indicate increases rather than declines: the average duration (in calendar days) of strikes was 18 to 19 days in the 1950s, stabilized in the low to mid-twenties from 1960 to 1973 and continued to rise after that to a high of 33 days in 1978. With respect to the actual number of work stoppages: 4,800 in 1950 to a low of 3,300 in 1960, after which the number of stoppages fluctuated in the 5,000s throughout the 1960s up through much of the seventies; in 1974 it reached a high of 6,000 and plummeted to 4,200 in 1978 (U. S. Bureau of the Census 1975b:373, 1980a:431).

Findings similar to these are reported on a broader scale for ten major industrialized nations including the United States, Canada, Japan, and the countries comprising much of the European economic community. The data, in the form of workdays lost per thousand wage and salary workers, likewise cover the period from 1950 to 1970 and show few overall declines in strikes (Hibbs 1976:1036–37):

It is apparent . . . that despite the substantial growth of postindustrial, service oriented sectors of the economy in all of these nations, and notwithstanding the supposed decline of ideology and *embourgeoisement* of the working class, there has been no "withering away" of the strike in the postwar period. The strike volumes of most of the nations . . . simply do not exhibit any pronounced downward trend. Indeed, *long run* trend analyses reveal that substantial declines in aggregate strike activity are found only in the smaller democracies of northern Europe and Scandanavia. The evolution of postindustrial social structure, then, does not seem to have resolved the grievances or reduced the militancy of wage labor.

These data are consistent with the more sweeping generalization that affluence in highly industrialized societies does little to reduce conflict. If comparisons are drawn only between industrialized and nonindustrialized nations, then it is likely true that industrialized nations do have less conflict (Trieman 1970:226–27). This has been shown with respect to political instability (Bwy 1971:224–25; Feierabend and Feierabend 1971), civil strife (Gurr 1971:224–25), and a traditional (albeit questionable) indicator of conflict—Communist Party membership (Benjamin and Kautsky 1968).

If attention, however, is confined to moderately and highly developed nations, then the data are more uniformly consistent with the labor strike data previously reported. Dogan (1960), for example, finds no relationship between Communist Party support and income among the states of Western Europe. Marsh and Parish (1965) similarly show a weak association between economic development and Communist votes and almost no association at all between income inequality and Communist votes. Korpi (1971) has speculated that Communist Party support may have more to do with the hardships provoked by the economy than with per capita income as such. In his own research, Communist support was more strongly related to the percentage of a nation's labor force in agriculture (a possible indicator of economic duress) than to income as such.

Nor has the hypothesis linking affluence to class action fared better in analyses across time. Snyder and Tilly (1972), for example, in research on collective violence in France from 1830 to 1960—a period representing a transition from a basically agricultural economy to a full-scale industrial economy—found violence to be more closely correlated with governmental repression than with indications of economic hardship. In a similar vein, Rose and Unwin (1969) report no recent trend toward a reduction in support for working class parties in Western Europe, in spite of a general swell in prosperity. Hamilton (1967) has similarly noted no decline in radical politics corresponding with the increase in affluence in post–World War II France.

In brief, the evidence on the wider scale of conflict generally or labor strife particularly strongly suggests that the general volume of conflict does not decline as the affluence of industrial societies increases. This is consistent with the theme I have already expounded. Societies such as the United States are structured to permit and facilitate the growth and development of the capitalist enterprise. The *Klasse an sich* that Marx observed more than a century ago is omnipresent. This structure favors the use of surplus funds for capital growth rather than for wages and equality. It likewise favors the persistence of conflict, particularly in highly industrialized societies where worker mobilization is extensive and sophisticated mechanisms for monitoring economies are widespread. It is in this sense that I reject as naive the consensus theorist's view of industrial harmony. Yet, at the same time it is unclear whether rejecting the consensus position of necessity lends credence to the Marxist position.

Labor Conflict and Change: Summary Judgements. The persistence of labor conflict has obvious relevance to Marxism and to conflict theory generally. Marx saw labor conflict as a first, albeit unsuccessful step in the development of a class-conscious working force. More recent theorists (Birnbaum 1969) see militance as a new phase in class development, where specific unions become the arm of the working class. Other contemporary Marxists have abandoned the prospect of mobilizing the impoverished and look to unions as a major revolutionary force in contemporary society (Gorz 1971). Still others hold out hope that an increase in the complexity of labor conflict will have "domino effects . . . [which] might eventually bring industrial politics into the larger political arenas" (Goldman and Van Houten 1977:111). The target in these comments is not merely the traditional proponents of the industrial harmony theme but also the less traditional proponents who see contemporary labor conflict as institutionalized and lacking in ideology.

Whatever the merit of these positions, they do not reach the heart of the matter, with respect either to Marxism or to conflict-consensus generally. After all, from the point of view of understanding stratification structures, conflict by itself only reflects tension points in social arrangements. Conflict reveals malaise and the capacity for its expression. But the promise of conflict (and the Marxist interpretation of it) holds something else, whether or not conflict indeed alters anything—that is, whether it portends actual change in the social structure. I distinguish here between "conflict," sanctions to condition the behavior and activities of opponents; and "change," alterations in the structure of rights and obligations between groups. It may be true that the utility of conflict analysis lies in reflecting the configuration of the class structure and the opposition it breeds. But conflict analysis or Marxism cannot stop there: are businesses likely to share their affluence? Is labor's share increased? Is the class structure in fact altered? Because of its obvious relevance to the institutional division of economic surplus, the referent here is exclusively business-labor shares.

My broader contention is that labor conflict operates within the constraints of the decision-making principles of efficiency and equality. That is, worker demands for higher wages are effective only insofar as they protect the profitability of corporate firms and their long-range plans for growth and development—plans themselves designed to maximize profits by minimizing risks. This can be seen from a variety of perspectives. The most simple view is in terms of the dual loyalty of workers. This irony, from a Marxist perspective, is poignantly captured in Tannenbaum and Kahn's (1958) observations regarding union members who see their destiny tied not merely to the union but to the success of the corporate enterprise as well (see also Wedderburn and Crompton 1972).

The structural analogue of the dual loyalty syndrome is cemented in sectorial alliances—alliances given more play in the popular press than in the sociological literature. These alliances take the form of labor and business marching in unison to Capitol Hill to lobby for protective legislation to benefit the industry as a whole. Business does so under the guise of maintaining employment opportunities; labor, under the guise of maintaining the viability of industry. But there is little question what constitutes the interests of each. Indeed these interests are reminiscent of Marcuse's (1964) comments on the one-dimensional society: given the Marxian conception of money exchange as the critical bond in capitalist society, the interests of potentially antagonistic groups are blurred in the pursuit of economic advantage.

The frequent liaisons between business and labor are not to deny labor's offensive stand with regard to wage increases or business' unwillingness to readily grant such increases. The rule of thumb is this: as wages fall relative to standards of living, the call to strike occurs. This makes a good deal of sense and indeed has been supported in a variety of studies: as in Snyder's (1975) finding that post–World War II strikes in the United States can be predicted most potently by declining wages relative to aspirations; or as in Hibbs' (1976) more general finding that wage expectations considered over time predict strikes in a variety of industrialized nations, the United States included.

The critical issue is whether such strikes portend changes in the relative shares of business and labor. Or, to put the matter differently: does conflict jeopardize profits? The answer to this, while not exact, is likely no. To understand this suggestion, it is necessary to understand the nature and timing of strikes, which reflect, in my view, labor's militant rather than radical intent. A classic study by Albert Rees (1952) pointed to a significant association between strike activity and prosperity, indicating that strikes increased under prosperity. Similar findings were reported for more recent times for the United States (O'Brien 1965; Weintraub 1966; Snyder 1975), Canada (Walsh 1975), and a sample of other industrialized nations (Hibbs 1976).

In terms of the short-range goal of securing wage hikes, strikes in prosperous times make sense. Businesses are vulnerable in periods of prosperity for the simple reason that inventories are usually low when demand is high. Other advantages also accrue at such times: prosperity brings overtime after strikes, and this on top of good strike insurance means that labor will not hurt if the threat to strike is carried out. Furthermore, from business' vantage point demand is high, sales brisk, and wage increases can easily be absorbed into high profit margins or otherwise be passed on to consumers. Yet, it is the timing of the strike that is important from our view: geared to extract wages without disturbing profits. In essence, the timing reveals how the efficiency-equality principle operates as a means of simultaneously seeking wage demands and staying within the confines of the profit margins business identifies as necessary.

This much is obvious, but must be said: strikes during prosperity make sense only as a means of successfully extracting wage hikes. They make no sense in terms of radically altering the structure of capitalism—which might best be accomplished in depression economies when businesses are vulnerable. This latter possibility has been endlessly noted in Marxist visions of stimulating crisis in the capitalist order. The Marxist idea is simply to cut into the underbelly of capitalism by aggravating its precarious financial state. Presumably, touching nerve centers will cause the collapse of capitalism, and the road to radical change will be cleared. Yet the evidence on strikes in prosperity rather than austerity suggests this Marxist vision to be little more than faint hope. The fact that labor is more or less inert during depression reveals its motivation pure and simple: to secure high wages within the confines of a prosperous profit ledger.

In this sense, the conflict in labor strife is not indicative of change in the relative shares between labor and business. And in fact labor economists have found little evidence to suggest that unions are a major factor in reducing inequality. One study, for example, examined the growth in union membership and changes in labor's share of wealth and found no stable relationship between the two variables (Fleischer 1970). Another study similarly observed little association between historic growth spurts in union membership and labor's share of wealth (Phelps Brown 1968). The conclusion suggested is that inroads into business profits in the United States have yet to be made by unions. This is consistent with Rees's (1973:220) summary observation on existing evidence that "no union influence on labor's share can be detected."

What, then, of the militance of labor? It is true, as I previously contended, that union militance persists. All is not reduced to bureaucratic details of collective bargaining. At the same time, this militance is not of the kind traditional

Marxist theorists envisioned. It is a demand for high wages, to be sure, but in the context of the surplus funds deemed necessary for the capitalist system. As for consensus theorists, they also may have been misguided in their estimate of declining militance in the industrial state. But their observations on the absence of "visionary aspirations" is, for the moment, right on target. Hence conflict—but conflict without change.

Business Motivation and Government Response: Future Trends. The logic behind equality-efficiency decisions is a buffer against radical action. Labor allows business to accrue capital funds when the economy is in a downswing; when boom cycles appear, labor strikes to recoup past losses. And these gains are granted by corporations capable of otherwise sustaining stability in profits over costs. But whether these trends can continue without rupture is anyone's guess. For the high and persistent rate of inflation may shatter the convenient arrangement of business and industry in a way so as to completely transform the politics of the future. Unfortunately, so short is America's experience with spiraling inflationary cycles that how (and whether) politics will be transformed is at the moment simply unknown.

One thing is clear: the necessity of dispensing with shibboleths in understanding what is at stake in the business community. Any notion of business-labor alliances, or of business ever being willing to accommodate labor demands, is naive and simply will not do. Even so conservative a spokesman as James Schlesinger (*Minneapolis Tribune* 1977:1) recognized that "Greed is the virtue that drives the free enterprise system, the desire to acquire substantial profits. It is profits which are at issue—and there is every reason to believe business will be relentless in their pursuit."

Nor will estimates of "business security" be any more useful for understanding corporate motivation. Commentators such as Galbraith (1977) are likely correct that subsidies, government support, and government contracts are effective hedges against bankruptcy for large corporate conglomerates. But the issue here is not bankruptcy as much as profit certainty in what is seen as a continually threatening environment, with respect to nationalization abroad, government regulation in the domestic market, foreign competition, technological innovations elsewhere, war—or any other factors wrapped in the perspective of risk and of an "unhealthy business climate." That is, business is never assured of the absence of risk. Any challenge to stable costs, such as wage hikes, is met with skepticism and minimized.

Perhaps the most serious issue pertaining to contemporary business interests—and the symbiotic alliance of business and labor—is the advent of double-digit inflation. The issue is not whether this alliance will persist under inflation but rather whether the alliance will sustain inflation. The symbiotic ties between business and labor are, after all, part of what inflation is about.

In focusing on this alliance, I depart from the usual economic interpretation of inflation. The traditional wisdom points to a surfeit of dollars: excessive demand chases short supply, thus driving up the price of goods and services. This view is part of the politically popular recommendation that inflation be thwarted by "cooling off" the economy. Interest rates are raised to reduce business investment, to cut back production so as to decrease employment, consumer spending, and demand.

The evidence in support of the traditional view is not entirely clear. But what does exist does not overwhelmingly favor this position. First, inflation spirals may persist in recessions. High unemployment and rising prices apparently are not incompatible, as was dramatically shown in the recession of 1974. Second, there has been no recent, widespread shortage of consumer goods as suggested by the position on excessive demand. The only case to the contrary concerns fuel and the unquestionable impact it exerted on inflation. But in some cases that shortage may be more contrived than actual. Furthermore, when the entire range of goods and services is examined, there has been no discernible drop in supply.

My speculation is that inflation is more closely tied into the wage-price cycle of core industries than traditional economists are willing to admit. The connection follows from my assumptions that wealth and profits are scarce, valued, and uncertain. If these assumptions are valid, then both business and labor should be continually engaged in tactics to offset risk against future contingencies. This means persistent pressure for higher wages and profits. When productivity is high, business offsets wage demands by drawing on surplus sales. But when this is not the case, as is currently the situation, costs are increasingly passed on to consumers (Hong 1978; Wachtel and Adelsheim 1977). These costs, in turn, are benchmarks for further wage demands—thus the familiar wage-price cycle.

This reasoning suggests that inflation (and much else) can be traced to the ancient issue as to who gets what. In the absence of explicit debate and policies, the issue is unlikely to be resolved soon. This means that inflation may well become a way of life in the United States in the same way it has in many nations throughout the world, particularly in South America. My speculation is that at varying times, administrations will tinker with this cycle through wage-price policies. As yet, however, few have had the confidence to do so in a forceful manner. Yet one thing is clear: while the free market is usually seen as a force resolving economic problems, the opposite effect may be occurring with respect to inflation. The long-range implications spell a persistent source of inequality with core industries and core workers on top.

Democratic Government

Governments are important considerations in both the conflict and consensus perspectives. In the consensus view, the chief factors pertain to democracy and representation, which provide through the franchise a vehicle for extending the economic interests of the working class. In the conflict view, democracies are little more than a legitimized battlefield for business domination. To paraphrase Marx's acid observation: governments are the executive arm of the bourgeoisie.

These views are more broadly tied into a diversity of opinions crossing the political spectrum with liberals seeing big business influence behind every tree and conservatives scorning huge welfare expenditures proposed by urban legislators. Furthermore, such views have spawned a variety of theoretical positions dominating contemporary sociological thought on government activities: Lenski's (1966) conception of the redistributive role of government; Mills's (1956) conception of the power elite; as well as a host of other positions surrounding the conventional phrasing of elitist vs. pluralist positions (Kornhauser 1966). These views have emerged in a voluminous literature on who governments "really" represent—business or a broader diversity of interests. Yet, there has been no real resolution of this issue.

Part of the reason for the lack of resolution may lie in the complexity and ambiguity of the data, variously supporting both the elitist and the pluralist position. Lieberson (1971) has judiciously drawn a parallel between this debate and the issue of hereditary and environmental influence on socialization. His position, which I will discuss further in this section, attempts to outline the conditions under which pluralistic or elite interests dominate an issue. The position I will advance takes a slightly different point of departure. I will argue that both pluralist and elitist positions have a limited view of influence in the public sector, and in fact omit a major actor: the government itself. This essentially Weberian perspective, while given nodding acceptance in a variety of writings in the area, needs further consideration as a means of resolving the pluralist-elitist debate.

The resolution of the pluralist-elitist debate is necessary

for my argument. In the previous chapter I portrayed considerable stability in institutional inequality. The question I raise here pertains to the roots of the status quo. Is it a simple function of a stalemate among pluralistic interests, or of the ineffectiveness of elites in manipulating a more favorable balance? While both may be possibilities, my position stresses the government as an active and willing partner in maintaining the status quo. There is decided usefulness in seeing the government as a self-interested party in its own activities. For it allows these activities to be seen not as simple responses to domestic interests but more broadly as a function of a range of concerns tied into international politics and the nationalist thrust for world domination. More than simple representatives of business elites or pluralistic mosaics, governments are complex mechanisms for continually monitoring environments: giving emphasis and funding to the economic enterprise in periods of production slack and recession; providing insurance and welfare nets to sustain living standards, however minimal, for the deprived—but always with an eye toward (and within the constraints set by) America's position as a world power.

Few would deny the powerful role of the government with law, prestige, and vast financial resources at its disposal. Whether (and for what reasons) it assumes a role in furthering equality or efficiency is central to my concern with inequality and conflict. For this reason I turn first to a more detailed review of the adequacies and inadequacies of the consensus and conflict positions on government, and then to a consideration of the Weberian position previously alluded to. My argument is that the United States generally favors efficiency norms, not necessarily catering to a business elite as much as to its own set of nationalistic concerns; given these concerns, and the constraints placed on them, there is only remote possibility that it will alter the scales favoring business norms, affect further equality, and thereby shift the existing status quo.

Consensus Theory: The Democratic Hope. The consensus position turns on the issue of citizenship in the industrial state. In Marshall's (1965) view, citizenship provides three principal kinds of rights to individuals: legal, political, and social. Political and legal rights extend avenues of expression through the courts and parliamentary system. The hope is that conflict would be politicized and consequently expressed in the halls of parliament. As for social rights, they presumably extend a life free from economic hardship and insecurity. These rights presume a sequence of activities: that workers put pressure on governments to act in their behalf, and that governments in turn actively and successfully intervene in the economic process to redistribute income more equitably.

This view is based on a more or less pluralistic understanding of government, in which the public sector is responsive to the needs and interests it represents (Dahl 1967; Rose 1967). In tying political to social rights, the view assumes commitment by the electorate to greater equality as well as the existence of a governmental organization to reflect and carry out this commitment. Whether such optimistic assumptions are justified is not clear from the research literature. Existing studies are simply ambiguous as to the precise role— if any—democratic governments play in assuring equality (Cutright 1967; Jackman 1974; Ward 1978). The ambiguity suggests that the pluralistic hope of a committed electorate and a responsive government might itself be based on faulty understandings and assumptions. I have little doubt that this is in fact the case, and that consensus theorists have bought a version of democracy based more on textbook ideals than on sociological understanding.

A first and perhaps most implausible assumption drawn by consensus theorists pertains to commitment to equalitarian programs. Simply put: does the electorate want greater equality? In spite of much rhetoric to the contrary, there simply is no groundswell of evidence to suggest that inroads in inequality are deemed desirable. In this, I am in agreement with Tilton's (1974:570–71) comment that:

The most essential condition for radical reforms . . . the existence of a powerful popular movement—is nowhere in sight, nor does it appear likely to develop. Without this essential prerequisite the United States will not modernize in the direction of a more decent society. . . .

The evidence for this conclusion is well known and generally consistent with observations on the absence of equalitarian ideology among the American working class. On even so neutral an item as voting for slightly more liberal candidates, blue collar workers are hardly distinguishable from their white collar counterparts. No more than 15 to 20 percentage points traditionally separate manual from upper strata occupational groups in their choice of candidates (Cantor 1975). This reflects not so much the erosion of liberal values under affluence (Guest 1974) as the absence in the working class of significant commitments to any ideology resembling equality. One exhaustive review of the literature concluded that the ideological patterns in the working class were "positively schizophrenic, with a large proportion of the electorate operationally liberal but ideologically conservative" (Mann 1970:432). Many want collective bargaining but reject equality. Others see specific management practices as contrary to worker interest but conceive of management-labor relations as harmonious. Still others see inequality as just— you get what you work for (Rainwater 1974).

These points are consistent with my view that mobility politics and mobility concerns dominate the American electorate. The consensus position that democratic government allows the translation of working class interests into programs pertaining to equality are illusory. The electorate, in fact, plays no such simple role. Given the opportunities previously noted in regard to income mobility, radical (or even less radical) economic solutions have never been a chief concern of the American electorate. This is surely one of the reasons why the United States is among the more unequal in its income of nearly all industrialized nations (Lydall 1968), and why in addition it lacks elementary programs related to equality:

public control over investment, over property ownership, and over income distribution.

The problem of translating working class economic interests into public law is further compounded by the uniqueness of the American party structure. Consensus theory assumes a governmental apparatus responsive to conflicting political demands. For change to occur, such responsiveness is mandatory (Tilton 1974). Yet it is a commonplace observation that the American political structure is without a party dedicated to working class interests. Rose and Unwin's (1969) review of the political structure in the industrialized West noted the presence of class-based parties in 15 of 17 nations. The two exceptions were Ireland and the United States. The absence of such a structure may reflect the absence of a clearcut working class movement—or merely the unique historical circumstances surrounding the development of the party system during the years of the Civil War (Lipset and Rokkan 1967).

Whatever the reasons for this absence, the American political structure is without an important mechanism for mobilizing worker sentiment and influencing political behavior. One study of Norway and the United States, for example, noted higher political activism in Norway in spite of a more rural context—an activism the authors attribute to the clarity of socialism as a divisive issue in Norway's party structure (Rokkan and Campbell 1960). If parties themselves divide on and clarify economically based political issues, this will draw out or at least offer the opportunity for schisms between rich and poor to gain expression. It is little wonder, then, that class-based political voting in the United States, in contrast with England or Germany, for example, is not high (Janowitz and Segal 1967; Alford 1963; Abramson 1975); in spite of a rough linkage between the rich and the Republicans or the poor and the Democrats, there is simply no major party identified with economic class issues as such.

The absence of a political structure conforming to clear economic interests minimizes the opportunity to mobilize these interests and translate them into the political arena.

But even were this possible, there is some question as to whether such interests would exert decisive influence on political elites. The classical understanding is that electorates with distinct interests seek out and vote for representatives with similar interests who in turn represent their constituent's views in government. In practice, as Schumpeter (1962) has noted, the causal connections are often the other way around: voters seek representatives on such nonrational bases as their symbolic themes or personalities. The representatives then define the issues and in turn influence and mold the opinions of the electorate. It is thus the governmental elite who are the linchpins in the political processes of democracy.

It is quite understandable, therefore, that discrepancies may appear between the opinions of representatives and their constituents. This has been shown in a number of studies which have all matched either the opinions or the actual voting records of elected officials with surveys of the opinions of their constituents. One study of over 100 congressional districts showed that officials poorly estimate their own electorate's opinions in areas pertaining to social welfare and foreign involvement; the only area with more accurate perceptions pertained to civil rights (Miller and Stokes 1963)—but even here the overlap in opinions between constituencies and elected officials was minimal (see also Segal and Smith 1970).

These discrepancies raise a broader issue with respect to the consensus perspective and its pluralistic assumptions: what indeed are legislators reacting to? It is clearly too simple to think they are just fleeing off on their own, voting according to personal whim and fancy (Kingdom 1967; Cnudde and McCrone 1966; Sullivan 1972). More likely than not, they are engaged in setting priorities in terms of what highly organized interests see as vital in their district, and trading off votes on issues that are non-vital and of low priority. Lieberson (1971) has correctly noted that on issues of little concern to a broad range of interests legislation can easily be passed as votes are bartered and negotiated. On issues of great concern, alternatively, matters may become more difficult. Here, if legislation is to be passed, compromise may have to be effected.

And if it is, the result may be legislation sufficiently watered down to satisfy everyone and offend no one. Hence the art of compromise becomes tantamount to the maintenance of the status quo. And the pluralistic model emerges as a model of blocked change. What, then, of the consensus view that governments champion the cause of the working class through redistributive efforts?

This portrait may be overly pessimistic and somewhat overdrawn. Obviously, legislation of an equalitarian nature does get passed—and this in spite of influential interest groups. Yet our review of consensus theory suggests two possible characteristics of the legislative process which weakens even enacted legislation: on issues easily passed into law, there is minimal commitment; on vital issues there is controversy and opposition. This issue takes on significance in what may be one of the more important but least explored links in the consensus position on democratic government: the capacity to translate legislation into concrete change.

The central problem is that significant inroads into inequality will probably fly in the face of established interests. This is not a situation especially conducive to following up on legislation and seeing that its desired effects are indeed realized. Furthermore, much legislation concerning equality does not have a politically active constituency. An interesting insight into this difficulty is given in Edelman's (1967) discussion on the symbolic nature of legislation. Laws, from Edelman's perspective, are gestures or tokens of awareness that particular interest groups exist, and are deserving of notice and protection. Minority groups lobby for civil rights; labor groups for minimum wage laws; poverty groups for welfare legislation. Each group deems the passage of particular legislation necessary. But beyond the substantive content of law is the symbolic gesture implied in passage which may, Edelman reasons, merely appease the interests in question. The risk run is that if these interests (and the politicians concerned) see the passage of legislation as more important than its enforcement, the legislation will have only symbolic consequences. For everywhere, dissension exists and means to subvert or ignore legislation may be found. If this is the case, the status quo prior to legislation will be maintained. And it will be maintained, Edelman argues, unless the pressure group lobbying for the legislation has an organization sufficient to monitor legislative effects and feed them back to the courts or legislative bodies. Suffice it to say, few groups maintain such organizational capacities.

Edelman's comments raise questions beyond the obvious issue of the capacity of corporate wealth to seek means of altering the aims of legislation. First, do government agencies possess the apparatus for monitoring social change? That is, is there a system of accountability to legislative standards? Second, if accountability were high, would there be at the same time sufficient knowledge to effect social change—particularly with respect to inequality? The issue here is not a simple matter of taking money from corporate coffers or the wealthy and distributing it to the poor. What system of incentives, if any, is necessary for production and economic growth? Is economic growth necessary for full employment and reasonable wages—and if so, at what rate? How can the excessive sums targeted for national defense, sums which strip the national government's financial flexibility to deal with issues of welfare, be dislodged at minimal cost to workers in military-related industries? Beyond any attempt to alter structures, one additional point must be kept in mind: the objects of change are not themselves static. Attempts to decrease inequality in some spheres may merely transfer the roots of inequality to new contexts.

Business-Government Alliances. The view of government championing the equalitarian causes of the working class is open to question on several grounds: the commitment of the electorate, organizational responsiveness, and the capacity to affect change. Nor is labor likely to be more effective in this regard: on the one hand striking for increased benefits and on the other aligning themselves with the long-range interests of the business community. Against this backdrop, social scientists have considered alternative views of government, not as a champion of the working class but an arm of business and wealth.

In this and the following sections I will consider this latter view in detail. I have previously described American society as structured according to the class interests of business. At this time, I attempt to give more precise meaning to this concept by distinguishing between a society structured *for* business interests and a society structured *by* business interests. My contention is that while the former distinction may hold, the latter need not. Although some may argue that this is distinction without a difference, I will attempt to show how this distinction points to powerful influences on governments over and above business as such. I turn first to the issue of a business-government alliance raised in the Marxist tradition. My overall conclusions suggest that while the Marxist view is more realistic than the consensus view, it too fails to account for certain long-range trends in inequality.

Marxism holds that social, cultural, and political life are culminations of the inequalities conditioned by the means of production. From this view, governments may be considered as mere extensions of capitalist interests. Governmental policy grows out of such interests and ultimately is designed to nurture and protect them (Giddens 1976a:124–25):

> The Marxian conception treats the state essentially as an 'expression' of the class relationships in the market. . . . Marx's treatment of the state is very much steeped in that tradition of nineteenth-century social thought . . . which regards the state as subordinate to society, and which consequently tends to consider the former as capable of being 'reduced' to its conditions of dependence upon the latter—in Marx's case, to class relationships. This is why there is in Marx no recognition of the possible existence of the state as an independent force. . . .

While the identity between government and business interests has not been accepted in its entirety, there have been a variety of attempts to work out the influence of business on government. The most important of these is contained in Mills' (1956) conception of a power elite. A power elite is an amalgam of class-related elites with elites in politics and the military. Mills' argument focuses on the coincidence of interest among elites in government, business, and the military—an identity which virtually forges the elite into a more or less monolithic group with broad agreement on major principles. In addition, he discusses the interchange of personnel between major institutions. Others have likewise documented patterns of informal interaction binding an elite together (Domhoff 1967).

On a broad and most general level there are obvious coincidences of interest between business and government. Business demands highly qualified technical personnel, and mass education is virtually guaranteed, at little or no direct cost to the student. Likewise, high levels of employment, as well as a variety of subsidies to the poor, provide the consumer environment necessary for sustained business growth.

But beyond such obvious and general coincidences of interest, there is simply an overwhelming array of evidence to favor the view of a government tipped toward business prerogatives. I spelled many of these out in chapter 2 with respect to inordinate economic concentration in commerce, industry, and finance, as well as monolithic corporate control manipulated through the intricacies of interlocking directorates.

Against this backdrop of inequality and massive economic concentration, elite theorists have considered what appears to be a reasonable conclusion: how can so lush and flourishing an environment for inequality and concentration be created without active government support? That government support is present is true, in my view, without question. But the additional inference—present in Marx, latent in Mills—that business controls government is debatable.

If business indeed controlled government, one might question why a virtual status quo has been effected on certain key dimensions of inequality over the last century of American experience. Unless one ascribes to elites some basis for satiating demands, the status quo is hardly suggestive of business omnipotence. Lenski (1966), for one, has indeed argued for the principle of the satiation of elite demands in industrialized nations. As previously noted, however, at least with respect to the corporate structure there is no simple basis for satiation. Profits, economic expansion, new markets for alternative sources of revenue—the search is boundless. Each aspect is seen as a hedge against an uncertain future. In a society where wealth is idolized, it would be surprising indeed to see corporations restraining their eternal quest. As for the wealthy generally, the evidence here is more ambiguous, but from the perspective of business influence on government less important as well.

A second difficulty in the Marxian view and in Mills's writings as well is that they attribute an identity of interest to economic elites. Elites, of course, do share certain common desires: supportive governments, favorable tax breaks, a public with sufficient purchasing power. But beyond these generalities, is there a unified economic elite? And if there is not, can we properly speak about business influence on government—as if business were a unitary actor?

There are probably decided schisms within the economic elites, each seeking its own advantage even at the cost (if necessary) of the others. Mining interests are not necessarily the same as manufacturing interests. Nor are nuclear interests identical to interests in electronics. Many writers of Marxist and non-Marxist persuasion have generally rejected the view of a monolithic elite controlling government policy (see Gold, Lo, and Wright 1975a, 1975b). I am in agreement here with Giddens' (1976b:171) observation that:

Mills' *The Power Elite* . . . greatly exaggerates the degree of harmony within the 'higher circles' of the American society in general, and within the economic elite in particular. Struggles and clashes between different factions are the rule rather than the exception in the higher echelons of the economic order; nothing is more out of accord with reality than to present a 'conspiracy' picture of an unbroken cooperative consensus (as critics of Western society, like Mills, have tended to do . . .)

In fact, statistics on large corporations reflect consider-able fluidity in the composition of the top group—suggesting something less than omnipotence in business control over gov-ernment decisions. Were business control over politics sub-stantial, one might expect more stability in corporate struc-tures. But this is not the case. In their analysis of business liaisons with the military, Pilisuk and Hayden (1965) note substantial turnover in top defense contractors. Of the 100 top contractors in 1940, for example, only 18 remained on the list two decades later. Government support for these corpo-rations is simply pulled out in response to changing techno-logical demands. As the authors note (ibid.:87–88):

the constant pattern in American society is the rise and fall of temporarily-irresponsible groups. By temporary we mean that, out-side of the largest industrial conglomerates, the groups which wield significant power to influence policy decisions are not guaranteed stability.

Less dramatic but still substantial turnover is likewise indicated for manufacturing corporations generally. For ex-ample, of the 50 largest corporations in 1947, 24 were in these ranks in 1977, 13 had fallen by 1977 into the 51–100 largest corporations, 5 others to the 101–200 category and the re-maining 18 to below the 201 ranking (U. S. Bureau of the Census 1981b:8). This is considerable turnover for only a twenty-five year period. It may in part reflect shifting con-sumer tastes and technological demands. Yet whatever the cause, the turnover must be evaluated against the standards implied in the thesis of monolithic business influence over government. If indeed business influence on governmental decisions were substantial, then government policy should be able to protect the interests of large-scale industrial enter-prises fully over less than a generation.

This heterogeneity of interests leads to another consid-eration concerning a government-business alliance—one dis-cussed previously. That is whether the organization of the Congress permits any group to ram through legislation im-pinging on the vital interests of others. To be sure, there are issues on which business may stand united, as, for example, general taxation or tariff policies. Likewise, there are others on which a particular industry may literally have the nation over a barrel, as evidenced by write-offs for exploration into new sources of fuel. Nonetheless, the checks and balances implied in the pluralistic conception may thwart not only welfare legislation but pro-business legislation as well. As Lieberson (1971:578) has aptly noted: "legislation beneficial to a specific interest must not at the same time create too great a loss for the majority of other interests." "Otherwise," Lieberson adds, "a concerted effort to combat the legislation will occur."

In general the evidence on these three issues—stability in inequality, heterogeneity of interests, the partially pluralistic organization of Congress—while by no means definitive, does not overwhelmingly support massive business control over political decisions. Yet at the same time, on balance, the economic environment has been and remains favorable to business growth and development.

One possible resolution of the paradox, and one alternative to consensus and Marxist positions, is to see the role of the government itself as more active and independent. Perhaps governments are not influenced by capitalist interests so much as they pursue pro-capitalist policies in their own interests, on their own behalf. That is, governments may conceivably be more than passive recipients of outside pressures. They may be active innovators in pro-business, pro-capitalist legislation. This alternative may explain the instability observed with respect to industrial corporations generally and defense contractors specifically. Pro-business policies may be enacted by varying administrations. But since such policies are not the result of particular business interests, no one business firm necessarily profits, although business in general does well. These ideas, of course, relate back to the conceptions previously discussed: of the status quo and of efficiency and equality as alternate bases for government decisions. I should add that over the past decade various theorists have introduced similar conceptions into the stream of contemporary Marxism, as in Poulantzas' (1973) discussion of the relative autonomy of the state or Offe's conception of governments selecting out pro-capitalist policy alternatives (Gold, Lo, and Wright 1975b).

Efficiency, Equality, and Government Choice. That governments assume interests of their own is a Weberian notion frequently suggested as an alternative to Marxist precepts. Bendix (1974:155), for example, has commented that governmental officials

can interpose their judgment between any decision and its execution. Their ability to do so is a major organizational reason for the decision making capacity of government, even when the pressure of interest groups is great. Actions of government have a momentum of their own. They are more than mere enlargements of tendencies already existing in the society.

By interpreting government as a straightforward extension of class interests, Marxism locks together two variable terms: the interests of classes and the interests of governments. The Weberian perspective is an alternative to this alleged identity of interests.

Whether governments will in fact act independently depends on the development of separate concerns in addition to those in the private sector. Social scientists have not studied this issue at great length, but it seems that separate government interests lie in two related areas. The first of these is the "health of the economy," which means business investment in modernizing plants, in lively consumer demand, in economic growth, and in rising productivity. The assumption here is that a healthy economy lends a firm base for attacking a myriad of other problems, from education to unemployment to revitalizing decay in urban centers. The second lies in preserving and enhancing the United States' role as a leading contender for world power. This interest is in no small part an outcome of the cold war mentality, which imbues the quest for power with a sense of urgency and self-preservation. World power rests not on symbolic gesture or ideological commitment alone. Since the world system is itself a stratified order (Wallerstein 1974), America's competition for ascendance rests on the traditional bases for advanced status: wealth, in the form of economic domination, and power, in the form of military might. These, in turn, require that the economic machine be well tuned—a nationalistic concern which cuts across party alliances. These areas of interest, I should add, are not necessarily at odds with similar interests held in the business community. Yet two points must be noted: that government interests are not necessarily intertwined with the long-range interests of any particular sector of the economy; that such interests flourish not because of capitalism as such but because of the linkage between international power and economic development—a point I will turn to in the final section of this chapter.

As a consequence of this presumed linkage, key issues in American society come to be defined around the efficiency of the marketplace. The nation's stature, its health and viability are seen in large part in marketplace terms. This perspective is not, in my view, the work of a small economic elite pressing governmental agents into certain perspectives. Rather such perspectives are inherent in the government's adopted role in a capitalist system. In this role, the government seeks to mold and stimulate the business enterprise with the resources at its disposal (Okun 1975:32):

the functioning—indeed, the very life—of the market depends on the coercive power of political institutions. The state uses these powers to establish and ensure rights in the marketplace, directly supply some essential services, and indirectly generate the environment of trust, understanding, and security that is vital to the daily conduct of business.

This attitude is translated into the myriad facilities at the government's disposal: from tax breaks to outright subsidies. If the economy is "sluggish," credit policies are eased by the Federal Reserve Board to stimulate capital investment, tax breaks are given to ease depreciation write-offs, government contracts are awarded to stimulate growth in key economic sectors. Federal agencies continually monitor critical economic indicators to suggest what ought to be pruned here or nurtured there.

If there is any consensus, then, which pervades American society, its core is a healthy economy mirrored in a proper climate for business growth. If this is a contention of consensus theorists, then I am in agreement with that segment of their position. Commitment to the long-range health of the economy does not mean that the impoverished necessarily suffer as a consequence—but it does mean that the lion's share of attention goes toward priority business goals. Obviously, legislation benefiting the lower strata, of the sort discussed in chapter 2, does get passed. My point here is that welfare legislation represents a variable commitment that is low priority and consequently contingent on economic circumstances. If, for example, inflation is unduly high, and dwindling purchasing power reduces consumer demand and business investments, then unemployment and welfare spending simply suffer to keep inflation in check. The consequence here is obvious as well: stability with respect to trends in inequality.

These postures take on added meaning in regard to the realities (and assumptions) of fixed economic resources. The fixed nature of such resources limits government choices for dealing with items of secondary priority—such as legislation to improve the plight of the poor. This has been noted in studies in other nations which suggest limited latitude to affect change, even among administrations of varying ideological persuasion (Fried 1976). Might not a similar point be raised about national commitments in the United States? In 1975, for example, six out of every ten dollars in the national budget were locked into two items: national defense and social security. No administration will—at least in the near future—alter these in any dramatic way. The initial 1982 budget proposed by the Reagan administration, though it attempted some cutbacks in the escalating funds for social security, met with sufficient resistance to be buried as politically inexpedient; the revised budget continued the commitment to social security and further expanded national defense spending. Other fixed-cost items further limit governmental freedom. What this means is that lower priority items, such as welfare and poverty legislation, are competing for funds which are not vast in the first place. That they could be made more vast is, of course, another issue, although the previous discussion of public commitment to equality does not encourage optimism in this regard.

The dominant concern with business means also that when swords are crossed, governments are careful to preserve the status quo: whatever is taken away with one hand is given back with the other. Hence suggestions by the Carter administration to cut back on business tax preferences and fringe benefits and to increase employer social security contributions had another, less publicly touted side to them (*New York Times* 1978a:28):

Under the Carter plan, corporate income taxes would be cut by $6 billion. The investment tax credit would be expanded to encourage capital spending, worth an additional $2.4 billion. Telephone excise taxes and unemployment levies would be reduced, generating a further tax break of about $1 billion for business. That adds up to a hefty $9.4 billion tax cut for corporate America, and all of it could be in place for the 1979 tax year.

As the *Times* piece concluded, the total package would "leave business where it started." These decisions are not atypical of other administrations.

This emphasis on government's active role in implementing programs related to efficiency (and secondarily equality) offers a better perspective on the realities of American society than is afforded by the other hypotheses reviewed. Unlike either the consensus or the pluralistic model, it goes some way toward explaining persistent inequality and the lopsided attention given to the business share of the ledger. And unlike the view stressing the influence of economic elites, it can account for a pro-business orientation which nonetheless allows for substantial instability among firms—without alluding to rumors concerning conspiracies, deals, kickbacks, bribes, and so forth (however frequent they may be). The fact of the matter is that most Americans and government officials share the conviction that capitalism, profits, and high economic growth are desirable features of the United States, and no allusion to the obvious power of American business need be made to explain this. The government actively purveys these values and hence is a responsible agent in maintaining the status quo in regard to efficiency and equality outcomes.

There is no implication here that in regard to monitoring issues of efficiency and equality the principles guiding American economic policy are principles in the scientific sense. There is no necessary reason, for example, why a trade-off between efficiency and equality must occur, as Okun maintains. Nor is it necessary that equality issues need be viewed as unproductive investments. Like all ideologies, equality-efficiency notions limit choices of action to prescribed and traditional thought. Hence the formula answer to sluggish growth is more capitalism: greater leeway for protected market operations, greater availability of funds for capital investment, and more liberal tax laws to permit investment at minimum costs. These are the primary choices pursued. Of course, they all leave business wide latitude in terms of concentration, merger, and investment.

Furthermore, I by no means want to suggest that this view on capitalism is shared by all, that it is eternal, or that it represents a new stage in any evolutionary scheme. Such views prevail as long as they appear to work. As with any ideological precepts, however, they dominate decisions for long periods of time and are difficult to shake off. Ideologies limit the pursuit of choices. In part, as I have noted, this ideology gains structural support from institutions such as labor unions and government, who are themselves implicated in the bipolar decisions of efficiency and equality. In part, however, it is also possible that support for this ideology is sustained by the economy of other nations which are likewise engaged in efficiency-equality decisions.

A Brief Note on Cross-National Pressures. It is easy to see the unabashedly capitalistic profit structure of the American economy as the sole and motivating force behind efficiency principles. Whatever the merit of this idea, it is necessary to point to an additional, obvious fact: that less capitalistic societies engage in similar decisions, and each such decision influences and reinforces policies pursued in the United States. Furthermore, given the increased interdependence of all economies, a fact evidenced in the United States by soaring trade figures (U.S. Bureau of the Census 1975b:798, 810), whatever decisions are made in the USSR, in France, or in Japan will have far more influence on the American economy today and in the future than was true in the past.

This interdependence may not be a simple picture of American capitalism facing countries with a more socialist orientation—with greater hesitancy to compete for goods and services. On the contrary, these countries also may be implementing efficiency principles and may show little hesitation at slicing welfare spending for purposes of economic competitiveness. To the extent that other nations cut back wages or welfare to make production easier and more efficient, the United States is under constraint to follow suit. More broadly, I suggest that economic growth as it pertains to capital investment and international competitiveness is a worldwide phenomena, and has striking appeal to the images of national grandeur which governments of varying political persuasion routinely pursue.

A classic example can be seen in decisions made by the Labour Party in Britain several years ago. By all standards Great Britain has long been a model of the welfare state and of nationalized industry, with approximately 10 percent of industry under state ownership. Recent years have shown substantial slippage in Britain's economic status. A *New York Times* (1976:69) article summarized Labour's response as follows:

Prime Minister James Callaghan gave notice last night that his Labour Party government was relying on private enterprise to pull

Britain out of its economic mess. To this end, he said, capitalism will get "absolute" priority over the traditional objectives of socialism.

Mr. Callaghan has already rejected the pleas of the left wing members of his party to cure Britain's ills by socialist methods. "We must adhere to the industrial strategy . . . which aims at giving absolute priority to industrial needs ahead of even our social objectives."

"We must ensure that industry is profitable and industry must respond by investing, modernizing and finding and exploiting export markets."

In the late 1970s Callaghan's plan was brought to fruition with the entry of Margaret Thatcher as Prime Minister.

Nor does it appear that the presence of nationalized industries or leftist ideological preferences are obstacles to the national push for efficiency. Italy is one case in point. To curb industrial inefficiency and soaring budget deficits, the Christian Democratic government, with Communist Party support, committed itself to selling a substantial number of nationalized industries to private investors (*International Herald Tribune* 1977c:2). France is another case in point. Rumors during the preelection campaign of 1977–78 suggested that a reconciliation of the Communist and Socialist factions was put off by Communist fear of an inability to deliver higher income to workers during a period of inflation and sluggish economic growth. The specter here again is the desirability of industrial efficiency at the cost of wage equalization. Likewise, French Socialists apparently admitted that increased wages would indeed bankrupt many industrial concerns, and earmarked $6 billion to make up this deficit (*International Herald Tribune* 1978d:7). Whether such deficits would indeed jeopardize competitiveness and increase demands for efficiency is yet unknown. Mitterrand's election provides an interesting test case of what accommodations the Socialists can provide between worker equality and industrial growth.

Admittedly, these examples are unsystematic and offered in a speculative vein. Nonetheless, they suggest that commitments to socialism or communism are no obstacles to the rush for dominance in foreign trade competition. This is consistent with evidence previously cited that labor conflict does not wane under socialist regimes—the implication being that workers may be ignored under a variety of ideological convictions.

I do not suggest that change with respect to inequality is impossible. Obviously, there is major variation in inequality across industrialized nations, which indicates possibilities for change. What these comments are meant to suggest is that competitiveness in international markets is a dominant concern of most major governments. Regardless of the direction of influence, they represent an additional factor contributing to the pro-business posture of the American government. And further, to the extent that efficiencies are typically viewed as trade-offs with respect to welfare spending, programs concerned with equality will suffer. These trade-offs are not necessities in any economic sense; nor is international competition for markets the only way of ordering world trade and power. But as long as these conceptions predominate, they provide additional mechanisms for implicating governments in the status quo.

This conclusion appears justified: as long as institutions hitch their star to economic growth, inroads into inequality will not necessarily be made. In the first place, if economic growth is viewed as a trade-off against welfare expenditures, then growth priorities preclude declines in inequality. In the second place, any conception pertaining to the automatic dividends for equality derived from economic growth—such as the "trickle down" hypothesis—is simply fallacious.

In fact, as we have already seen, the income business derives from growth trickles down only under very specialized circumstances: when businesses can pass added labor costs on to consumers and when labor is sufficiently well organized to constrain them to do so. But at best, this affords economic benefits for a very select portion of the labor force. In the following two chapters we turn to two groups typically omitted from the "consensus" between organized labor and big business: black Americans and the old middle class. We will examine how the reactions of each cannot readily be understood from either a consensus or class conflict perspective—and how the theme developed in the first chapter, of mobility and conflict, does more justice to the reactions of deprived marginal groups.

Case Studies
in Economic Conflict

THE PRECEDING SECTION expanded the term "class conflict" by distinguishing militant from radical forms. In the present section, my concern lies more in the "class" than the "conflict" component of the term. Difficulties in the use of the class concept have dominated critiques of Marxism. Suggestions from abandoning the concept altogether—and focusing instead on the individual pursuit of mobility—to a shift in emphasis on organized pluralities of interest groups are sprinkled throughout the literature.

Each suggestion has its deficiencies. Those advocating the substitution of individual status terms for class terms miss the widespread emphasis in all industrialized societies on organization and mobilization to achieve collective aims. The analysis of interest groups is a more realistic thrust in emphasis. Yet the literature in that area has developed primarily so as to explain the evolution of organizational tactics and resources rather than link these tactics to the general economic conditions underlying protest (Gamson 1975).

In evaluating these views, it is necessary to question whether the basic and useful insights of Marxism have been abandoned prematurely. The undeniable utility of Marx is insight into the insatiable quest for profits under capitalism and the recalcitrance of capitalist elites to share their rather substantial slice of the pie. While Marx's critics may be partially correct in pointing to difficulties in applying class terms, there is no reason why insights into the economic structure need necessarily be restricted to classes. After all, the capitalist quest for economic growth and profit stability has wide-ranging consequences: for specific categories of workers in industries displaced by competition from abroad or by changing technology; for status groups singled out for economic discrimination; for groups outside the wage-dependency relationship, such as a petty bourgeoisie made inefficient by waves of concentration in the economy.

Since these groups are not classes as such, it is tempting to evoke special understandings of their activities—or to ignore the economic conditions underlying their reactions and concentrate on explaining protest tactics alone. Yet it is probably unwise to dispense with general economic considerations. Clearly, a large variety of groups are concerned with advancing claims for mobility; and the potential for realizing these claims is in turn conditioned by and implanted in the wider economic environment. Whatever merit specialized theories might have, is it not reasonable to consider first and foremost explanations which draw on a more general understanding of economic behavior?

Among Marxist revisionists, there is a long-standing tradition of using economic interpretations as a more general phrasing of class analysis (Bernstein 1965). In the present context, this general understanding of economic behavior refers specifically to the variables and relationships noted in previous chapters: (1) to the issue of mobility opportunities and elite resource monopolization; (2) to the internal differentiation such opportunities introduce; (3) to the use of conflict to maintain existing advantages and thereby solidify the status quo. My contention is that economic conflict is a collective reaction pertaining to a wide variety of groups—including the class of wage workers who are key players in the Marxian drama.

In arguing for a more general conception of economic conflict, I open the possibility of considering economic variables to be central to a large variety of groups—larger, unfortunately, than can be possibly covered in the confines of this book. Accordingly, I turn to case analyses of two particular groups chosen with these criteria in mind: that they were implicated in major forms of conflict in recent American experience and that they have been widely analyzed in terms of some highly restrictive, specialized theory.

The two groups selected are blacks and small businessmen, the conflicts refer to urban riots and McCarthyism, and the alternate theories are variants on colonial and mass society perspectives. In the following two chapters, I discuss each of these cases with a view toward arguing the generality of economic conflict analysis—and to showing why traditional Marxist and consensus perspectives (of which the specialized theories are a piece) are inadequate to the facts.

CHAPTER FOUR

Black Americans—
Protest and Economic
Differentiation

THE SAGA OF the blacks in the United States is well known and stamped on the national conscience. It is a history of slavery, of years of servitude in a technically free political context, of widespread social and economic deprivation. The last decades have seen an alteration of this history and a possible turning point in destiny: a resurgence of racial consciousness in the form of freedom marches and economic boycotts, of riots which flamed cities and national attention. But whether this turning point will materialize—quickly and completely—is less well known. Recent years have been marked by political quiet against a background where few Americans are aware whether and if the promise of political change and economic well-being have in fact come to pass.

How are the politics, the economic gains and losses of blacks to be explained? In this chapter I will maintain that neither the consensus nor the traditional conflict view propounded by Marx are wholly adequate to the task. Following the ideas on inequality and conflict previously discussed, I will attempt to show how black gains, losses, and politics may be more comprehensively understoood as an economic mobility movement, nurtured on conflict and on partial gains.

Central to my position are some remarkable examples of structural stability behind the ballyhoo of black economic change in the preceding several decades. In spite of the hue and cry following the long hot summers of the 1960s, in spite of the liberal call for dramatic change, one fact remained clear: the activities of the sixties benefited a select group of middle status persons but left the magnitude of black poverty intact over the span of several decades.

This outcome is characteristic of economic mobility movements. Such movements typically involve highly differentiated groups, with multiple problems partly relevant to various members. With respect to blacks in the 1960s, for example, two distinct economic groupings and economic problems were at stake: discrimination facing employed blacks in their access to high-status occupations and to incomes befitting their jobs; poverty and unemployment facing an underclass of blacks, problems which were less the result of contemporary attitudes than a legacy of older forms of discrimination. These latter issues of poverty and unemployment were in turn bound to broader problems of the capitalist state: whether the economy could at once maximize the pursuit of profits and at the same time provide individuals with reasonable life chances.

The differentiation of economic issues makes both class and consensus analysis problematic. The consensus view cannot handle the possibility of certain groups remaining outside the umbrella of national affluence. Likewise, class analysis cannot easily handle the possibility of somewhat less deprived individuals wanting little more than a secure spot under the umbrella of affluence—without any hidden agenda to alter institutional priorities.

This bifurcation of problems characterized black America on the brink of the 1960s. The politics of the sixties involved: (1) an attempt to alter the status of select individuals (2) within the existing parameters of the capitalist structure, (3) with the consequence that some benefited while the problems of others were left unexpressed and unresolved. Mobility movements, as noted previously, do not preclude threats, violence, and force—and all this was characteristic of black activities in the last decade. In fact, the use of violence unquestionably dramatized the black plight and brought about selective opportunities. At the same time, confrontations and other pressure tactics were by no means expressive of a unified racial group bent on resolving the dilemmas of capitalism to which their problems were intimately linked. If anything these politics simply illustrated the successful tactics of high status individuals, able to mobilize their activities effectively and make vocal their discontent. In this way inequalities within the black community were not merely perpetuated but increased.

In the following sections I will deal with three issues: (1) economic differentiation up to the brink of the sixties; (2) the political activities characteristic of that decade; (3) the consequent effects which benefited some but left the position of others unchanged. My argument is simply that such outcomes are typical of economic mobility movements, and inconsistent with both consensus and class conflict analysis.

Economic Factors:
Differentiation Before the Sixties

Resource Monopolization. Mobility movements operate in partially adaptive settings. In the public domain, adaptiveness may be reflected in governmental considerations of equality and efficiency; in the private domain, adaptiveness may be seen in the wage hikes granted by monopolistic industries to a militant labor force for purposes of appeasement and control. Whatever the motivations of the respective institutions may be, the activities afford a partial basis for improving life chances. And it is this which sets the stage for militant (rather than radical) conflict.

The first question in analyzing mobility movements, therefore, must address the extent of differentiation in access to life chances. One view, clearly inadequate to this task, is the consensus emphasis on the widespread benefits accompanying economic growth. Whatever can be said about the merits of the consensus view, this much should be clear: blacks do not fit the mold of clear, simple, and gradual assimilation experienced among minority groups in America's past.

Yet it is unclear whether drastic and opposing indictments of American society have any more merit. One popular view, set around the idea of colonization, depicted blacks as uniformly subject to total deprivation, exploitation, and subordination. As was literally the case in colonies, elites totally monopolized resources. Clearly if this or similar views have merit, then attempts to apply economic mobility models may be misplaced. For mobility movements gain impetus from differentiated groups in which life chances are unequal rather than homogeneous groups in which life chances are uniform— and meager.

The colonial perspective gained popularity during the race riots of the sixties, which were themselves taken as acts of rebellion by an exploited population. The perspective shares a more general contention that while racial and other differences may have splintered the working class, the internal solidarity of the separate, splintered groups increases in the process (Fogelson 1969; Blauner 1969). The analytical model, however, draws not on class relationships but on the relationships between colonial powers and their subordinate colonies. In contrast with the prophecy of harmony advanced by the consensus view, the colonial position speaks of either continued exploitation of one group by the other or the development of a dual society with parallel structures for majority and minority sectors.

The development of colonial structures has been variously discussed. Hechter (1971, 1973, 1974) for example, sees these structures as typically arising in isolated, poorly developed regions of a nation. Underdevelopment sets the stage for a vicious circle of underrepresentation patterned on majority attitudes of discrimination and prejudice. With time, differences between regions become cultural differences, persistent and normative, and are locked into inequality through continued association with the occupational division of labor. Poorly paid jobs and industries rooted in menial labor become the property of certain minorities in particular areas. Subservient jobs and cultural differences reinforce each other: they make it difficult for the minority to advance; they allow discrimination and exploitation to persist. In the long run, these developments lower potential for change.

Unfortunately, underdeveloped regions with distinctive minorities may persist in spite of widespread economic growth in the remainder of the society (Hughes 1961). Myrdal (1957), for example, argues for a model of circular causation: labor, capital, and services move from economically backward regions to more advanced regions. This movement in already backward regions causes a deteriorating labor supply and poor services to spiral downward, in turn increasing the risk of capital investment and industrial development. If particular ethnic or racial groups are caught in underdeveloped areas, they may well remain in extreme poverty and maintain a unique cultural profile. Hechter (1973), has illustrated, for example, how the Celtic fringe in Great Britain has long contained victims of poverty in spite of the development of a large-scale industrial nation (see also Schwartz 1974; Green 1969).

The colonial model and others similar to it are important statements stressing elite monopolization of resources. Were these models accurate estimates of the black condition, unified radical activity among blacks would be more than a remote possibility. Yet, whatever its radical appeal, the colonial model is inadequate for explaining the life chances among blacks today. If anything, these models are really applicable to extreme economic conditions, as, for example, those pre-

vailing in the rural South of the nineteenth century—where
the agricultural system was decidedly labor intensive, where
few if any opportunities existed for black economic advancement, and where blacks were literally maintained as a cheap
labor alternative to costly mechanization. But these feudal
conditions simply do not represent recent experience. Few
persons are involved in agriculture, and blacks are not
overrepresented in these activities—indeed, the reverse is
true (U.S. Bureau of the Census 1975b:360). Nor, for that
matter, are blacks distinctively southern or rural (ibid.:18,
28). Furthermore, the South—a key region for analyzing a
colonial pocket—can hardly be classified as "backward." Industrialization has markedly attenuated differences between
the South and the rest of the nation (McKinney and Bourque
1971; Williamson 1965; but see also Glenn 1967). While income disparities between southern blacks and whites may be
somewhat more than in the North, these regional differences
are also more quickly diminishing, particularly in younger
households (U.S. Bureau of the Census 1975a:36–40).

Even in the urban ghetto, a colonial model does not make
complete sense. As Robert Fogelson (1969:33–34) noted:

For all their grievances, Negroes have greater opportunities to enter
the middle class and exert political power than colonial people
do. . . . The ghetto is not a colony—unless by a colony is meant
nothing more than a dependent neighborhood, a definition which
would include nearly all of the modern metropolis. The ghetto is
exploited, but not so much by the whole society as by fragments of
it. . . . These differences . . . do not mean that the Negro problem
is less serious than the colonial situation, only that it is quite different.

Fogelson's comment on black opportunity questions the
position of total subservience implicit in the colonial model.
I will take this one step further: precisely what advantages
accrue to capitalist elites who reserve and protect higher
wages for whites rather than blacks? In systems of slavery,
the answer is obvious: blacks are a cheap labor supply. Even
in more industrialized settings, the use of blacks as strike-

breakers keeps wages low and fragments white claims for union power. Nonetheless, legislation guaranteeing labor's right to organize (Bonacich 1976) minimizes the benefit in using strikebreakers. It also increases pressure on unions to mobilize black workers. In fact, as Hill (1974:509) has pointed out, economic discrimination in the labor market under monopoly conditions may in fact increase costs to capitalists:

Racial discrimination results in fewer blacks hired by whites. Therefore, discrimination will cause: (1) the income of white labor to rise since there is less labor competition within the white sector; (2) the income of white owners will fall since they will have to pay higher wages to white labor than would be dictated under competitive conditions. . . . Discrimination . . . is opposed to the economic self-interest of white owners of capital. . . .

The point may be somewhat overdrawn. But the fact of the matter is that the color line in labor markets is not so distinct that adverse effects on blacks will not also be to the detriment of whites, albeit to a lesser extent. The colonial position portrays distinct advantages to whites from racial employment discrimination. Yet this is not clearly the case. Reich's (1971) analysis of wages in metropolitan areas, for example, showed a close connection between black-white income disparities and income inequality for whites generally: in areas where black-white income differences were large, the coefficients for income inequality among whites were large as well. Reich argues that these patterns illustrate a typical feature of generally exploitative labor markets; employers keep white income down with the argument that blacks will take jobs held by whites. The data presented by Reich do not really support this argument directly—that is, there are no real indications of employer activities. But they do at least suggest that while low wages are most peculiar to blacks, everyone is in some sense affected by employer attempts to minimize labor costs. Implicit in the colonial model is the contention of white advantage resulting from black subordination. Yet this is not strongly supported in existing research.

Economic Differentiation. An alternative to the view of monolithic economic subordination is to give greater recognition
to the differentiation of opportunities in the black community.
My understanding is that blacks were in fact clearly differentiated into distinct economic strata on the brink of the sixties, and this differentiation as much as anything influenced
the course and direction their politics would assume. To be
sure, real and high levels of poverty existed. But this was
blended into a mosaic of a proportionately small but numerically substantial group of middle status individuals and a
somewhat larger proportion of industrial workers with stable
employment. Recognition of these differences is not tantamount to a celebration of black progress. Rather, it is an indication of the discontinuous movement to black-white parity.

It is not necessary to spell out here the detailed record
of economic change in the years preceding the 1960s. Yet
several factors are worthy of mention. The most important of
these is the mechanization of agriculture. This fact alone
changed the shape of poverty from the largely rural emphasis
characteristic of the nineteenth century. For blacks, mechanization meant a push out of low-paying agricultural jobs into
work in industry, into cities, and into the North. As late as
1940 nearly 80 percent of the blacks resided in the South;
twenty years later that number was reduced to 60 percent
(U. S. Bureau of the Census 1975b:28). Likewise, with respect
to rural-urban differences, the 3 to 1 ratio among blacks of
rural to urban dwellers was in 1960 completely reversed
(Baran and Sweezy 1977:251–52; U. S. Bureau of the Census
1975b:28). These trends reflected the demise of an agricultural
economy and of patriarchal race relations which bred household servants and hired hands. In the brief period from 1940
to 1960 the percentage of black workers in low-paid service
and agricultural pursuits was cut in half.

Migration into the cities and the North did not translate
into an unblemished record of economic assimilation. Blacks
were poor, easily exploitable, unskilled, and widely used as
strikebreakers. These factors reflected their availability as a

cheap labor supply. Yet, availability was not readily trans-
ferred into use. The most important obstacle, as Bonacich
(1976:45) has noted, was the passage of the National Industrial Recovery Act and related legislation in the 1930s. This
legislation emphasized minimum wage rates and banned employer interference with unionization. It also made it un-
profitable for capitalists to play on cheap labor supplies in the
black community. For, as Bonacich (ibid.) has commented,
New Deal legislation made it illegal for

employers to use blacks as strikebreakers or strike insurance, denying the legitimacy of the company union and taking away the
advantage to be had in paying blacks lower wages for longer hours.
Protective legislation ideally made the price of labor equal regardless of race.

While discrimination in unions of course persisted, their
new legitimacy put pressure on labor to organize entire industries—blacks included. Only in this way could strike effectiveness be maintained. Statistics on the history of black
union members are lacking. But contemporary estimates show
in 1960 an equal proportion of black and white union members
(U. S. Bureau of Labor 1966:70). Thus, between 25 and 30
percent of the black labor force had entry into union jobs. In
spite of a legacy of labor discrimination, black income reflects
this access to union organization, for blacks' wages are clearly
superior in unionized as compared with nonunionized urban
areas (Hill 1974).

In addition to the demise of agriculture and the entry of
unionized black workers in the labor force, a number of other
trends contributed to economic advancement. The most important of these was the general rise in human capital skills,
symbolized in educational training. In the decades prior to
1960, black-white educational differences declined at the
same time as the level of education increased for the population as a whole. Hence in 1940 the ratio of white to black
median educational attainment was 1.5 to 1; in 1960, the
differences were cut to 1.28 to 1 (U. S. Bureau of the Census
1975b:118).

One source of demand for skills came from the black community itself. At a rate substantially greater than the white majority, blacks numerically increased nearly 50 percent from 1940 to 1960 (U. S. Bureau of the Census 1975b:30). At the same time, segregation in residence by no means declined (Taeuber and Taeuber 1969; Lieberson 1963). This created a substantial black community cut off residentially from the larger white community, with needs of its own for health, legal services, commerce, and so forth.

On top of this was the dramatic rise in demand for workers in the government sector—a rise in which blacks fully participated. For example, the percentage of blacks in government employ doubled in the decades from 1940 to 1960 (Baran and Sweezy 1977:263). Whether this was a product of universalistic criteria in government hiring practices is unknown, although that is a reasonable assumption. Nonetheless, one of every ten black workers were employed by the government in 1960. And although the proportion of white collar workers who were black stood at no more than a third of those who were white, 16 percent could be classified in this stratum as of 1960 (U. S. Bureau of the Census 1975b:360).

These statistics are hardly cause for celebration. Furthermore, they fail to reflect a rate of unemployment approximately twice as high as that of whites and a rate of poverty nearly three times as high (U. S. Bureau of the Census 1975a:42, 64). The point to be emphasized is the increased income differentiation in the black community, not the total subordination some conflict and colonial perspectives suggest. In the decade 1950–60, for example, white family income inequality was generally declining. In contrast, income data for blacks show slight increases in income inequality for families and dramatic increases for unrelated individuals in the period 1948–60 (U. S. Bureau of the Census 1963). These statistics suggest diverse and uncoordinated trends folded one on the other: a huge underclass of the poverty-stricken and unemployed with unionized industrial workers on top of them and a handful of blacks in more prestigious white collar jobs.

My contention is that this income differentiation shaped the conflict of the sixties and splintered it into multiple fronts of confrontation. On the one hand there was the explosion of hostility from hard core poverty in the urban ghettos. On the other, the more organized confrontations—sit-ins, voting rights drives, boycotts—from blacks with education and skill but without matching income advantage. These latter individuals spearheaded a series of political confrontations which had serious ramifications for their own advancement but left intact the proportion of blacks in poverty as well as the context which nurtured this poverty to a level of national disgrace. These outcomes, as I will point out, are traditional consequences of economic mobility movements: securing privilege for those already advantaged; reinforcing the status quo in failing to alter the structural conditions underlying poverty and unemployment.

Political Mobilization

Parallels exist in the economic and political conditions of the black community. In neither situation, for example, is the consensus position defensible. Consensus theorists stress the widespread availability of opportunities for altering life chances, through democratic government in the political arena and through organized labor in the economic arena. The assumption here is simply that elites could be pressured to favorably expand economic opportunity.

But hindsight makes clear the futility of these channels for blacks in the decades prior to the sixties. Democracy is meaningless if participation is denied. In the early sixties, only 100 blacks were elected officials at the national and state level (U. S. Bureau of the Census 1975a:151). Furthermore, representation alone is no guarantee of effective power. Democratic decision-making is based on win-or-lose outcomes. Unless minorities can mobilize effective coalitions, there is no clear reason why democratic access can easily be translated into economic gain. As for gain in the marketplace, this too was limited. In terms of representation at bargaining tables, there is no institutional apparatus for effectively arguing the case for status groups as such. Whatever gains were made by blacks were simply part of the gains of unionized labor generally. The institutional mechanisms discussed by consensus theorists were simply ineffective or absent.

An additional and perhaps more relevant parallel in the analysis of the economic and political conditions of blacks pertains to the questionable assumption of homogeneity. This issue is frequently stressed in conflict theory's emphasis on black political unity. The idea has roots in a more general conception of the differentiation of the working class (MacDonald and MacDonald 1962; Harrington 1972): fragmented by racial, religious, and ethnic differences which rip the potential for working class unity but at the same time reinforce the internal solidarities of the separate groups involved. That is, through common values, common residences, and high in-group interaction, blacks may be more unified than the working class could ever be.

Whatever the popularity of such views, political unity among blacks is largely a myth. For as the working class generally was bifurcated into "haves" and "have nots," so too was the black community. The problems of the 50 percent of blacks defined as below government standards of poverty were not wage discrimination or voting rights or segregation or access to public facilities—but merely jobs with a regular wage. Furthermore, the differential advantages of the "haves" to mobilize their claims increased the likelihood of a quicker and more effective organizational thrust, a thrust directed toward a more secure spot under the umbrella of affluence.

The consequence of these differences was a bifurcation of political activities, at least in an informal sense. Given the organizational capacities of the middle stratum, their politics were furthered in political marches and direct confrontations. This contrasted with the rioting characteristic of the poverty-

stricken urban ghettos. The somewhat greater rationality in
the politics of the middle stratum was not necessarily a constraint encouraging moderation—if by moderation is meant
the lack of force. In fact the threat of force and civil disruption
was a characteristic weapon in these confrontations. What
was moderate was the demands: the abolition of job and wage
discrimination as well as segregation. But for the impoverished and deprived, wage discrimination was less important
than jobs, and segregation was less important than housing.

The organizational capacities of the middle stratum, and
the willingness of business and government to accede to moderate demands, meant that the outcome of the conflict-torn
sixties would likely benefit those already advantaged. More
radical solutions necessary for alleviating poverty and unemployment were infrequently vocalized and not seriously
considered by existing elites. Hence these problems remain,
and this in spite of a decade of conflict which ripped into the
very fabric of American society. Outcomes benefiting the advantaged are precisely what characterize economic mobility
movements.

In this sense some of the predictions of consensus theorists
are partially correct. Some years ago Lipset and Rokkan
(1967) argued that industrialization increased functional (i.e.,
economic) cleavages and undermined traditional (i.e., racial-
ethnic) cleavages. That is, as minority groups were assimi-
lated into the wider society, general economic interests would
prevail over traditional ethnic or racial loyalties. The final
stage in this process, from Lipset and Rokkan's view, is the
incorporation of minority groups into mainstream society.

I agree with this perspective—with two important pro-
visos. First, assimilation may be neither smooth nor gradual.
Instead it may be abrupt and associated with overt and violent
conflict. Second, assimilation into the economic mainstream
may be partial and discontinuous, leaving in its wake unresolved and unbroached problems of poverty. Yet Lipset and
Rokkan are probably correct in their basic observation: mobility into affluence can be more magnetic than racial unity.

There is irony in this. Mobility is a wedge separating those with common traditions and heritage. Ironic or not, the notion of a unified black movement, acting in solidarity to solve a totality of problems, is a myth. Yet the question of black unity has been repeatedly suggested in the conflict literature. In this and the following section I will show how the politics of the sixties were spearheaded by middle status individuals and how the consequences of these politics primarily benefited them, leaving untouched the large reservoir of blacks in hard core poverty.

Superimposition: Residence and Black Unity. In spite of substantial differentiation in life chances and economic goals, the idea that the black community would solidify into a united front is a pervasive theme in the literature. The idea parallels the hope for unification of the working class generally, in which the superficial differences separating workers would be cast off in favor of labor solidarity. Among blacks, the axis of solidarity was simply the ghetto. For the segregated boundaries of residence were thought to increase communication, interaction, and whatever else was necessary to nurture organizational unity. The emphasis on ghetto living contributed a uniquely racial component to this perspective.

This view on residence and racial unity was expressed in a widely reprinted and influential piece on America's unique class politics. In it the author, Norbert Wiley (1967:540), put the matter as follows:

The organization of propertyless elements for purposes of collective action has usually centered around type of job and place of work. But the Negro protest movement is showing that this organization can occur outside of the labor market, on other bases. There are indications that the Negro poor can now be organized and made a political force more easily than the white poor, for the Negroes have found an organizational weapon lacking to the Whites. This weapon is skin color itself, and it is backed up by the residential ghetto with its many small organizations, its grapevines and other communication networks. Color and segregation give a unity and an organizational potential which the White poor do not have. We are not saying these mechanisms are a sufficient condition for the Negro protest movement. Rather, they are organizational resources which are intensifying a movement which began for quite different reasons. Negro organization is building on these unifying bases, much as the industrial labor unions were built on the unifying elements of the factory itself and its working conditions.

Wiley's conception of the relationship between race and residence is linked to a broader conception of social problem development. In this view, problems are multiple, related, and intensified. The antagonisms from one dimension reinforce antagonisms from other dimensions. In this way, a group's internal unity is reinforced but the antagonisms between it and other groups are deepened into broad social cleavages. Dahrendorf (1959) has referred to this category of problems as instances of superimposition—literally the placement of problems one on top of the other. In his view, racial or ethnic characteristics are sources of differentiation which represent potentials for societal cleavage. These cleavages are likely to come to pass if—as is frequently the case—ethnic or racial groups are not randomly scattered. Instead, they may be integrated by common residence and in a way that makes the racial or ethnic group at once the victim of social prejudice and of economic discrimination. In this case, the effect of superimposition is to influence and reinforce a multiplicity of problems. As Dahrendorf (1959:213–14) put it:

there may be an undetermined number of conflict groups and conflicts arising from antagonisms other than those based on the authority structure of associations. In fact, of course, this extreme scattering of conflicts and conflict groups is rarely the case. Empirical evidence shows that different conflicts may be, and often are, superimposed in given historical societies, so that the multitude of possible conflict fronts are reduced to a few dominant conflicts. I suggest that phenomenon has considerable bearing on the degree of intensity and violence of empirical conflicts. . . .

You might suppose that in a given country there are three dominant types of social conflict: conflict of the class type, conflict between town and country, and conflict between Protestant and Catholic. It is of course conceivable that these lines of conflict cut

across each other in a random fashion, so that, e.g., there are as
many Protestants among the ruling groups of the state as there are
Catholics and as many town people in either denomination as there
are country people. However, here, too, you might suspect that dis-
association and pluralism are empirically rather unlikely to occur.
One would not be surprised to find that most Protestants live in
town and most Catholics in the country, or that only one of the
denominations commands the instruments of political control. If this
is so, we are again faced with the phenomenon of superimposition
in the sense of the same people meeting in different contexts but in
identical relations of conflict.

Implicit in Wiley's and Dahrenforf's conception is an emphasis on the effects of common residence in heightening organizational potential. The key mechanism here is differential association—the idea that persons associate more
frequently with some than with others. Persons with common
characteristics sharing common residential areas are more
likely to direct their interaction and positive bonds toward
one another. This has a dual effect: it ties together groups
with common characteristics, and it severs bonds to the majority population. This situation is a key condition for polarization and conflict: a group internally well integrated but
cut off from ties with the wider society. The internal integration heightens capacities for political mobilization; the sev-
erance of ties with the wider society means that in any given
situation, pressures from the majority population are likely
to be discounted (Davis 1959; Coleman 1957).

It is indeed conceivable, as Wiley implied in his comment,
that particular ethnic or racial groups may have within them
the unity necessary for political action. Ethnic or racial groups
are frequently communities marked by similar cultures, life
styles, and at times, common language (Lieberson 1970).
These commonalities reinforce positive feelings and at the
same time minimize cross-pressures from the wider society to
moderate demands. In extreme form, community contexts may
be "institutionally complete," containing their own economic,
social, and religious institutions which make interaction with
majority group members unnecessary (Breton 1964). The residential area resembles a society in miniature.

The question of whether residential communities solidify interests rests on two related issues: the degree of segregation and the effects of segregation on homogenizing attitudes. The first issue takes on importance in light of Wiley's observation on the role of segregation and the ghetto as keys to understanding political soliarity among blacks. Poor whites are also victims of residential segregation, but this differs from black segregation in two important respects: the degree of segregation is less severe among whites; as whites advance in the occupational structure they leave inner city residences to settle in suburban settings. Contrary to the general trend with respect to other minority (and majority) groups, however, blacks do not migrate heavily from inner city areas to the suburbs as they gain in occupational status. While residential differences among blacks do conform somewhat to lines of occupational status, these differences appear less dramatic than they are for whites (Martson 1968).

The unique residential status of blacks is borne out in existing research. Data indicate that poverty alone is not a determining factor in accounting for black segregation— hence reinforcing the idea that racial factors may be as or more relevant than economic conditions. As one leading authority of residential segregation put it (Taeuber 1968:112): "The blunt fact is that poverty has very little to do with racial residential segregation. If Negroes were housed according to the spatial patterns of Whites with similar incomes, racial segregation would not be noticeable."

Blacks from all income levels tend to be more segregated than whites. This means that whatever occupational gains have been made in recent decades, such gains have not been readily translated into the breakdown of ghetto residence. It is difficult to tell with certainty how much, if at all, segregation has decreased for the simple reason that reliable records generally were not kept until recent decades. Yet where trend data are available, they suggest no substantial decline in segregation by residential sector. Lieberson (1963) has shown, in an analysis of ten major cities, that from 1910 through 1950 residential segregation among blacks was in-

creasing—in contrast with lower segregation figures for foreign immigrant groups. Likewise, Taeuber's (1968:106) analysis of segregation in Cleveland suggests a general upward
trend from 1910 to 1940, at which point segregation leveled
off, with minor fluctuations, to 1965. These trends may not
be typical of all cities, but they do indicate the inertia against
which integration proceeds. Furthermore, although there may
be some indications of black flight to the suburbs with better
jobs, these trends are not nearly so dramatic as they are for
whites. What is important, however, from the superimposition
perspective is not the fact of segregation alone but its consequences for increasing solidarity within the black community and blocking integration into the wider mainstream society.

Specifically, does segregation create a racial "unity and
organizational potential that the white poor do not have"
(Wiley 1967:540)? There is some indication that on broad and
highly general points of identification, such unity does surface. For example, a review of eight national surveys concluded that "Negroes have a political affiliation as a racial
group rather than dividing between Democrats and Republicans on the basis of their socioeconomic position" (Janowitz
and Segal 1967:610). Unlike whites, then, high income blacks
are more likely to maintain liberal voting preferences. As for
general class identity, this does not follow traditional patterns; middle income blacks, for example, do not see themselves as "middle class" (Jackman and Jackman 1973). On
exploitation, research on a sample of approximately 1,800
persons in four middle size New England communities found
that with respect to exploitation, race was generally more
relevant to blacks than occupational position. Blacks in any
occupational position were more likely than whites to feel put
down economically and manipulated politically (Hurst 1972).

That blacks at any level of income feel more exploited
and express this is understandable. But the issue of racial
unity goes beyond this: can common residence and heightened
in-group interaction create solidarity on the complex economic

fronts blacks have faced—both in terms of job and wage discrimination and in terms of the more deep-seated issues of
poverty and unemployment? That is somewhat more questionable.

In the first place, research on interaction and segregation
effects has never convincingly shown that heightened in-
group interaction creates homogeneous attitudes among diversified groups (Allardt 1954; Howells and Alexander 1968;
Rosenborough and Breton 1968; Kerr and Siegel 1954). Political homogeneity, of course, may be partially predicated on
physical proximity (Duncan and Schnore 1959). But the reverse is not necessarily the case: proximity is no guarantee
of homogeneity. What is more likely is that segregation is
only one of a set of unrelated factors contributing to solidarity
and a homogeneity of views (Nelson and Grams 1978; Bulmer
1975).

In the second place, segregation even in the ghetto does
not approximate an "institutionally complete" community,
that is, an enclave separate and distinct from the white majority. Studies reported by the Institute for Social Research
(1975) suggest that even in the early sixties blacks were not
nearly so isolated from whites as whites were from blacks.
And although exact figures are not reported for blacks, significant proportions of whites have cross-racial ties. A study
of integrated and segregated areas in Los Angeles (Ransford
1968) found low interracial contacts among 43 percent of those
in segregated areas and 29 percent in integrated areas. Cross-
racial interaction was defined in terms of social meetings,
home visits, and common leisure excursions. These figures,
while dramatic in themselves, are hardly in keeping with the
residentially distinct enclave. In the third place, ghetto or not,
economic distinctiveness remains even under segregation, for
the ghetto by itself does not block differences in economic
achievement (Jibou and Marshall 1971).

Common residence alone, then, is not likely to produce
a unity of views. And it is probably insufficient to provoke
most middle status blacks to rally around radical demands

necessary to alleviate poverty and unemployment. Interaction is simply not that substantial. Even when organizational potential is present, residential effects are not apparent. An illustration of this is given in Street and Leggett's (1961) research on two black areas in Detroit's inner city. One area had numerous political groups and was organizationally "dense," with a high number of neighborhood clubs per person. Another was more isolated, as reflected in the absence of voluntary organizations. These differences correspond to Wiley's "organizational potential." Aside from this, the areas were demographically similar. When asked to characterize their response to social and economic stress, persons in both areas were as likely to suggest collective political action as individual action. The differences between areas were minute. The role of organizational density in unifying ghetto attitudes is not pervasive.

This conclusion is likewise supported by research on neighborhoods in the Los Angeles metropolitan area. Ransford (1968) questioned blacks on the use of violence to obtain their rights. There were differences between those with high and low histories of cross-racial interaction. But the differences were restricted primarily to those dissatisfied with the racial situation who at the same time felt powerless to affect the course of events. These findings conform to my previous characterization of interaction as only one in a set of factors contributing to the development of homogeneous attitudes. The role of residence and interaction has probably been overemphasized in allegations of racial solidarity.

Wiley also commented on the leftist attitudes associated with a class of propertyless blacks. The above studies do not include such detailed perceptions of the social order. Even when such perceptions are examined, the unity—or the radicalness—suggested in the literature is not apparent. One author, for example, speaks of the black worker as a potential agent of the working class (Leggett 1968:5–6):

Many analysts dismiss the views of Negro workers, labeling their opinions as petulant and regarding them as irrelevant for American politics. Others say these attitudes and actions represent a loss of faith in government and capitalism. This loss is bad, they add. That Negro workmen have unwisely abandoned their sense of respect for political authority and private property is, to these critics, the major concern. Thus, they regard the problem as one of restoration of loyalty and not redistribution of wealth.

Both these interpretations overlook the possibility of rational pursuit of working-class objectives. Furthermore, they create a stereotype that ignores the sources, content, and consequences of class consciousness.

In support of these remarks, the same commentator marshaled evidence to suggest that blacks were more likely than whites to engage in picketing, to support the view that economic booms benefit the rich, and generally to reflect leanings toward a leftist perspective.

But such support was neither startling nor widespread. In fact, greatest leftist support in Leggett's study came not from the general population of blacks but in the deprived quarters from which they were expected: to wit, among the unemployed. Furthermore, there is a real question as to whether Leggett's respondents would select these same themes of class exploitation if other perspectives were made available. There is some indication that they would not, for the hue and cry surrounding black protest in the sixties did not turn on unity with exploited labor.

Some indication of the perspectives blacks do select when given an array of choices is suggested in a study by Form and Rytina (1969; also Form and Huber 1971). The authors presented the following statements to a sample of 175 residents of an industrial community in Michigan. The respondents were asked to select the statement conforming to their own opinions (Form and Rytina 1969:22):

Political Pluralism Model. No one group really runs the government in this country. Instead, important decisions about national policy are made by a lot of different groups such as labor, business, religious, and educational groups, and so on. These groups influence both political parties, but no single group can dictate to the others, and each group is strong enough to protect its own interests.

Power Elite Model. A small group of men at the top really run the government of this country. These are the heads of the biggest business corporations, the highest officers in the Army, Navy, and Air Force, and a few important Senators, Congressmen and federal officials in Washington. These men dominate both the Republican and Democratic Parties.

Dominance Model. Big businessmen really run the government in this country. The heads of the large corporations dominate both the Republican and Democratic Parties. This means that things in Washington go pretty much the way big businessmen want them to.

The authors interpret this last statement as closest to a Marxist understanding of political affairs, and blacks are consistently more likely than whites to select it. In the lowest income group, where class persuasion might be thought of as higher, 33 percent of the blacks select the economic dominance model as opposed to 23 percent of the whites. In the middle-income category black-white differences are somewhat greater, with 40 percent of the blacks selecting the economic dominance model as opposed to 17 percent of the whites. Lest this be taken as an indication of racial unity on leftist views, one other trend in the study must be cited as dominant: among blacks (and whites) of any income category the pluralist model is the most preferred choice. Sixty percent of the poor and middle income whites and 52 percent of a comparable group of blacks favor the pluralistic view. The findings hardly lend overwhelming support to the presence of class or Marxist leanings among low and middle income blacks. Nor do they favor the interpretation of leftist unity which Wiley and others speculated would emerge from ghetto residence.

Mobility Movements: Deprivation in the Middle Strata. The politics of the 1960s largely reflected the mobility aims of middle status blacks. My reference here is not to the urban riots, which indeed were cries from the depths of poverty—a point to be dealt with in a later section. Rather I refer to the confrontations and marches on issues of equal access to public facilities, on economic discrimination, and on the right to vote.

These were not priorities dominating the consciences of the economically down and out so much as they were obstacles to middle class economic assimilation. Because of their education, middle class blacks were able to command organizational resources to articulate their moderate position—a simple demand for entry into the middle ranks of the majority. The long-term trend in politics is for minority groups to moderate the priorities of change as the credentials of mobility become available (Knoke and Felson 1974). I doubt that blacks are an exception to that rule.

In this section I illustrate the mechanisms for middle status domination of some part of black protest in the sixties. In a following section I will detail how protest worked to the advantage of the more affluent black. These issues are intended to illustrate the meaning of mobility movements: (1) carried out by a partial sector of a group (2) to advance their own claims (3) without altering a structure linked to unemployment, inequality, and poverty.

There were several bases for deprivation among middle status blacks. Perhaps the most important of these was the greater racial income differential for those with advanced educations and more prestigious jobs (Siegel 1970; Miller 1971; Farley 1977; Hauser and Featherman 1974). Greater racial equality had been expected to follow on more substantial credentials, but the outcome was just the reverse. Another basis of deprivation pertained to mobility. Blacks were more likely than whites to be downwardly mobile and less likely to be upwardly mobile (Blau and Duncan 1967:209). Furthermore, whatever occupational advantages blacks gained had less payoff for the mobility potential of their children (Duncan 1969). This suggests considerable intergenerational slippage and inadequate resources to transmit attained status from one generation to the next.

I do not argue that a discrepancy between attained status and anticipated reward suddenly widened in the sixties, with direct implications for conflict and protest. Such positions have been suggested around the theme of "rising aspirations." Yet mobility movements do not burst out in one particular historical moment to attain a place in the sun. Furthermore, the theme of rising aspirations ignores the organizational resources a group has at hand. To search for the seeds of protest purely in deprivation is an error. Since the deprivational argument has attained popularity, it is necessary to briefly review the futility of the position.

The deprivation argument revolves around the concept of discrepancies in changing expectations. Adverse change brings about a realization that the future need not follow the past. Change conditions expectations, and expectations, in turn, create tolerance limits for estimating desirable states of affairs. In periods of expansion and affluence, expectations are raised, but they may be raised beyond the possibilities of fulfillment. From this view, then, heightened political activity is preceded by periods of affluence and rising expectations. However, if affluence declines, a point may be reached where expectations cannot be fulfilled. The gap created between expectations and fulfillment become intolerable. Revolution or protest then follows (Davies 1962).

This model has been widely quoted in the literature on race relations. Pettigrew (1964), for example, reviewed evidence to suggest that black aspirations are high and rising quickly. He draws on a study in 1955, the period preceding the spread of protest behavior, which showed blacks to be more likely than whites to expect things to be better in the next five years. He concludes with the observation that "Negro aspirations have risen far more swiftly than Negro advances" (ibid.:179). Broom and Glenn (1965) similarly conclude that the closing of the racial gap in education during the 1950s was not matched by a closing of the income gap. This, of course, was most critical for highly educated blacks. It is not coincidental, from this view, that one study found dissatisfaction highest in the educational category where black-white income differences are greatest, that is, among high school graduates without a college degree (Killian and Griggs 1964).

Yet it is an error to search for the causes of heightened political activity in deprivation alone. In the first place, not

all studies have supported equally the notion of special obstacles to the achievement of aspirations in the 1960s, the era
of heightened political activity. Trend data during the riot-
torn sixties indicated no perceived downturn. Morgan and
Clark (1973), for example, report responses to the following
Gallup poll question to blacks: "On the whole would you say
you are satisfied or dissatisfied with the work you do?" The
percentage of those satisfied with their jobs showed a gradual
increase over two decades, with no dips in satisfaction coin-
ciding with the era of political protest. Other studies on deprivation have been ambiguous. Grofman and Muller (1973),
for example, in research on a riot-prone town in Iowa, concluded that blacks who perceived positive *or* negative changes
in their achievements were more likely to want to arm themselves in crises than those who perceived no change at all.
Bowen and Bowen (1968) similarly observed a link between
the discontinuity of experience and protest: upwardly *or* downwardly mobile blacks were more likely to be riot oriented than
stable blacks. Caplan and Paige (1968), however, were not
able to discern differences between rioters and nonrioters to
the question, "Are things getting better or worse for you over
the last several decades?"

An additional difficulty in searching for wholly deprivational causes of heightened political activity lies in the implication that something special happens to aspirations—that
they are suddenly thwarted or turned downward. It is simply
unclear whether "unsettling aspects of change" or intolerable
gaps between expectations and rewards are actually felt by
blacks or are posited by researchers to rationalize understandings of behavior (Lupsha 1971; Tilly 1961).

Suffice it to say that deprivation among middle status
blacks may have been long-standing, and that heightened
political activity during the sixties was simply an extension
and culmination of a drive for greater mobility gains among
an increasingly large group of highly educated blacks—who,
because of their education, were able to command organizational resources to articulate their position. This interpreta-

tion seems reasonable, given the absence of differences in feelings of economic subjugation between low and middle status blacks (Hurst 1972). Furthermore, we must note that while status in the middle ranks under specific conditions may be a deterrent against radical activity, it is no deterrent against militant activity. The rich organizational ties of middle status blacks stimulated their forceful entry into the political arena. And it is precisely in the middle strata—not among the poverty-stricken or the entire black community, as Wiley suggested—that organizational ties flourish.

It is now firmly established that higher status individuals are more likely to participate in voluntary organizations than lower status individuals (see Erbe 1964 for a review). This participation, furthermore, should be heightened whenever common interests coincide with shared residential areas (Greer and Orleans 1962). And this is indeed the case among high status blacks. Although whites may participate somewhat more than blacks, this is little more than a reflection of gross status differences. As an illustration, Olsen (1970) reported participation rates in community activities to be virtually identical between blacks and whites in the lower strata; in the middle strata, 40 percent of the blacks and 21 percent of the whites were found to be high participants; in the upper strata, these differences increased to 72 versus 39 percent— to the black sample's advantage (Olsen 1970:690). While this research was confined to one urban area, Indianapolis, the general direction of the results has been replicated in other geographical contexts (Orum 1966; Williams, Babchuck, and Johnson 1973). Taken together, these studies suggest a rich and flourishing network of organizational ties among middle and upper status blacks.

The importance of such ties is in heightening political involvement. Organizational ties increase interest and sensitivity to issues, stimulate political efficacy, and increase the organizational skills necessary for mobilization. Given, then, the greater richness of such ties among higher status blacks, as well as the independent effects of status per se, it is little wonder that many were thrust into the political arena.

TABLE 3.   ATTITUDES TOWARD PROTEST BY RACE

	Percent Agreeing	
Protest Attitudes	Black (N = 246)	White (N = 331)
Demonstrations are better than voting in this city because demonstrations are about the only way to get your point across.	24%	4%
Demonstrations and mass marches are one good way to get the city government to listen to you.	69%	23%
It's sometimes important to take part in demonstrations because that's one way to make your voice heard.	73%	29%

ADAPTED FROM: Eisenger (1974:596)

The participation of higher status blacks has been amply demonstrated. For example, the pioneering "Freedom Ride" movement in Baltimore drew supporters overwhelmingly from the middle class (Pinard 1967). In the initial attempts to desegregate public facilities, Matthews and Protho (1966) similarly observed strong middle class representation. This finding was more generally replicated in Gary Marx's (1967) analysis of protest in four metropolitan areas. Marx defined militants by their agreement with the following kinds of statements: "The government is moving too slowly on integration"; "More demonstrations are needed"; "Negros must be served at restaurants." Consistent with other findings, advocates of these views tended to have more education and more prestigious occupational positions. They were also more likely to be organizational participants. Not coincidentally, in the Indianapolis study mentioned above, organizational participation was highest among those most strongly identified with blacks as a minority.

But even these studies do not clearly illustrate the dramatic thrust into politics and protest for middle status black Americans. Some indication of black-white differences is shown in table 3, where responses are reported to questions on protest from a cross-racial sample of Milwaukee residents. The data indicate a potential for protest activity among blacks nearly three times that of whites. As we will see shortly, these attitudes in combination with some sense of being able to slow down and reverse economic discrimination laid the foundations for black protest.

And who were these blacks? Were they the poverty-stricken discussed by Wiley? Were they bent on "theft" or given to an "outbreak of animal spirits"—as Banfield (1970) suggested in his infamous book *The Unheavenly City*? Eisenger's (1974:599) profile of the Milwaukee protesters is instructive:

Other data suggest that black protesters not only resemble the socioeconomic norm in the black community but that they are also drawn disproportionately from its more integrated, stable elements. Black protesters are more likely than black nonprotesters to own or to be in the process of buying their homes. Among whites, however, the pattern is reversed: protesters are more likely than nonprotesters to be renters.

Black protesters and nonprotesters also tend to resemble one another in terms of the average length of time they have lived in the city. The average for the former is 13.6 years, for the latter, 15 years. White protesters have lived in the city an average of 11.4 years compared to the white nonprotester average of 24.2 years. . . . They . . . add to the evidence that black protesters seem more centrally located in or integrated members of their racial community than white protesters do of theirs.

Black protest and militance occur in the higher echelons of status. This theme parallels the mobility thrust of organized labor discussed earlier—the greater prevalence of unionization among the advantaged—no doubt partly because organization breeds advantage. But there is another parallel important for an understanding of mobility movements. Mobility pushes occur primarily when the organized can win. Organized protest does not necessarily occur in a context of futility. Successful strikes, for example, are most likely against monopolized industries where the wage bill is low and higher wage demands can be easily effected. Strikes are also likely in periods of prosperity when demand is brisk, inventories low, and corporations vulnerable to labor.

These considerations are important means of placing mobility movements in a context of calculated and rational extensions of interests. They take away the aura of militant protest as something exotic or extraordinary. Militance is thus a normal extension of political activities.

Protests among blacks can be understood in these terms. After all, black protest is an effort to widen opportunities for advancement. When these opportunities present themselves, protest is more likely to emerge. Some evidence for this view is suggested in an analysis of protest in 43 large metropolitan areas (Eisenger 1973). The author coded protest behavior from newspaper accounts of marches, sit-ins, demonstrations, pickets, and so forth. At the same time local city governments were classified into three categories: mixed, opened, or closed. The purpose here was to link the presence of opportunity to the potential for protest. Closed governments, for example, had nonrepresentative and nonelected managers whereas opened governments had elected mayors, city councils, formal representation of blacks, and other indications of responsiveness. Mixed governments possessed combinations of the two. Overall, the author found support for what he termed the "curvilinear hypothesis": protest was most likely to occur in cities with mixed characteristics, where the doors of opportunity were already partially open. The presumption is that closed governments are repressive, with little potential for success. More open governments, alternatively, may already contain ingredients for change. But in situations with an ambiguous mix, the potential for protest to effect change is clearly present. And this is where protest is likely to occur.

The parallels between these findings and those on labor movements are not exact. But the overall implications are similar: militant protest is a calculated drive to enhance mobility; it is carried on by middle status individuals in settings affording the possibility for success. This is in contrast to radical class movements, which occur under conditions of monopolized resources. With mobility movements, resources are infrequently monopolized, so that opportunities are open for the already successful to further their claims for advanced status.

Riots: A Brief Note. The urban riots in the sixties were significantly different from the political confrontations just discussed. In fact, it is in connection with the riots rather than the confrontations that the factors stressed by Wiley—the residential ghetto, the grapevine, the informal communication—probably had an effect. Riots, after all, are explosive behaviors mediated through networks of interaction: incidents cluster, behaviors become magnified, and violence spreads by contagion.

The riots clearly dramatized the differentiation and basic lack of unity in the black community—illustrating on the one hand the enormous passion and depth to which black feelings in the ghetto ran, and on the other the failure of middle status black militants to mobilize discontent into concrete demands and political activities. This failure reflects the irony of mobility movements: they leave unorganized those in dire economic need. In the same way that much of the labor movement left untouched large segments of the poor, so too the political activities of the sixties left the problems of black poverty intact.

Little else could realistically be expected. For the root issues of black poverty were never fully expressed in the sixties. The problem of poverty extends to the heart of capitalism as an economic structure: specifically, in an economy designed to maximize business growth and profit, who besides the individual assumes responsibility for providing jobs, livelihoods, adequate standards of living? Certainly this issue was not expressed in the emphasis in the middle strata on access to better housing and public accommodations. In fact, adequate housing was beyond the economic reach of black families strapped by poverty. The issue for them devolved on jobs and income.

The failure to articulate black poverty meant that riots

would be ill-defined and badly understood. This further contributed obstacles to a solution. Interpretations of riots were
entangled with financial estimates of property loss. Issues of
law and order introduced another agenda, deflecting attention
from the problems at hand. Social scientists—most notably
Banfield (1970) in *The Unheavenly City*—attributed riots to
"an outbreak of animal . . . spirit" where "the motive is theft."
Nor was the public better equipped to understand what riots
were all about. Responding in part to the media focus on riot
activity, a vast majority of the whites in the mid-sixties registered support for the sentiment that "civil rights leaders are
trying to push too fast" (Institute for Social Research 1975).
A study of white reactions to the Watts riot showed that approximately 50 percent of the white population sampled did
not define it as expressive of protest activity (Jefferies,
Turner, and Morris 1971). A Harris poll conducted in 1967
similarly showed whites to be half as likely as blacks to attribute disorders to grievances over jobs, education, housing,
police, and inequality (Sears and Tomlinson 1968). Even
within the black community, discrepancies in understanding
occur: in Newark, New Jersey, for example, nonrioters were
less likely than rioters to attribute disorders to social injustice
and discrimination than to personal factors related to voca-
tional inexperience and inadequate training (Caplan and
Paige 1968).

It cannot be determined with certainty whether liaisons
with the middle strata would have contributed understanding
and other solutions. But this much is known: that riot sites
were based in ghettos rather than more affluent residential
settings; that few middle status persons participated; that the
brunt of hostility was targeted against ghetto merchants and
police, rather than against an economic system that was
surely at the root of the blacks' plight. The riots then were
an opportunity lost. They left the issues facing the poor un-
articulated and unresolved (Oberschall 1973:231–38). In this
regard I am in agreement with Jacobs and Landau's (1966:26)
contention that "The masses of poor Negroes remain an un-

organized minority in swelling urban ghettoes, and neither SNCC nor any other group has found a form of political organization that can convert the energy of the slums into political power."

Whether the differentiation in the black community had a more immediate and direct bearing on riot behavior is unclear. One point of speculation is whether black occupational advantages dramatize the deprivation of the poor. Lieberson and Silverman's (1965) classic study of minority riots (covering the years 1913–63) indeed showed that riots were more likely in cities with blacks in superior economic positions. These findings have been extended to cover more recent activities in the sixties (Bloombaum 1968). Morgan and Clark (1968) considered riots for the year 1968 and likewise found occupational inequality between blacks and whites to be related to racial outbreaks: the lower the inequality, the higher the probability of a disorder. The reverse of this was curiously true with respect to housing inequality (see also Wanderer 1969). Since it is unlikely that middle status blacks themselves participated in the rioting on any scale, the implication is that achievement dramatized economic disparities for the poor.

Yet the inferences required in positing perceived disparity, as well as ambiguities in other studies, lower confidence in extending the differentiation argument to a direct cause of riots. Downs (1968) found that riot cities usually have greater unemployment than non-riot cities; but more detailed investigations of riot sites indicate their importance in some instances, as in Newark, but not in others, as in Detroit (Caplan and Paige 1968). Other research has identified even less in the way of relevant community characteristics. Spilerman (1970, 1971), for example, in a detailed analysis of some 341 spontaneous riots found no support for a link between riot cities and traditional indicators of economic position: unemployment, median black income, black-white income differences, and occupational status. The relationships uncovered in the study were more a function of region or size of the

minority population than economic conditions as such (Spilerman 1970:645):

we conclude that differences in disorder-proneness among communities cannot be explained in terms of variations in the objective
situation of the Negro.
    Instead, an explanation which identifies disorder-proneness as
an attribute of the individual would seem to be in order. . . . I would
argue that although different communities are not equally prone
to racial disturbance, the susceptibility of an individual Negro to
participating in a disorder does not depend upon the structural characteristics of the community in which he resides. As for the community propensity, it is an aggregate of the individual values—the
larger the Negro population, the greater the likelihood of a disorder.
Little else appears to matter.

Spilerman's estimate of causation at the level of individuals may be overdrawn. But his data on the differentiation
argument are clear enough. Too many things were happening
in the sixties—including the mounting war in Vietnam and
the anticipation of "long hot summers"—to expect a clear link
between a community's economic profile and the onset of riots.
    Regardless of specific causes in any one city, the broader
implications of status differentiation should be clear. The failure to mobilize the energies of the black poor increased the
likelihood that little change would occur in this group. One
is reminded here of *Germinal,* and of Zola's lightning account
of labor strife in northern France: in spite of a tumultous era
of strikes, riots, murder, suffering, the conditions of desper-
ation remained virtually unchanged.

Aftermath: Gains and Losses

Following the riot-torn sixties, massive changes altered the
position of blacks in American society. These changes crossed
the entire spectrum of the social structure, in economic and
political gains as well as in widespread social acceptance. Yet,
as I will argue in this section, these dramatic, almost revo-

lutionary changes primarily benefited a burgeoning middle strata, leaving an underclass of blacks as numerous and disadvantaged as ever.

From my view, this outcome is no anomaly. Mobility movements are instruments of individual gain. Aimed at enhancing the status claims of those already advantaged, these movements operate within the existing parameters of wealth and profit. The massive redistribution of economic surplus necessary to alleviate inadequate living standards remains beyond the pale of mobility politics. The structural bases of inequality remain in force. The status quo persists.

The widening economic opportunity of the middle strata worked to the disadvantage of the impoverished. For if some blacks were able to solidify their economic advantage, then as Wilson (1978) has noted, the poverty of others could hardly be seen as a necessary consequence of race. Wiley and others suggested the ease of mobilizing poverty sectors with common racial ties. Yet gradual slippage in the liaisons between race and poverty makes such mobilization increasingly problematic. Hence the double threat posed by the ascendance of a black middle stratum, indicating on the one hand the partial and incomplete nature of economic assimilation, and on the other hand, the possibility of some blacks slipping into what Harrington (1968) has called the invisible nature of poverty.

Gains: Economic, Social, Political. Black gains have been widely touted, ballyhooed, and made cause for national celebration. And the gains are certainly dramatic in themselves. But they are even more dramatic when seen in the context of massive stability among an emergent underclass: economic gains in the midst of widespread poverty, social acceptance, but the persistence of the ghetto. I will turn to these paradoxes after a review of the gains registered over the past decade. Since these gains are widely known, they merit only brief comment.

Even the most casual observations suggest overwhelming assimilation of blacks into formerly tabooed areas: in the increased interracial nature of advertising, television, sales contacts. While some of these shifts can unquestionably be charged with "tokenism," the fact of the matter remains that blacks overwhelmingly support moves toward cross-racial contacts and integration: few favor residential segregation, question the right to share public facilities equally, or deny the power or right of government to enforce integration (Institute for Social Research 1975). These goals are consistent with the avowed aim to achieve acceptance into "mainstream society."

There are definite indications that assimilationist desires have been partially realized. Blacks report decided increases in contacts with whites over the years, suggesting both motivation and capacity to sustain cross-racial relationships (Institute for Social Research 1975:6):

The black people interviewed in these surveys also saw the racial situation as changing during the 1964–1974 period. In some respects their perceptions of change paralleled those of whites. Like white people, they reported more cross-racial contact at the end of the decade than they had at the beginning, although the pattern of change over time was somewhat different. There was a sharp drop in the number of black people describing their neighborhoods, their local schools, and their friends as all black during the 1960's and no consistent change in the years thereafter. The proportion of black respondents reporting working in an all black situation declined moderately throughout this period, reaching a low of about one person in seven in 1974.

As this quotation implies, increases in perceived contacts were not the fantasies of those bent on social assimilation. Whites also report sharp increases in cross-racial relationships. These reports, furthermore, are accompanied by significant and dramatic changes in the attitudes of whites toward blacks (Institute for Social Research 1975). In 1964, 81 percent of the whites interviewed answered yes to the question, "Are your friends all white"? In 1974, 53 percent answered yes. Or, in response to the question, "Are you in favor of strict segregation?" 25 percent of the whites answered yes in 1964 but only 10 percent in 1974.

These shifts reflect the changing alignments of race and

class. For if blacks were increasingly accepted as friends and neighbors, it was partially because of the fading of a stereotype: the black as lower class. Hence changes in social attitudes were probably preceded by dramatic changes in economic status.

Indications of the nature of economic advancement may be seen through sample comparisons from the sixties to the present. For example, the number of blacks in white collar jobs more than doubled from 1960 to 1979. In 1960, 16 percent of the black labor force was in white collar jobs; in 1979 this figure was 38 percent. The corresponding increase during the same years for whites was from 47 to 52 percent. Likewise, with respect to education: in 1960, 2.7 years separated blacks and whites in the median years of school completed; in 1979, the difference dropped to 0.6 (U. S. Bureau of the Census 1980a:149, 421).

On top of the decline in skill differences, there was also a decline in the "cost of being black"—that is, in the income loss attributable to race when skill and experiential differences are held constant. Farley (1977) reports a drop of approximately $500 in this cost from 1959 to 1974 for black males. For females there was an even more dramatic drop—$900; in 1974 black women with the same characteristics as white women were likely to make $750 more.

Another area of mobility, into positions of power, has likewise shown substantial gains. One survey showed that in the private sector, 17 percent of a group of manufacturing firms and 28 percent of a group of nonmanufacturing firms reported blacks on their boards of directors (*International Herald Tribune* 1977a:9). Whether these statistics represent an increase is not indicated, although common sense suggests that they do. In the public sector gains are both more easily documented and more profound. While blacks have not achieved proportionate government representation, the Voting Rights Act of 1965 appears to have altered dramatically the frequency of black elected officials. Most of this has occurred on the state level. In 1977, there were only 1 senator and 16 representatives in Congress, but at the state level, the number of black legislators and executives more than tripled between 1964 and 1977, from 94 to 299. The available data for mayors and other elected officials date back only to 1970, but even during these years, representation increased: from 48 to 162 mayors during the years 1970–77; and during the same years a tripling—from approximately 1,200 to 3,800—of other elected officials (U. S. Department of Commerce 1979:156, 179).

There can be little dispute as to the facts. They reflect sharp changes in less than a decade. The point of contention is the meaning of such changes. Do they benefit only a small segment of blacks? Or are they more widely dispersed over the entire black community? This is difficult to tell. For however dramatic these changes may appear, the quest for racial parity moves at a snail's pace. Blacks more than doubled their numbers in the white collar labor force from 1960 to 1979; yet approximately the same proportion of whites had white collar jobs in 1940 as blacks in 1979. Likewise, the "cost of being black" has narrowed in recent years; yet the purchasing power of black families in 1974 was approximately equivalent to that of white families in 1954 (Farley 1977).

One interpretation of these paradoxes is this: change proceeds on a miniscule base of past black achievement. Hence dramatic shifts do not substantially alter the black's position in the community. There is an alternate view: that the distribution of mobility opportunities is bimodal. Some are advancing rapidly; others, hardly at all. This latter view is consistent with the mobility movement theme, and I turn to this issue next.

Losses: The Underclass. The major legislation passed during the sixties was of little direct benefit to poor blacks. In terms of voting, the poor in urban ghettos were mostly franchised, and this was not a dominant concern. In terms of federal discrimination, poor blacks were simply not competitive for most government positions; furthermore, the impact of affirm-ative action programs is probably open to question (*New York Times* 1978b:D9).

The issue of federal intervention that had potential sig-nificance was the "War on Poverty," mounted primarily under Johnson. Aside from poor administration and the eventual depletion of funds to support the debacle in Vietnam, the poverty program was typical of the American stance on pov-erty: attacking symptoms rather than causes. The brunt of the program extended job training and remedial education under the assumption that individual earnings were a func-tion solely of skills and personal resources. If skills and per-sonal resources were increased, earnings should follow.

Under optimum conditions, this argument may have merit. But the legacy of slavery and discrimination left a large portion of the black labor force vulnerable to structural trends in the economy: massive unemployment, a shrinking market for unskilled labor, and, where that marked existed, generally inadequate wages. Clearly, unless skilled jobs were available with reasonable wages, increasing the skill level of blacks would not substantially alter their numbers in poverty. At best then, the war on poverty, if successful—which it was not—might have merely created a skilled labor force without adequate employment. Altering the supply of skills may do little if the demand for these skills is not simultaneously changed.

In light of my remarks on efficiency and equality in the preceding chapter, it is no surprise that the government did little to expand employment opportunities. Nor could the cap-italist enterprise be counted on to do this on its own. In fact, by pursuing its own profit interests, the corporate enterprise may have an adverse effect: decreasing the demand for un-skilled and semi-skilled labor. Under the banner of minimiz-ing rising labor costs, corporations have increasingly sought to automate production or use cheap labor supplies in less developed countries. How many jobs have been lost in this process is largely unknown (see Barnett and Muller 1974).

But regardless of the exact numbers involved, the consequence is clear: a drop in demand for unskilled and semi-skilled labor, with the result that the very market in which blacks were competitive has been partially depleted.

Bonacich (1976) has wisely seized on these trends with a view to explaining the soaring rates of black unemployment. Her argument illustrates the greater ratio of black to white unemployment to be of recent vintage; as of 1930, for example, the ratio was reversed to the blacks' advantage. The cause of this turnabout lies in minimum wage legislation—which, in her view, inflated wages for the unskilled and led to a search for alternative sources of production. Whether minimum wage laws necessarily have this effect is unclear. Yet Bonacich's (1976:47, 49) remarks, in this situation, may have merit:

At least three options were open to the capitalist class. (Of course, not every capitalist had all three alternatives available.) First, they could relocate part of the industrial process overseas to make use of cheaper foreign labor. Second, they could relocate internally to those sectors of the economy where organized labor and/or protection had not yet penetrated. And third, they could mechanize, displacing jobs which had previously been performed by "cheap labor." These processes all had a negative impact on black employment. Protective legislation equalized the . . . price of labor, leading capital to seek cheaper alternatives. As a result, black labor has been by-passed for machines and other cheap labor groups, here and abroad, creating a class of hard-core unemployed in the ghettos. This reality took a while to emerge after the New Deal and only became full-blown in the mid-1950's when black unemployment reached its current two-to-one ratio.

This argument puts at center stage in discussions of black unemployment and poverty the capitalist quest to maintain profits in an uncertain marketplace. Until this quest is altered or until the government assumes more radical policies in the marketplace, the number of blacks in poverty may be remarkably stable, in spite of the furor of the sixties, and in spite of the economic progress of a middle stratum. Hence the possible stability of an underclass in American society, with blacks as its most numerous member.

There is nothing in Bonacich's argument which ties current discriminatory practices into unemployment in the black community. As a result of a legacy of discrimination, however, blacks may now be squeezed by a corporate effort to minimize labor costs. The importance of this view is in preventing overemphasis on "last hired, first fired" notions—and other attempts to link the black's plight to employer discrimination—at the expense of deeper, structural problems.

Countless research efforts have tied the economic status of blacks into the general vitality of the economy. Anderson (1964), for example, estimated that a 5 percent growth rate in per capita income would result in a 2.5 percent growth rate in black income; if per capita income was at a standstill, income among blacks would decline (see also Batchelder 1964). Yet Bonacich's position is less sanguine: that the market for unskilled employment is declining and may continue to do so regardless of long-term trends in the vitality of the economy. Indeed, the lesson of recent economic history suggests the compatibility of economic growth with less than full-scale employment.

The stability of unemployment and poverty is clear from statistics over the last two decades of experience—the period which reflects from several views an era of black progress. In 1960, 10.2 percent of the blacks were unemployed in comparison with 4.9 percent of the whites. In 1978, 12.2 percent of the blacks were unemployed in comparison with 5.3 percent of the whites. In 1960, the ratio of black to white unemployment was 2.1:1; in 1978, it was 2.3:1—virtually unchanged (U. S. Department of Commerce 1979:69, 209). While it is sometimes mentioned that black unemployment is generic to the young, the fact of the matter is that the racial ratio of imbalance in unemployment appears in all age groups and for both males and females (U. S. Bureau of the Census 1975a:65). Age statistics may aid in accurately describing black-white differences but they do not totally explain why these differences occur.

Nor is poverty any more reflective of change than unemployment. Of course, if one were to believe government statistics, the proportions of black families in poverty appear to have dropped drastically from 1959 to 1977, from 55 to 31 percent (U. S. Department of Commerce 1979:49, 201). Even so careful an observer as Oberschall (1973:236) has fallen prey to this myth: "The absolute number of blacks living below the poverty line decreased. . . . The first such reversal of this trend in a decade." The implication is that "the underclass is diminishing."

Yet, as formerly noted, government statistics on poverty hold the unrealistic position that persons in poverty ought to maintain living standards prevailing more than a decade ago while others enjoy the fruits of affluence. This view perpetuates the fiction of a decline in poverty. Although the fiction is widely understood in government circles, little has been done about it (U. S. Department of Labor 1970).

If, in lieu of government standards, a definition of poverty as half the median income is used, something different is suggested. As noted in chapter 2, there is ample support in the literature for defining poverty in relative terms (e.g., Townsend 1974; Miller and Roby 1970). When this alternate definition is used, and family size differences are ignored, income data show that 43 percent of black families earned less than half the median income in 1960 as compared with 40 percent in 1979 (U. S. Bureau of the Census 1980a:450). By any criterion, this decline is meager. Furthermore, even with government poverty standards, there is no indication of blacks moving out of poverty more quickly than whites. In fact, the reverse is true. On a percentage basis, the black-white ratio for individuals in poverty was 1.30:1 in 1959 and 1.88:1 in 1979; for families the ratio was 3.39:1 in 1959 and 4.10 to 1 in 1979. Nor are the statistics more impressive if alternate government standards are used—as, for example, those below 125 percent of the low-income poverty level: the ratio of blacks to whites here was 2.50:1 in 1959 and 3.05:1 in 1979 (U. S. Bureau of the Census 1980a:465). Again, a slip backward.

Unemployment and poverty may have additional, more indirect influences on access to life chances. The case can—and has—been made that poverty and unemployment generally debase the traditional male role. The consequence of this may be seen in the larger proportion of female-headed households among blacks. In 1979, for example, 37 percent of existing black families were headed by women in contrast to 12 percent among whites (U. S. Bureau of the Census 1980a:48). Furthermore, there are indications that this ratio has been widening—and also indications that black female-headed households have had more children to support in recent years than in the past (U. S. Bureau of the Census 1975a:106–7). The absence of a potential wage earner naturally puts families at an economic disadvantage. Farley's review of black economic gains shows that family income has not paralleled rises in individual income (Farley 1977:199): "If family income is the criteria of status, there is no evidence that the pattern of improvement which was seen in the 1960's continued into the 1970's." Census data show some minor equalization but little in the way of a dramatic trend over three decades of experience: black to white family income ratio was at 0.54 in 1950, rose to 0.65 in 1975, and dropped back to 0.60 in 1979 (U. S. Bureau of the Census 1980a:451).

These data, on family income, on poverty, on unemployment highlight the stagnation or deterioration in the black condition. Each of these three factors is a key determinant of access to life chances. And all of this, surprisingly, occurred during an era with narrowing black-white differences in occupational status, education, and individual income. The conclusion is inescapable: an underclass of blacks may be becoming increasingly differentiated within the larger black community. Furthermore, there is no hint here that prejudice in the contemporary marketplace is wholly responsible for black poverty. The legacy of discrimination created a resevoir of semi-skilled and unskilled blacks squeezed into a market of contracting demand. Unless market developments are reversed or the government activates large-scale programs to offset poverty and unemployment—through adequate welfare or through attacking this problem at its roots—the differences among blacks and between a black underclass and more affluent whites may become painfully more dramatic in the future.

Conclusions

The stability of blacks in poverty is an ironic consequence of a successful mobility movement: a middle stratum able to press its demands; a lower stratum caught in more complex economic straits. Neither consensus views nor conflict views espoused from a Marxist perspective adequately handle these events.

Consensus notions turn too heavily on negotiation and compromise, whereas bitter confrontations and violence were integral to the fight for black rights. These facts in themselves signaled the failure of democracy and the corporate economy to extend benefits to all. Marxist views hold up somewhat better, particularly in their depiction of poverty as a consequence of the relentless quest to minimize labor costs so as to maximize profit. But in the contention of a *Klasse für sich* Marxism fails. Capitalism was not made a dominant issue in the struggle for black rights; the gains sought were compatible with the existing parameters of the capitalist structure. From the point of view of the economic system, no radical changes were sought, nor for that matter was any such change activated by the government. The structural bases of inequality continued. The changes that were extended were simply in line with America's definition of opportunity. Given equal opportunity, everyone can succeed.

Unfortunately, opportunity does not extend to all. As I noted in the preceding section, blacks in poverty remain as numerous as before the inflammatory outbursts of the sixties. Two things work against an immediate resolution of this problem. The first is the possibility that black leadership may be partially satisfied with some of the legislation in the sixties and therefore unwilling to take up the cause of the impoverished. Symbolic satiation is always a potential. Certainly, there is no dominant, widespread national concern over the plight of blacks today in spite of the persistence of economic disadvantage.

A second factor is the increased differentiation within the black community. If the assimilation of middle stratum blacks into positions of affluence continues, then the poverty of other blacks can hardly be considered a racial issue alone. This robs the situation of its inflammatory quality. Increased differentiation may also undermine the possibility of a coalition between a lower stratum and a middle stratum which might take up the cause. I should point out, however, that coalitions of this type are increasingly prevalent. Certainly some of the black protest in the sixties was aided in wealthy, liberal circles.

But even if the problem of blacks in poverty were solved, what precisely would a solution mean? The fact of the matter is that the issue of blacks in poverty goes beyond the issue of race. The issue, as I have argued, is connected to the larger problems of the capitalist structure: whether an unplanned economy dedicated to growth and profits can at the same time provide a livelihood for all members of society. Capitalism may well exploit minorities—although it would just as well underpay all persons who lack the power to demand more: the aged, rural people, migrant workers. There is litte question that Marxists are correct in their view of the exploitative nature of capitalism. My point of contention, however, is that the solutions sought to problems of poverty in America are typically couched in mobility terms. This means that while various groups may be displaced from poverty, poverty itself remains.

This is not to minimize the importance of the black problem or to deny its unique racial characteristics. But I do argue for the utility of seeing racial problems in the context of eco-

nomic inequality generally. As long as inequality exists, there
will be both advantaged and disadvantaged. At any point in
time, different sectors may fall into the economically subordinate group: minorities, workers displaced by technological
change; migrants; victims of failing industries. From the perspective of our current knowledge, which groupings fall into
the slots of poverty may be indeterminate. But until the broad
problems of capitalism are broached and resolved, the differences between the advantaged and disadvantaged persist.

Small Businessmen:
Economic or
Psychological Reactions?

MOBILITY AND CONFLICT shift the fruits of affluence and the burdens of deprivation. But the underlying structure of inequality persists. In illustrating this point, my perspective is essentially in agreement with Marx's characterization of business, in the relentless pursuit of profits and the conflict emerging from this pursuit. Yet I depart on two points: whether the economy offers partial mobility opportunities; whether these opportunities encourage conflict to advance status claims, at the cost of keeping the status quo intact. The use of conflict for mobility may well describe any variety of groups implicated in the capitalist economy and not merely the general category of wage workers which is the centerpiece of Marxist analysis.

In this chapter, I further illustrate the mobility argument with reference to small businessmen. This choice provides an opportunity to discuss mobility analysis in economic and political arenas different from those broached in previous chapters: with respect to the political right rather than the left;

with respect to individuals outside the dependency relationship of business and labor. Furthermore, the case allows examination of McCarthyism—which, with the race riots of the
sixties, represents one of the major rifts in post–World War
II America. But most generally, the choice of small businessmen brings into focus an important variant of consensus perspectives, the theory of mass society. Consideration of this
perspective is vital to my contention that neither consensus
nor Marxist views are wholly adequate to explain conflict in
contemporary American society.

Specifically, as considerable ink has been spent on fitting
racial conflict into Marxist and similar views—stressing resource monopolization and racial unity—so too much ink has
been spent on reconciling the consensus position with rightist
movements of a protofascistic variety. Small businessmen are
seen to be at the center of such rightist activities, responsible
for a diversity of political movements ranging from Nazi
power in Germany to Poujadism in France and McCarthyism
in the United States. Each is identified by mass society theorists as a revolution of the right, moving by authoritarian
means to return time to an era of laissez-faire capitalism.

My basic concern is to confront the thrust and terms of
mass society theory. The essence of the theory is simply put:
structural changes in the wider society have moved various
groups out from under the umbrella of affluence and prestige.
These groups tend to be isolated from ongoing relations, and
furthermore, alienated and distrustful of ascendent trends in
the wider society. Their resentments are expressed in extremist behavior, which represents a threat to order and stability—that is, to the very norms on which democratic consensus
is built. In the mass society view, such extremism underlies
the central path of facism.

In previous chapters I argued that an understanding of
mobility opportunities and aspirations is better able to account for conflict than the classical versions of Marxist analysis. In this chapter I argue the same point with respect to
the mass society view: that economic considerations are gen-

erally at the heart of most contemporary conflict; that such conflicts become comprehensible as the diverse meanings of inequality are considered, with respect to market situations and opportunity structures; and that the mobility goals of the groups in question can usually account for conflict. The implication here is that the special terms of mass society theory pertaining to economic marginality as well as to psychological considerations of alienation and distrust are superfluous and represent an attempt to rationalize away existing and persistent conflicts.

Mass Society Theory: An Elaboration of the Consensus Position

Mass society theory is a variant of the consensus position. It attempts to explain conflict situations left unresolved in the consensus framework—without considering Marxist alternatives. Four major terms are central to the theory: (1) extremism; (2) alienation; (3) participation; (4) marginality. In this section I review these terms within the context of the theory, and in following sections illustrate their inadequacies in the face of simpler explanations concerned with politics and economic mobility.

Extremism. Consensus theory is no naive denial of group differentiation. From the consensus view, conflict in industrial societies persists, though minor in form compared with the revolutionary challenges of a former era. Business interests work for more profits, labor for higher wages and fringe benefits. But these differences are neither incompatible nor divisive. Instead, the differences provide an agenda for institutionalized compromise through the forum of unions and democratic government. As compromise is effected, the course of industrial societies toward political stability and order is charted and reinforced.

Critics of the consensus view have noted that democratic mechanisms do not preclude conflict (Gamson 1975). Institutional procedures may break down. The positions involved in conflict may be too far apart. Or the mechanisms themselves may be faulty, giving too much weight to financially or numerically powerful groups. At this point dissident groups may take direct action to force their position on others, or otherwise sanction powerful majorities.

To handle this possibility, mass society theory adds to the consensus framework a distinction between conventional and extremist conflict. Conventional conflict involves the usual array of pressure group tactics: lobbying, bargaining, compromising, and so forth. Extremist conflict, however, is defined by two important traits: (1) a direct attack on opposing groups through nondemocratic channels; (2) a position maintained without possibility for compromise (Selznick 1952). Kornhauser (1959:45) discusses this distinction as follows:

At times, people may act directly by grasping those means of action which lie immediately at hand. They may employ various more or less coercive measures against those individuals and groups who resist them. . . . For example, when large numbers of people feel that taxes are intolerably high, they may engage in quite different types of action. On the one hand, they may seek to change the tax laws by financing lobbyists, electing representatives, persuading others of their views by means of discussion, and so forth. These types of action are mediated by institutional relations, and are therefore subject to rules concerning legitimate modes of political action. On the other hand, people may seek to prevent others from paying their taxes and forcibly impede officials from collecting taxes. . . . This is direct action.

Direct action in this view is extremism. It is tantamount to a denial of democratic process and legitimate opposition. Since this is a threat to the order of industrial society, its sources—the reasoning assumes—must lie among those handicapped by the industrial economy. That is, the proponents of extremism must be economically marginal. This is an important way mass society theory shunts conflict to the side—attributing it to persons outside the nearly (but not totally) comprehensive umbrella of affluence.

The link of marginality to extremism is explained in terms of the process of social change—specifically, uneven industrialization and urbanization. Kornhauser (1959:150, 157), for example, speaks of "marked discontinuities in social organization" brought about by "the very rapid expansion of cities and industries." Change is also partial. Because of outmoded production or other failings, certain groups are incapable of adapting to the industrial order. Without recourse to whatever fruits the industrial society may bear, these groups support extremist movements, which, symbolically or otherwise, promise a place in the sun. Mass theorists are thus able at once to conceive of industrial societies as relatively free of social conflict and to account for extremist activities. Extremism is a vestige, a leftover of a prior class-ridden society.

Implicit throughout mass society discussions is the judgment on the desirability of order. References are made to the importance of maintaining "institutional procedures," "rules," "majority choice," "minority rights." These phrases refer to the rules of the game which weigh on democratic procedure regardless of the decisions reached. The procedures which regulate democratic activities are vital to preserving order and stability. For when all is said and done, the minority of today may be the majority of tomorrow. But it can only be a majority if alternate positions are not shut off and access to democratic procedure is preserved. In this way, the pluralistic balance of interests which contributes to democratic government can be maintained.

This is a reasonable interpretation of democratic theory and in fact may sound like a textbook celebration of democracy. But matters are more complex than this. Simply put: mass theory views with suspicion departures from conventional interest-group politics. These departures play havoc with the social order, undermining the very foundations of democracy. Overt and violent conflict is then an extraordinary event. Its presence signals the necessity of bringing to bear terms other than those applied to more conventional tactics. Hence the array of verbal distinctions underlined by mass theorists: alienation, extremism, marginality.

But is there anything really extraordinary about conflict occurring beyond parliamentary debate and negotiation? Probably not, since conventional politics may be without desired effects. Critics of the mass position argue that values favoring order have little place in scientific theories, and in fact restrict understandings of protest (O'Brien 1972). These critics point to the plight of various minority groups for whom democracy simply does not work. Does democracy demand that blacks postpone radical action for another day and moderate their outrage? Are the urban riots of the sixties best viewed as casting democracy aside or as an attempt to alter its course by advancing mobility claims of the deprived? Is it reasonable to anticipate that democracy must (or will) bind individuals to its rules—even when these same individuals suffer from the way democracy is run (Gusfield 1962)? Furthermore, although intense and violent conflict indeed denies the legitimacy of opposition, this is true of many forms of political change (Bottomore 1970:22): "There is nothing at all undemocratic in popular movements which aim to get rid of those interest groups whose activities are harmful to a majority of the population, even if this involves reducing the plurality of interest groups. . . ."

To the extent that the "normal channels of protest" are conservative and adverse to change and risk, many groups will continually be jeopardized economically—and led to seek solutions through conflict of an overt and potentially violent nature. The probability of conflict extending beyond democratic channels, then, is continually high under capitalism. This is not an extraordinary outcome to be examined with special terms. Rather it is quite compatible with the more traditional concepts used in analyzing the quest for mobility in restrictive economic settings.

Furthermore, little is gained from alluding to marginality—unless one is willing to expand that category to include the deprived generally. Unemployed blacks, workers in peripheral industries, persons without marketable skills have no better prospects for long-range gain than small businessmen or others identified by mass theorists as marginal. In fact their prospects may be less. In addition, the term "marginality" portrays the roots of conflict among those excluded from the fruits of economic affluence. I have shown previously and will argue here that the reverse is frequently the case: conflict is bred not among those with much to lose, but among those with much to gain.

Alienation and Participation. To the terms marginality and extremism another set of phrases are added: participation and alienation. The contention here is that the failure to participate fully in the rich life of interest group politics further estranges and alienates individuals. In this climate of psychological suspicion and distrust, the stage is set for irrational attacks on existing institutions. The alienated become pawns of the facist appeal.

The concern with integration and social stability reflects the influential hand of Durkheim in functionalist sociology. Nearly all Durkheim's writings express concern with societal intgration and order. In *The Division of Labor* (Durkheim 1960:353–73) and later in *Suicide* (Durkheim 1966:241–58), this concern focused on the particularly vulnerable aspects of industrial society: specifically, the upheavals in the economy and their repercussions for individuals and classes. Disillusioned with the prospects of either the family or religion as moral authorities, Durkheim turned to occupational associations out of the belief that they were available to all for participation, stable beyond the lives of individuals, and important agencies proximate to a potentially disruptive economic marketplace. In Durkheim's view, the occupational group was as an adjustive mechanism permitting individuals to withstand societal crises and reduce felt alienation.

Mass society theorists take up and enlarge Durkheim's concerns. Extremist responses not only reflect the failure to use existing channels of protest but are themselves a product of isolation from ongoing interest groups. Interest groups, in the mass view, provide a forum for discussing current events and for linking the implications of these events to everyday life. In the absence of a forum, events in the wider society become difficult to comprehend (Kornhauser 1959:65):

> People who do not participate in organized activity are less likely to understand distant events, so that a major crisis which suddenly thrust such events into personal situations finds previous non-participants readily available for highly irrational and extremist interpretations of them.

Irrational actions, of the extremist variety, are a possible outcome.

Peculiarly, the logic used in this argument reverses the connections usually drawn between conflict and organizational participation. In the mass view, participation restrains overt conflict by directing discontent into normal political channels. Yet the evidence discussed in previous chapters suggests a contrary view: that the propensity for conflict is greatest among those least isolated—union members, blacks tied to voluntary organizations, and so forth. As Pinard (1968:684) has put the matter:

> What constitutes a major shortcoming of mass theory is its failure to recognize that secondary groupings can also exert . . . mobilizing functions. . . . By this, we mean that certain intermediate groups, because of their positive orientations to the means and goals of a social movement, can be a strong force acting to motivate and legitimate individual as well as group participation in a movement.

The failure to tie protest to organizational life further reflects the resistance in the mass view to understanding conflict as integral to ongoing social activities (Coser 1964). This is further reinforced by the use of the term alienation, which partially shifts the burden of explanation from economic to psychological grounds. Conflict, in this view, is not merely a product of deprivation, but also a product of those psychologically out of step with society: the distrustful, the suspicious, the powerless, the confused. Again, the questionable link of adjustment to consensus and order.

Mass society theory must be credited with going beyond consensus theory in evolving a framework for analyzing conflict. Yet, in my view, this framework must be judged inadequate. By attributing conflict to the marginal—defined in economic, interactional, and psychological terms—mass theory at once explains conflict and explains it away. In the following sections I will show: (1) that alienation has little to do with marginality, and instead can be traced to the position of businessmen in the productive process; (2) that some of the attitudes identified with extremism are not rallying points for a rightist revolt as much as a standard part of business ideology—and indeed are distinct and separate from the more authoritarian, "facist" attitudes of the alienated; and (3) that the business ideology, which has been connected to support for McCarthyism and other seemingly facistic movements, is espoused not by the alienated or the marginal but by the standard bearers of the community's status quo: business members of local chambers of commerce. My purpose is simply to illustrate conflict as an anticipated outcome normally associated with collective reactions to economic interests.

Small Business:
The Structure of Partial Opportunity

The demise of the old middle class, as evidenced by the marginality of small businessmen, is a critical case in the mass society framework. For the small businessman is said to exemplify the loss of power and the futility of hope for success in the contemporary industrial world. He is literally the mar-

ginal man of the marketplace—displaced by the soaring capacity for big business to monopolize control of the economy.
In this context mass society theory spins its scenario of the
small businessman's reaction to increasingly restrictive economic opportunity: heightened alienation, the absence of long-
term possibilities for success, the turning of political support
to authoritarian, facistic regimes so as to assure (and rees-
tablish) a place in the sun.

I have previously noted the utility of this logic for the
mass society position. By conceptualizing the small firm as
an anachronism in contemporary capitalism, a vestige from
a former era, mass theory is able to create an aura of consensus
marred only by forces out of tune with social and economic
change. Yet there is some question whether these highly restrictive understandings of opportunity are reasonable.

The point of contention in this section is the accuracy of
the judgement on marginality: the literal absence of long-
range possibilities for securing adequate life chances (Trow
1958). The judgment of marginality and deprivation—sub-
jectively and objectively defined—is fashionable in many
forms of conflict analysis. For it sets up a clear framework of
motivation for understanding the radical alternatives posed
by dissident groups. But in so doing, conflict analysts may be
buying a highly rigid and restrictive notion of social change:
that change moves in a clear manner to totally displace the
functions of certain economic groups. Technology advances
and displaces the wage worker. Concentration advances and
displaces the small businessman. But another view is also
conceivable: new functions are added yet old ones are not
necessarily displaced. The new and old rest side by side. One
does not necessarily and inevitably displace the other (Gusfield 1967).

In this section I argue this case with respect to the persistence of small business opportunity. The impetus for this
is in part to dispel the description of increasing marginality
among small businessmen, and with it the explanation of
conflict as attributable to marginal and displaced elements.

This parallels the discussion of mobility opportunities for wage workers and blacks, although here my reference is to entrepreneurial activities rather than wage gains in the context of the corporate structure. Yet the purpose is similar: to reduce casual inferences from deprivation to the origins of conflict.

More specifically, I maintain that while businesses may grow and concentrate, this is not necessarily and inevitably at the cost of the small business enterprise. By recognizing this possibility, and the mobility opportunities it may afford, I direct explanations of conflict away from marginality. Instead attention is directed toward an understanding of conflict as integral to the recurrent functions of the small business enterprise in capitalist economies.

Market Contraction. The growth and concentration of industry and finance are not open to question. This is widely recognized and hardly needs to be recounted here. Economic giants dominate retailing and industry; the record of mergers and acquisitions, though variable and erratic, shows no long-range trend toward decline—the reverse indeed being the case (U.S. Bureau of the Census 1975b:487–508).

What is at issue is whether and in what way these trends threaten the existence of small businesses. Assumed in the mass society position are mutually exclusive courses of organizational development and survival: the growth of big business means the demise of small business. Little attention is given to the possibility that big and small businesses may exist side by side, where the presence of one need not necessarily and inevitably affect the success of the other.

The threats posed by growth and concentration, real as they may be, have probably been exaggerated. In the first place, there is nothing in trends on industrial concentration which necessarily threaten all small business enterprises. Large firms gain advantage through an increase in scale: in capital investments, in smaller marginal fixed costs, in product innovation, and so forth. On these grounds, larger businesses can and do provide products at more competitive rates, hence squeezing small businesses from the marketplace. But small businesses are threatened by larger ones only to the extent that they represent higher marginal costs per product. In many areas large and small businesses do not compete with respect to products. Small businesses cannot (and do not) make cars and refrigerators on any scale. And even in areas where there is product competition, other bases of competition are refocused on a host of sundry services. Furthermore, small businesses frequently function as high risk, limited investment outlets to capitalize on specialized consumer minorities. This is particularly evident in exotic art, home decorations and furnishings, specialty food, clothing, antiques. Again, competition with big business is not direct. Finally, many professional and service related activities have traditionally maintained a small business basis of organization.

By focusing on the limited instance of direct competition at higher marginal costs, mass society theory exaggerates the risks for small businesses implied in economic growth and concentration. Past estimates of risk are difficult to come by and not precisely comparable with contemporary statistics. Yet, limited as they may be, they suggest small business enterprises to be as much a risk in the past—when industrial concentration was less exaggerated—as they are today. Mayer (1947), for example, covered historical records in Worcester and Boston for the year 1840 and found that for a total of 56 businesses, 20 percent were suspended within five years, another 20 percent in ten years, and yet another 20 percent within fifteen years. Likewise, Oxenfeldt and Oxenfeldt (1951) report that of 539 retailers who started businesses within the state of Colorado in 1927, 80 percent failed within eight years. These figures are slightly higher but not incomparable with more recent estimates of business failure (Mayer and Goldstein 1961; Bechofer et al., 1974). Rosenbluth (1959:197), in reviewing the Dun and Bradstreet failure record states that over a fifty-year period dating back to the turn of the century, the evidence "suggests that there has not been any long run tendency towards increased mortality among small firms. In fact, the opposite trend is suggested by the figures." More recent data, from 1935–1974, largely bear out this conclusion (Dun and Bradstreet 1976). Incomplete as these data may be, they do not point to excessive increases in economic marginality of the small business enterprise.

A similar conclusion can be drawn with respect to the number of new businesses started each year. Unquestionably, fewer persons are engaged today in small businesses than was true in the past, although how much so is a point of speculation. Mills (1951:63) estimates that in the early nineteenth century four-fifths of the labor force was self-employed compared to about one-fifth in mid-twentieth century—although this included agricultural workers. More to the point, however, are estimates of business enterprises as a percentage of all gainful workers. Phillips (1958), for example, notes that when only nonagricultural concerns are considered, the relative number of small businessmen remained constant over the seventy year period 1880–1950. The same is true of the number of small business enterprises: it was approximately 22 per thousand of population in 1900 and 26 per thousand in 1955 (Mayer and Goldstein 1961). Between 1950 and 1977, the census lists an absolute increase of 65 percent in the number of individually owned businesses (U. S. Bureau of the Census 1980a:556; see also Rogers and Berg 1961). In part this reflects population growth; in part also it reflects the curious persistence of small businesses, even in the context of massive economic concentration.

Risk and Economic Well-Being. Dun and Bradstreet's (1976) extensive annual review of some 9,000 business records shows failure to be a direct function of size of assets: firms with more than $1 million in assets fail at the rate of 4.3 percent a year; firms with assets of between $5,000 and $1 million dollars fail at a rate of approximately 33 percent a year. The only exception to this pattern of relationship is the almost tiny businesses with capital investments of under $5,000 dollars; here the failure record is only 3.1 percent. While Dun and Bradstreet do not further describe this category, I surmise that it is made up of either artisans (e.g., painters, carpenters) or those moonlighting on a second job, but in any event those with little capital investment to incur any risk from possible failure.

The implication of mass theory is that the high margin of risk is a function of business growth and concentration. Yet the statistics suggest this not to be clearly the case. Furthermore, existing studies ascribe small business failure more to irrational practices than to industrial trends—with the implication being that failure rates may be stable throughout the course of industrialization. Were this the case, the displacement argument given by mass theorists would be open to question.

A variety of research has documented a connection between small business failure and the absence of commercial rationality. One study reports in pathetic detail the utter commercial ignorance of many new enterprises (Mayer and Goldstein 1961:117–33). Irrational practices abound. The details are ludicrous, ranging from restaurants with no food to serve, major repairs made without charges, working capital of no more than $17.00. Furthermore, the reasons given for opening a business have little to do with expertise. A British study cited the desire to be independent, "one's own boss" as the chief reason for entering business (Bechofer et al. 1974). Likewise, Mayer and Goldstein (1961) note that working for oneself was the primary reason for entering business, and making "real" money was the most important secondary reason.

Mass society theory depicts entrepreneurs as rugged individualists squeezed by forces of economic concentration beyond their control. But these same individuals are frequently nothing other than blue collar workers—searching for a lark, an avenue of escape. Some years ago, Chinoy (1955) observed how the hopes and aspirations of automobile workers hinged on the prospects of opening a small shop. Lipset and Bendix's (1952) interviews with manual workers in Oakland, California, suggested that 40 percent were connected at one time or another with a small business. These are not individuals steeped in the folkways of commercial success. The assumption typically made is that businesses run themselves. This is not the case. Failure is a likely consequence whenever lack of business acumen compounds the problems of an already risky venture.

While the risk is high, the payoff may be substantial, considering who these businessmen are and what they expect. The earnings of small businessmen do not, of course, match those of salaried managers or professionals. But if we use the census category of "self-employed managers" as an approximation of small businessmen, then annual earnings are on a par with sales workers, higher than those of clerical workers, and also higher than in all the major categories of blue collar workers (U. S. Bureau of the Census 1980b:249). Furthermore, there is little sign of slippage. Self-employed managers earned 76 percent of salaried manager's income in 1958, 64 percent in 1969, and 72 percent in 1976 (U. S. Bureau of the Census 1971:229, 1978:224).

These incomes are hardly reflective of dismal economic prospects. Given the fact that many small businessmen are of blue collar origins (Lipset and Bendix 1959) and are distinctly less well educated than all categories of white collar workers (as well as some categories of blue collar workers—U. S. Bureau of the Census 1973:788), their earnings can hardly be written off as indicative of bleak economic prospects.

Transformations in Ownership and Control. A further defect in the mass society characterization of small business prospects lies in the failure to recognize significant changes and developments in the small firm. The image projected is of the "mom and pop" store, but this is only partially accurate. Increasingly, small retail firms are involved in franchise systems which link individual owners to large-scale capital investments and enterprises. Mass society theory relates small firms to a former stage of organizational development and, by freezing their conceptions of these firms as vestiges of the past, cannot do justice to transformations in ownership and control.

The franchise system, much like the dual labor market, offers possibilities for the mutual pursuit of interests among actors with varying interests. Although riding a wave of recent development, franchises themselves are not new. What is new is their mushrooming growth, beyond traditional grocery and service station outlets. The exact number of franchised outlets is approximately 450,000, representing about 5 percent of all known businesses, large and small (U. S. Department of Commerce 1976). While modest, the percentage is likely indicative of trends to come.

Franchises provide precisely the information and rationality typically absent in independent small business ventures: access to capital investment; information on site location and regional market studies; advertising; promotional aids; bookkeeping instruction; managerial training; and the product itself. In turn, the parent firm, by charging a licensing fee, reduces its own risk and further, through product outlets and commissions, continues throughout the life of the franchise to reap substantial profits.

Importantly, the risk for the small businessman is thereby reduced. A U. S. Department of Commerce (1976:24) estimate gives the failure rate of franchises to be approximately 5 percent. This rate is not exactly comparable with the 10–20 percent estimates previously discussed for small businesses (Mayer and Goldstein 1961; Bechofer et al. 1974), in part because some unknown portion of the franchise data involve corporate holdings. Nonetheless, the magnitude of the difference suggests the franchise to be a more secure investment.

The franchise is no alliance between large and small-scale businesses—at least no more so than the dual labor market is an alliance of capital and labor. By placing the burdens of investment on individual entrepreneurs, the arrangement indeed may be little more than a ploy by big business to reduce initial costs and displace risk. While formal studies of this issue are virtually nonexistent, media reports suggest persistent pressure on franchising outlets to turn highly profitable sites over to the parent organization. Under the guise of maintaining quality product control, franchise owners are pressured to sell, and thus convert the outlet to a company store (*Wall Street Journal* 1979:1).

Nonetheless, the franchise system reflects adaptive arrangements juxtaposing large and small organizations. In evaluating the mass society position, this arrangement poses a critical test. Mass theorists contend that extremism among small businessmen is a product of inadequate access to the advantages of large-scale economic organization. Franchised small businessmen, however, have both the independence of the typical entrepreneur and access to the benefits of large-scale organization. If it can be shown that these franchised businessmen—who are central to trends in large-scale retail and marketing developments—are susceptible to the same political movements as other businessmen, then doubt can be cast on the link between marginality and conflict. In the following section I turn to this problem.

Alienation and Conflict

Mass society theorists connect support for extremism with economic marginality and its consequence, alienation and distrust of contemporary events. The small business opportunities noted in the previous section, however, are inconsistent with these bleak characterizations of economic prospects. Opportunities exist. While these opportunities are by no means limitless, they tend to result in earnings higher than for manual workers and less skilled white collar workers.

Small businesses thrive as much in the present as they did a century ago. Risk is high, but no more so today than in eras prior to recent surges in economic concentration. Moreover, marginality would be a fitting description if, and only if, the term could be extended to the other groups in the population which likewise share high risk—albeit through unemployment rather than business failure—and moderate income. But mass theorists have yet to make this case.

Because of these facts, a major premise of mass theory should be viewed with suspicion: that extremism among small businessmen is a function of constricted opportunities. In this section I consider the connections of marginality to alienation and extremism. I will argue that the activities interpreted by mass theorists as extremist may in part be attempts by the integrated and advantaged to espouse values consistent with their economic interests.

Mass explanations of small business support for extremism rest on a dual charge. Small businessmen are alienated and distrustful of contemporary society *and* desirous of a return to a nineteenth-century economic order symbolized by competition and laissez-faire ideology. This argument departs from ordinary explanations of politics in its specific concern with alienation, suspicion, and distrust. Yet there is real question whether this additional psychological consideration is meaningful in this context or merely confusing. Alienated individuals may indeed be disposed to extremist activities, as mass theorists maintain. Likewise, small businessmen may embrace ideologies favoring competition in a laissez-faire economy. But to place these two assertions into one package is unreasonable. For it assumes that economic interests partially flow from psychological factors. This confuses two highly different types of explanation, and has the added effect for the mass view of explaining economic difficulties in terms of psychological adjustment. I will point out, however, that viable as each of these separate explanations may be, they pertain to different segments of small businessmen which have been inextricably but mistakenly linked in the mass society view.

The specifics of my argument are as follows. First, alienation is not related to marginality—at least not in the sense implied by mass theorists. Businessmen with good long-range prospects for success are no more alienated than those without such prospects; alienation is related more to recurrent economic functions than to marginal prospects. Second, alienated individuals, while frequently opposed to contemporary trends, are hardly likely to support a competitive economic order. The alienated are persons of modest mobility orientations and modest income, and are unlikely candidates for spearheading fierce competition in the economy. Third, competitive values favoring a laissez-faire orientation are no more suggestive of radical change than welfare values as favored by labor. Rather than a rightist attempt to dismantle growth toward concentration, these values are best seen as little more than typical of business ideology. Fourth, and consistent with my previous comments on mobility movements, proponents of the so-called nineteenth-century economic posture are not down and out but rather psychologically integrated and socially active members of the business community, supporting values consistent with their interests. In brief, the link from marginality to alienation to extremism is ill founded. If anything can be found among the politics of small businessmen, it is this: a simple attempt to support values consistent with economic interests.

More generally, the thrust of consensus theory, of which the mass society perspective is a variant, is to argue and illustrate widespread agreement on liberal-socialist values in the industrial state. This translates into the rights of labor to welfare, the rights of business to profits, and the rights of governments to intervene and regulate these interests in a just and equitable manner. The implication here is that values pertaining to competition and laissez-faire ideologies are anachronisms, are indicative of *nineteenth-century* postures and are therefore supported by those marginal to society: in a social, economic, and psychological sense. My intention here is to argue that consensus on liberal-socialist values is largely illusory and that support for competition and laissez-faire ide-

ology is neither dead nor a product of marginality and maladjustment in the sense mass society theorists postulate. I
will turn first to the evidence these theorists present in defense of their position.

The Small Businessman as Fascist. Traditional thinking in
political sociology suggests that in times of crisis, labor moves
to the left and business to the right. The implication of mass
society theory for the reactions of small businessmen goes
beyond this traditional posture. It suggests first that the problems of small businessmen are not defined by crisis, by erratic
swings in the economy, but are defined instead by long-term
trends offering faint hope of economic success. It suggests
second that small businessmen support not merely the right
but those elements in it which violently attack existing leaders—with a view to denying order in the democratic process.

The evidence in support of this contention is culled from
three social movements: Nazism in Germany, Poujadism in
France, McCarthyism in the United States. The interpretation of these movements is informed, however, by some fundamental ideas about industrialization drawn from the more
general consensus position. Central to this view is an understanding of the partial and discontinuous nature of industrial
change. Organizational and technological developments give
primacy to some groups, but displace others. At any point in
time, the sweep of affluence implicit in this view of industrialization will simply bypass economic activities founded on
outmoded forms of commerce and production. And it is in
these outmoded activities that conflict evolves.

Throughout the argument there is the limiting assumption that economic development results in mutually exclusive
trends: displaced groups have hopeless futures and react with
protest; favored groups join in a societal consensus. Scattered
in these discussions are passing references to the minimal but
discernible casualties of industrial change: unmodernized
plants, outlying regions, strata which have not shared in

economic growth (see, for example, Lipset 1968). The core of society is thus conflict free while the perimeters are cluttered with marginal elements reacting to industrial change. Protest is thus placed in the context of a "pocket of resistance," and consensus is reserved for those covered by contemporary affluence.

Mass theory picks up this explanation and generalizes it to the entire category of entrepreneurial functions. That is, not merely regional markets or segments of small firms are uncompetitive but all small businessmen. By pointing to nearly complete closure in long-range opportunities for status maintenance and mobility, mass theorists set the stage for explaining alienation and support for extremist conflict among small businessmen. And on the surface, at least, a review of the three social movements—Nazism, Poujadism, McCarthyism—appears to support their contentions.

In each of these cases, the burden of analysis is to show how the precarious economic position of small businessmen, compounded by the absence of allies in big business and big labor, enhances susceptibility to fascistic appeals. Hence in the analysis of small business support for the Nazis in the late twenties and early thirties, emphasis is placed on the generally harsh economic conditions: the five million unemployed; the farmers and small businessmen unable to meet mortgage obligations; the rash of labor strikes which underscored the possibility of a Bolshevik takeover. On top of this, as Heberle (1945:3) has argued, was the frightening ascendence of the giant industrial trust and cartel:

The entire period from 1920 to 1933 was characterized by the growth of combinations, trusts, cartels, holding companies in manufacturing, in commerce and in banking. The old middle class of independent businessmen was deprived of its financial resources, was weakened by its economic influence and suffered severe shocks to its sense of security.

The evidence indeed suggests that small businessmen responded in kind by supporting the Nazis. Pratt (1948), for example, cites a substantial area by area correlation between the percentage of votes given to Nazis and the presence of business establishments with one person employed. Likewise, Loomis and Beegle (1946) also were able to establish that for farmers, more votes were given to the Nazis among owners of middle-size family farms than large commercial farms. There is evidence to suggest also that the number of proprietors in an area (in comparison to wage workers) became more critical for Nazi support as the depression worsened (Heberle 1945:118).

Similar results are shown in support for Poujadism, a grass-roots effort in France of the mid-fifties to denationalize the economy, cut taxes, relax economic controls, and do all these things through cries of conspiracy and threats of political assasination and violence (Hoffman 1956; de Gramont 1970). As mass society theorists note, Poujadist support was drawn from the least modernized, least industrialized, and most rural sectors (Kornhauser 1959:205; Hoffman 1956:205–8). And it is also probably true that within these areas, major support was given by the small businessmen. Lipset (1959b:235), for example, quotes data to suggest that merchants and farmers across the nation constituted 50 percent of Poujade's support. Even within the heavily industrialized city of Paris, small businessmen overwhelmingly supported Poujade (Stoetzel and Hassner 1957).

In each of these movements, there is little question of small business support for parties engaged in antidemocratic tactics. What is unclear is whether support was given because of these tactics or in spite of them. This issue is simply obscured by statistics on voting preferences. Presumably the Nazis and Poujadists were complex political movements with multiple goals. It is not clear whether persons who voted for them necessarily supported all their positions. Mass society theorists use the evidence cited to illustrate a connection may be less psychological—of alienated individuals smashing out at an established order—than economic: of small businessmen voting their economic interests. The Poujadists, for example, were a pro–small business political party. The Nazis were less so, but did try to woo votes with promises of restoring a receptive business environment. If support for these movements is alleged to be on grounds other than (or in addition to) these purely economic ones, then this must be explicitly shown. The data cited on these two instances fail to do so.

The third case cited by mass theorists, small business support for McCarthy, adds information to this issue but does not resolve it. A national survey conducted in 1954 showed one-third of the respondents interviewed to be in favor of McCarthy. Although a class by class breakdown indicated manual workers to be more supportive of McCarthy than nonmanual workers, small businessmen were among his most avid supporters (Lipset 1964).

Martin Trow's (1958) community study of Bennington, Vermont, puts this support into the context of economic marginality and disdain for the contemporary industrial economy. Forty percent of Trow's sample approved of McCarthy's methods of investigation. Trow found no substantial differences in support between blue and white collar workers until the latter category was further differentiated into salaried and self-employed workers: not unexpectedly, small businessmen gave greatest support to McCarthy. Among, for example, individuals with less than a high school education, 65 percent of the small businessmen supported McCarthy in contrast to 38 percent of the salaried workers; among high school graduates McCarthy support registered 58 percent of the small businessmen and 36 percent of the salaried workers. The small business category referred only to merchants and small proprietors and not to professionals or small farmers. Trow (1958:274) commented

that small businessmen in our society disproportionately tend to develop a generalized hostility toward a complex of symbols and processes bound up with industrial capitalism: the steady growth and concentration of government, labor organizations, and business enterprises; the correlative trend toward greater rationalization of production and distribution; and the men, institutions, and ideas that symbolize these secular trends of modern society. These trends and their symbols were, we believe, McCarthy's most persuasive targets.

To pursue these suggestions Trow reanalyzed McCarthy support on the basis of whether respondents were (1) for or against big business, and (2) for or against big labor. Those responding unfavorably to both big business and big labor were categorized as "nineteenth century liberals"—a position Trow saw as reflecting distrust toward growth and centralization within industrial society. Among respondents in this category, support for McCarthy was highest: 60 percent as opposed to 37 percent in all other categories combined. Furthermore, small businessmen were disproportionately represented within the anti–big labor, anti–big business group. Trow (1958:277) interpreted these findings as suggesting that:

> generalized fear of the dominant currents and institutions of modern society was an important source of McCarthy's mass appeal, not only among small businessmen, but perhaps especially among a group like small businessmen whose economic and status security is continually threatened by those currents and institutions.

This speculation emphasizes differences in the reactions of the salaried and the self-employed. Salaried white collar workers, from Trow's view, react to short-term economic crises—unemployment, severe inflation, or depression; self-employed workers, small businessmen in particular, react to the long-term trends of growth and concentration in the economy. Small businessmen, from this view, are always disaffected and persistently attracted to extremist right-wing attacks on the industrial order. Given, however, the paucity of their numbers, the politics of the small businessman are typically a rearguard action.

The broader understandings implied here are clear: extremism breaks with democratic process. And who else but the marginal and unintegrated would violate the rules of the game? This, at least, is the implication of Trow's remark (1958:279) that small businessmen are "always disaffected" and that the "tendencies which small businessmen fear—of concentration and centralization—proceed without interruption. . . ." But this thesis is plagued by the same inferences of interpretation present in discussions of Nazism and Poujadism: the failure to distinguish between economic and psychological bases of support.

Two pieces of evidence are relevant to these issues. The first is from an early study by Polsby (1960) suggesting Republican Party affiliation to be the very best predictor of McCarthy support. If, as is usually alleged, the Republicans are the party of business interests, is it any wonder that small businessmen were more likely to support McCarthy than other, nonbusiness interests in society? This is a simpler explanation of McCarthy support, and while not better on that ground alone, nonetheless merits further attention (see Rogin 1967).

A second piece of evidence relates to the psychological dimension. Mass theorists contend that support for extremism is drawn from those disaffected from contemporary society. While existing studies show that small businessmen may be somewhat more alienated than other white collar workers (although percentage differences are sometimes small), they are no more alienated than blue collar workers. Furthermore, they are not distinctly dissatisfied with economic prospects (Hamilton 1975; Bonjean 1966; Nelson 1968b). Hence their alleged support for McCarthy is not clearly explained on psychological grounds alone. This suggests some of the inferences drawn by mass theorists from these three historical cases to be without solid foundation. More data are necessary to firmly link economic marginality, alienation, and extremism. I turn to these materials in the following sections.

Alienation: A Brief Note on Risk Capitalism. One issue raised, but left unresolved, by these historical cases is the connection of marginality to alienation. Mass theorists assume that the lack of long-term prospects for economic betterment increases distrust and disaffection among small businessmen, hence disposing them favorably toward antidemocratic appeals.

An alternate view of the issue is that alienation is a reflection of certain economic functions which are recurrent characteristics of capitalism. Alienation is not a transient indication of marginal prospects but a stable indication of the continual risks imposed by capitalist economies. This parallels the logic of my previous discussion: that risk (and its consequences) must be viewed as continual, persistent, and integral to capitalism rather than as an anomaly apart from capitalism in the same way that a vestige is apart from its original state.

The existing evidence indeed suggests small businessmen to be more alienated than others in comparable positions. "Others" in this context refers to persons who also work in business, such as managers, but are salaried employees. Nolan and Schneck (1969), for example, report greater alienation among small businessmen than branch managers. This was likewise shown in an analysis of a middle-sized town on the Gulf coast (Bonjean 1966), and in a sample of Minnesota business owners and managers (Nelson 1968a).

These empirical generalizations merely extend the mass thesis to yet another issue: whether the businessman's marginality, that is, his lack of integration into the dominant trends of the industrial order, is at the root of alienation. Any stratification system incurs risks for the individuals involved, and alienation may be merely an expression of frustration among those incapable of coping with the risk of failure. Yet the mass thesis is explicit in attributing alienation and extremism not just to risk but to marginality in terms of the trends of industrial societies. In this way extremism (and conflict) can be viewed as erupting outside of consensus achieved by the industrial order, rather than as a product of that order itself. Kornhauser (1959:202) notes that

Small business . . . increasingly is marginal in modern society and as a result has been more susceptible to [extremist] movements. . . . Squeezed between the pressure of big business and big labor, the class interests of small business are inherently ambiguous, finding allies neither in the classes above nor in the classes below. The central difficulty facing small business is the relative absence of realistic possibilities for improving its long run economic position in a world increasingly dominated by large-scale organization.

The central source of alienation is inadequate access to bureaucratic power and industrial organization. Risk is shared by small businessmen with others of inadequate income; but, from the mass view, what is really at issue is integration into the agencies exercising power and control— in this instance, the large-scale industrial bureaucracy.

One test of the mass position would be to examine differences among small businessmen, with a view to sorting those with differential access to large-scale organizations. As I previously mentioned, franchised business provides a case in point—an example of businesses which have adapted their methods to gain advantage from large-scale organizations. This organizational feature suggests two different ways of characterizing the small businessman as distinct from others, such as managers, similarly engaged in business activities: in terms of the ownership or the management of capital; in terms of access to large-scale organizations or bureaucracies.

These ideas are illustrated in the figure. The comparisons in most studies involve categories 1 and 4: owners in small businesses versus managers of large businesses. In category 3 are owners with franchised business affiliations; in category 2, managers of small businesses—bakeries, candy stores, florists, and the like. In a survey conducted on some 650 businesses in varying communities scattered throughout the state of Minnesota, businessmen were placed in one of the four categories (Nelson 1968b). Franchise owners (in category 3)

DIMENSIONS OF ECONOMIC ORGANIZATION

Type of Economic Organization	Relations to Capital	
	Owners	Managers
Small enterprise	1	2
Bureaucratic organization	3	4

ADAPTED FROM: Nelson (1968b:185)

were engaged in the usual variety of activities: service stations, hardware stores, restaurants, grocery chains, and so forth. When compared on levels of alienation, the findings showed owners to be uniformly more alienated than managers; bureaucratic affiliations, however, exerted no effect on alienation scores. That is, individuals in categories 1 and 3 were uniformly more alienated than those in categories 2 and 4.

These findings provide scant support for the mass society view of exclusion from the large-scale corporate bureaucracy as an important source of alienation. What the findings do suggest, however, is that the pronounced alienation among small businessmen may be more a function of the risks involved in the ownership of capital than in marginal connections to the corporate economy. Hence the organizational dimension to the mass society view does not appear to make much sense. The "marginality" of the small businessman is not responsible for alienation so much as their recurrent function within the economy. That is, the risks of investment— which are at the heart of capitalism—are at issue here.

If marginality of small businessmen to long-range trends is not at the base of alienation, what then is? Countless studies have cited income levels as a straightforward explanation of alienation (see Erbe 1964; Dean 1961; Thompson and Horton 1960). This understanding reflects a simple principle of stratification: that alienation is a consequence of economic failure (Mizruchi 1964). The less successful the individual, the greater the frustration, the greater the disdain for and distrust of contemporary life—and the higher the alienation. Small businessmen should be no exception to this generalization. Yet, were this generalization indeed correct, some of the unique qualities ascribed by mass theorists to small businessmen would be lacking. For some small businessmen may share inadequate incomes with others in society—low-skill white collar workers or varying categories of blue collar workers, for example. Yet no one has made the case that these individuals are marginal to long-range economic trends.

In a previous section I recounted the opportunities available to small businessmen. The Minnesota study (Nelson
1968b) showed a decided relationship between these opportunities and alienation. The higher the levels of income, the
lower the alienation. In fact, only at the low income levels
were small businessmen decidedly more alienated than managers; at the high income levels, differences were virtually
nonexistent.

Small businessmen are not, then, uniformly alienated.
Nor are they uniformly more alienated than other occupational categories (Hamilton 1975). As in other occupations,
income is differentially distributed. But this is less a reflection
of the "absence of . . . possibilities for improving" economic
status and more a function of varying opportunities normally
found under capitalism. Hence the mass theory attempt to
explain away businessmen's alienation by attributing it to a
vestigial type of economic organization hardly seems con-
vincing. It may be more realistic to see such alienation as
instead integral to a capitalist structure normally productive
of income and opportunity differentials. And it likewise may
be more realistic to discard the marginality argument used
by mass society theorists to preserve the illusion of contentment and consensus.

Extremism: Psychological Dimensions. The connection, then,
between marginality and alienation is weak and open to question. So too is the connection between alienation and political
activity. In linking alienation to politics, mass theorists bring
to bear psychological and economic terms and compound them
so as to impart confusion and little insight into the plight of
small businessmen.

The merger of psychological and economic explanations
imparts the peculiar flavor of the mass society position. Small
businessmen, in this view, react not merely to long-term closure of economic opportunities but to anxiety and personal
crisis. Kornhauser (1959:112), for example, speaks of the mass

man as seeking "to overcome the anxiety accompanying alienation" and of participation in mass movements to reduce
"the pain of self-alienation by shifting attention away from
himself and by focussing it on the movement." To traditional
explanations of conflict are added irrationality, anxiety, de-
spair.

At issue here is the credence to be placed in psychological
explanations of politics. It is probably true that the alienated
may be disposed toward organizations with authoritarian tactics. It is likewise conceivable that many small businessmen
harbor competitive economic values. But to see these two types
as part of a larger whole is in part to ascribe economic conflict
to psychological maladjustment. This, in my view, represents
a questionable attempt by mass theorists to minimize the
dysfunctions of the economy. In this section I will illustrate
that while psychological and economic explanations of conflict
are viable, combining the two may be theoretically naive and
empirically incorrect.

My purpose in this is not to dispute the link between
alienation and participation in authoritarian political organizations. Countless studies, for example, have discerned symbolic protests of alienated individuals against an array of substantive issues: school bonds (Horton and Thompson 1962),
metropolitan government (McDill and Ridley 1962), fluoridation (Gamson 1961). Furthermore, there is good reason to
believe that the alienated reach out for more active participation in authoritarian political movements. For it is in the
context of tight authoritarian control that the anxiety mass
theorists posit might be checked and reduced.

In the Minnesota study, several measures of extremist,
authoritarian behavior were available with which to examine
this issue. One was a set of items referring to tendencies to
enlist in authoritarian organizations. "It is a good feeling to
belong to a strong organization to do what its members consider right"; "more businessmen should join organizations
which take a strong stand against communism"—these are
a sample of the issues broached. Not unexpectedly, highly

alienated individuals were more likely to want to join such groups than less alienated individuals—42 percent of the former and 27 percent of the latter. Alienation moderately disposes individuals toward participation in authoritarian groups. To the extent that such measures were integral to the appeal of McCarthy, it is likely that alienated small businessmen lent support to the symbolism of McCarthy's crusade.

But were these the same individuals with economic dispositions to reverse current trends in business and government? This is certainly what is implied in the mass society framework. Yet studies of the profiles of alienated individuals hardly suggest them to be at the vanguard of a movement to usher in an era of competition and rugged economic individualism. As previously mentioned, alienated small businessmen were typically low income individuals, those persons traditionally lacking in concern with dominant economic trends. Furthermore, given the predominantly blue collar background of small businessmen and the limited aspirations associated with persons of this background (Lipset and Bendix 1959), the press of upward mobility is unlikely to be strong (Bechofer and Elliott 1968; Bechofer, Elliott, and Rushford 1971). Nor is it clear that the alienated businessman has a psychological profile consistent with the sacrifice and dedication to job implicit in the commitment to "nineteenth-century liberalism." When compared to salaried employees in the Minnesota research, small businessmen were significantly less likely to alter set patterns for occupational advancement: to leave their friends, to learn new routines, to move about the country, to leave their community, and so forth. These were the very restraints shown in the Minnesota study to be at the root of alienation.

Mass theory strongly suggests alienated individuals to be the same ones as those desiring a return to a laissez-faire economy. This is a crucial link between marginality and extremist activity. Yet the data just cited on the characteristics of the alienated suggest that these inferences should be made with extreme caution. Unfortunately, the aggregate preferences collected in studies on McCarthy offer little leeway for distinguishing psychological from economic bases of support.

A not wholly satisfactory alternative is to dispense with a direct examination of McCarthy and extremist movements. Attention could be given instead to a more indirect examination: sorting out the coincidence of alienation and the cluster of economic attitudes suggested by Trow as critical to McCarthy support—nineteenth-century liberal views. Two items from the Minnesota study were useful in this regard, although they were by no means identical to Trow's measures. The first was a measure of economic competition; I presume here that the distrust in Trow's study of big business and big labor stemmed primarily from the view of size as exerting a restraint on free competition. The second item was a measure of attitudes toward government intervention in business affairs, an issue reflecting distrust of restraint on free market principles.

When tabulated with alienation, the results in each case were the same: the alienated were *least* likely to support the "nineteenth-century liberal syndrome." With respect to competition, for example, 14 percent of the highly alienated small businessmen were in favor of competition in contrast with 43 percent of the least alienated small businessmen. Similar statistics obtained with respect to governmental intervention: the more alienated the small businessmen, the greater the support for such intervention (Nelson 1968a). Small businessmen are not uniformly conservative, and it is an error to think otherwise (Hamilton 1975).

The inference of these findings is clear. Alienation is associated with dispositions toward extremism. But these same individuals are not party to rightist efforts to reverse economic trends. That the alienated may have supported McCarthy is not extraordinary—and certainly scant evidence for singling out small businessmen as unique. Small businessmen, for example, are no more alienated than manual workers (Bonjean 1968), and manual workers were no less likely to be supportive of McCarthy than small businessmen. In Trow's research

(1958:274), 52 percent of the small businessmen supported McCarthy as opposed to 49 percent of the manual workers; in the national polls reviewed by Lipset (1964:400), with a separate small business entry, manual workers were either as likely or slightly more likely to support McCarthy as small businessmen.

Nor was it unusual for "nineteenth-century liberals" to support McCarthy, given the previously noted Republican favoritism toward McCarthy's politics (Polsby 1960). What is unusual in all this is the persistent attempt to link such favoritism to the politics of the alienated, which, as I have mentioned before, is part of a strategy to preserve the illusion of consensus by attributing economic conflict to the psychologically maladjusted. Yet the materials cited offer little support for this view. If economic conflict exists, then it must be studied in its own right and not as something evolving from psychological disorder. Mass society theory has neither confronted nor admitted that possibility.

The Economic Bases of Conflict. The nineteenth-century syndrome may be little more than an extension of economic interests derived from organized business ideology. This view is in keeping with the position that conflict—channeled here into rightist support for McCarthy—is in part an attempt to maintain and advance mobility aims in the context of a restrictive economic environment. Although some of McCarthy's support may indeed have been triggered by alienation, to generalize this to all small businessmen is erroneous. In this section I will further illustrate the link between the nineteenth-century syndrome—the cluster identified by Trow as critical to McCarthy support—and the economic interests of small businessmen: first, by showing how this syndrome is linked to organizational affiliations central to the small businessmen's economic interests; second, by connecting support for this syndrome to those secure and unthreatened by the ominous economic trends Trow and others portray. My purpose here is to see conflict as an ordinary extension of economic interests rather than an extraordinary and irrational outburst from the margins of the economy.

Conventional perspectives ascribe the incidence of conflict to political organization. The failure to account for this link is a decided weakness in the mass view—attributable in large part to the pervasive influence of Durkheim. In Durkheim's (1960) vision, organizations were guardians of societal norms and primary mechanisms for societal integration. By connecting alienation and extremism to isolation from voluntary organizations, mass theorists assume the Durkheimian thesis to be accurate. Yet in so doing, they fall prey to the very dilemma posed by Durkheim's sociology (Coser 1964): the virtual denial of the possibility that organizational participation exists without corresponding support for the dominant norms on which social order rests. This denial precludes connecting economic conflict to effective organization.

Mass theory to the contrary, more orthodox perspectives on conflict stress how alternate, dissenting ideologies are nurtured and reinforced in organizational domains. Organizational participation simply reinforces shared feelings of deprivation and threat. While community-wide organizations may bring together diverse individuals who act as cross-pressures to moderate extreme positions, the same may not necessarily be true of economic or other limited-interest groupings. Labor unions increase worker militancy. Black voluntary organizations increase racial militancy. Likewise, local business associations or chambers of commerce may be rallying points for the anti–big business, anti–big labor ideologies Trow discussed and promote rather than reduce stands at odds with those of others in society.

The link between participation and extremist conflict has been widely discussed by mass society critics. Pinard (1968), for example, has noted that under conditions of strain, organizations facilitate political mobilization by diffusing information, providing channels for communication, and motivating individuals to act. If organizations have goals at odds with others, participation in such organizations may dispose their members to extremist action. In a like vein, Gusfield (1962:26) has noted that

Attachment to intermediate structures may indeed promote a shared sense of alienation of the group from the total political order. The more informal organization the group possesses, the more likely it is that politically extremist sentiments can be communicated and legitimated. In playing the game of politics, it is not only important whether one is able to play, but whether one is winning or not. This problem is not solved by the degree of access which the group has to political association.

Through normal organizational processes—such as information diffusion or socialization—participants may sustain what others identify as "extremist" or "anachronistic" attitudes (Von Eschen, Kirk, and Pinard 1971). Organizations do not of necessity moderate views to integrate members around any presumed societal consensus. They may instead stimulate behavior which in the long run furthers antagonisms.

Were these suppositions correct, the nineteenth-century attitudes identified as crucial to McCarthy support well may be valued by those frequently thought of as central to the community: members of the chambers and junior chambers of commerce. The Minnesota data suggested exactly this to be the case. The active participant rather than the isolated member championed this nineteenth-century syndrome. That is, support was drawn most strongly from those central to the business community. The more active the participant, the greater the support for economic competition and for laissez-faire (anti–government intervention) postures. Furthermore, with respect to each of these issues, it was not the alienated member who gave strong support to this factor presumably related to McCarthyism. The reverse was the case: strongest support for competition, for laissez-faire ideology was found among participants with little evidence of alienation (Nelson 1968a).

These outcomes are consistent with the anticipation that

the nineteenth-century syndrome is probably an extension of
economic interests derived from organized business policy.
While a measure recording support for McCarthy was unavailable in the Minnesota research, the inference is that
Trow's finding could be generalized: McCarthy preferences
would run highest among those favoring competition and laissez-faire ideology. McCarthy may indeed have drawn support
from the psychologically alienated and disenchanted, but
major support was likely drawn as well from integrated individuals—in both a psychological and an interactive sense.

In light of these data, is it fair to depict such support as
symbolic of an irrational protest against contemporary society? Need such support be seen in "nineteenth-century liberal" terms rather than as expressive of "twentieth-century
conservative" views? Do such views necessarily imply rolling
back time, a desire for reactionary change? Or do they merely
signal dissent from restraints on trade and excessive regulation—part and parcel of traditional business ideology? The
fact of the matter is that both the mass view and the wider
consensus position have painted an overly monolithic portrait
of support for liberal-socialist values in contemporary America. Those falling outside this view are suspect of being alienated, malcontent, or bypassed by the sweep of the industrial order.

Yet it is quite conceivable that in this vision of the progressive order, mass society theorists have given little attention to conservative viewpoints—viewpoints which are ideologically reactionary but at the same time associated with
traditional business ideology. The data from the Minnesota
study not only suggest nineteenth-century liberals to be integrated in an interactive and psychological sense. They also
suggest these same nonalienated participants to be among
those least threatened by trends in the economy. In response
to a sixteen-item scale posing alternative sources of economic
threat—from high taxes to chain stores to small margins of
profit—the nonalienated, the active chamber of commerce
participant, the individuals most supportive of competition

and laissez-faire ideology were least likely to register feelings of economic threat posed by contemporary developments (Nelson 1968a). This is hardly a firm footing for depicting McCarthy supporters as malcontents squeezed by the industrial order. And given these sentiments, it is difficult to believe that such small businessmen desire sweeping reactionary changes which dismantle either "industrial progress" or "big business" growth and concentration.

This is reinforced by the realization that the sentiments espoused by small businessmen on competition and laissez-faire positions are not so much the ideological province of small businessmen as they are the province of businessmen generally. In an analysis of 500 speeches of big businessmen spanning a generation, from 1934 to 1970, this classical theme of "nineteenth-century liberalism" was the most widely stressed (Seider 1974). In addition to its emphasis on profits, the theme spelled out the need for "the market system as a regulating force, not requiring artificial rules and agencies." Or, in the words of an elite businessman: "If our government is to be a fair umpire for private enterprise then it must not be a player in the game" (Seider 1974:807). While the syndrome identified by Trow has a distinctive anti–big labor–big business component, I doubt that it is more than a variant on a persistent conservative cry for individualism, competition, and free enterprise. Furthermore, most big businessmen would probably sympathize with Trow's respondents' views on large union organizations.

What this suggests—by inference—is that supporters of McCarthy were not so much the outraged and the disadvantaged, but those Americans who valued the populist tradition of individualism. To be sure, some support may have been drawn from the alienated, but small businessmen are not unique in this regard. As likely an explanation is the link of businessmen to the conservative viewpoints Republicans (McCarthy included) have long espoused. Not only was McCarthy support tied to Republican affiliation, but this support persisted during trying times. That is, when most abandoned McCarthy for his tactics, Republicans split evenly on McCarthy whereas Democrats were against him in a ratio of five to one (Rogin 1967:234).

Adherence to nineteenth-century liberal views is likely little more than support for traditional business ideology. Mass theorists, however, are so bound up in the fiction of a "liberal-democratic consensus" that they cannot see this support for what it is. Lipset (1964) has aptly noted that pro-McCarthy sentiment was related to positions typical of economic conservatives: against welfare, against strikes, against federal health programs, and so forth. From the consensus perspective, this indeed may be interpreted as attacks on all the industrial society can give. Yet if the consensus view is abandoned, these stands amount to little more than the arch-conservative position in the ancient debate on responsibility for the poor and down-trodden. These stands do not necessarily spring from the frustrated and the alienated. They spring instead from the elementary ingredients involved in nominating Goldwater, or in electing Nixon and Reagan.

Conclusion

This discussion reinforces my prior statement that consensus theory fails to account adequately for inequality and conflict in contemporary society. In this chapter I detailed discontent with the consensus view. By attributing reactionary politics to economic marginality, mass theorists attempt to preserve the twin visions of consensus and affluence. Yet on all counts this argument is lacking. The marginality of small business-men is open to question, as is the liaison between marginality to politics. Politics and conflict are ordinary outcomes of activities to solidify interests and gain economic advantage.

In accepting this possibility, there is no preference given to the Marxist alternative. While Marxists better understand conflict as a consequence of economic roles, they underplay existing opportunities and thereby fail to come to grips with the possibility that conflict is unrelated to change. Small businessmen, for example, are dismissed as a transitory stratum. Yet real opportunities may exist for them in franchised or noncompetitive activities—in the same sense that real opportunities exist for some workers in the dual labor market and for some blacks in the service sector. These opportunities are likewise highly variable (Hamilton 1975), suggesting the error in portraying these businessmen as a point of monolithic opposition to contemporary trends.

Conclusion:
Inequality and Conflict
in the Service Economy

THE CORE OF my argument emphasizes stabilities in institutional inequality. This position does not deny change. It stresses only how key institutions adapt and handle existing changes to maintain inequality in a steady state. Blacks may rise in the occupational structure, labor conflict may escalate, core industrial workers may reap the benefits of an inflationary economy—but the shares of business and labor remain relatively unaltered. It is useful to examine this stability as a prospect for future trends.

To place the generalities of "the future" into a precise context, I focus on the emergent service society, for at least two principal reasons. First, Bell (1973) and others are correct in emphasizing the importance of the transition to a "post-industrial society," with the proliferation of service functions as its chief economic component. This is a major change paralleling the shift from agriculture to industry. Second, much of the writing in the consensus and conflict traditions concerns the industrial state. Discussing stabilities in the context of a service economy provides an opportunity to further test and elaborate my ideas: specifically, with reference to the deadlock between profits and wages and its implications for inequality and conflict.

Regarding the relevance of this transition, my contention is that certain institutional stabilities are maintained behind a facade of change. By emphasizing certain stabilities I focus attention on the discontinuous and incomplete nature of change implied in the principle of dynamic equilibrium. Growth in the service sector does not radically alter the institutional order. Services are a different type of economic activity; they do not necessarily shift the way economic institutions operate. Businesses continue to seek profits; labor continues to minimize risk by escalating wage demands and deploying whatever tactics are necessary to make these demands felt. The service economy is after all part of the capitalist structure. This is the central thread of continuity in America's past and future.

Yet at the same time, growth in services represents an important source of economic and social differentiation. Shifts in the labor force and the organizations involved give a new twist to some old problems. The labor force in service is distinctly different from industry—in sexual composition, in occupational makeup, and in relation to the public sector. Services are likewise different from manufactured goods—in the level of demand as well as in the inability to stockpile services over time. Differentiation entails new opportunities for reducing risk and for maintaining imbalances and inequality, even though the same forces dominating these imbalances in previous eras may preside in the future as well.

My speculation is that the deadlock between profits and wages will continue and conflict will persist; but as a result of a more highly differentiated society, the parties involved and the issues broached will assume different forms. In considering these issues, I briefly address three concerns in this chapter: industrial relations in the service economy; labor force characteristics of service workers; oligopoly in service functions.

Industry in Postindustrial Societies

While change is frequently seen as total, with the new as dramatically different from the old, this is infrequently the case (Gusfield 1967). More often, change involves newer patterns placed next to older ones; the two interlink or simply exist side by side. This view of change, stressing its incomplete and discontinuous nature, is illustrated in the persistence of industry and industry-related problems in the emergent service society.

My concern in this section is to specify the implications of service based economies for the industrial sector. Will the problems in the industrial sector fade as the labor force involved in service activities increases? Or is something else suggested? From Marx to the present, treatises on inequality have been written with reference to the industrial order. The first point of business is to outline the meaning of the expanding service sector for issues traditionally related to industrialization—that is, to the issues broached in previous chapters.

Problems of the Industrial Order: A Brief Note on Their Persistence. The shift to a service economy is well known and does not require detailed documentation. In terms of the economic sector, 6 out of every 10 employed persons are engaged in service activities (U. S. Bureau of the Census 1972c:1–16). In terms of the related transformation of the occupational labor force, 5 of every 10 workers are employed in white collar jobs (U. S. Bureau of the Census 1977:418)—with soaring predictions for the future (Bell 1973).

Yet any conception of service economies heralding a new order, blessed with white collar affluence and devoid of inequality, is simply misleading. Many of the problems of the industrial order persist: with respect to industry, with respect to stabilities in the blue collar labor force (predictions to the contrary), and with respect to wages in and out of service activities. These points illustrate that changes in the service sector do not drastically alter the society; rather they provide a different context for similar problems to emerge.

First, the "postindustrial" society is not without an industrial base. Services do not displace manufacturing and industrial concerns. The economy is simply more differentiated with the service sector growing along side the industrial sector. Historical records clearly show the persistence of industrial activities over a century of American experience: in 1870 17 percent of the labor force was engaged in manufacturing, in 1900 22 percent, in 1920 26 percent, in 1940 22 percent, and in 1979 23 percent. The dramatic decline, of course, is not in manufacturing but in agriculture: from approximately 50 percent of the labor force in 1870 to 4 percent one hundred years later (U. S. Bureau of the Census 1975c:138, 1976:365, 1980a:406; Browning and Singleman 1978). There is little reason to suggest major alterations of these trends in coming decades.

Second, the inference that the proliferation of services will continue to transform the work force into a predominately white collar labor pool is likewise open to question. Although the proportion of white collar workers has been increasing, this increase gradually may slow down. The proliferation of services, as just noted, has been at the cost of agriculture. That transition is now complete. Agricultural workers make up only a minute proportion of the total labor force and that number will not appreciably alter in the future. The proportion of blue collar workers may decline somewhat, but given the historic stability of industry—as well as relative stability in construction and mining—probably not dramatically in the future.

Furthermore, increases in services do not necessarily involve increases in white collar jobs. There are more than twice the proportion of blue collar workers in manufacturing than in services; but in absolute figures, the service sector has slightly more blue collar workers. Even these figures, however, understate the case with respect to work experience and rewards. Approximately half of all white collar jobs are in sales and clerical positions. Many of these jobs are routine, unskilled, dull, and parallel the work experience of many blue collar workers (Braverman 1975). That these workers have been accorded "white collar status," symbolizing esteem, high financial reward, and rich working experience distorts reality. These workers are as much blue collar as those who work with their hands.

The above points to a third issue of contention: the likely persistence of low wages in the service economy. On the average, service workers make less than industrial workers (Fuchs 1968). This may seem anomalous given the proportion of white collar workers in service activities. Yet at the same time, these wage rates are understandable in light of the following: (1) the large number of females in services, (2) the routine clerical and sales jobs (previously alluded to), (3) the large numbers employed in retail sales (which ranks as among the lowest paid of all major sectors in the economy).

This suggests that many of the major problems discussed in previous chapters do not evaporate as services continue to unfold. I will turn in a further section to a more detailed consideration of the service economy, with particular reference to its labor force and market situation. It may be useful first, however, to digress somewhat and broach a slightly different issue. If the industrial sector remains, is there any reason to believe that its traditional institutional linkages will alter in the more highly differentiated context of the future? That is, as services come to dominate the economy, will the oligopolistic market control exercised in principal American industries shift, and throw into disarray the symbiotic ties of business and labor keyed to the core sector of the economy?

The Dual Labor Market: Future Industrial Trends. American dominance in the world order rests largely on the rate and quantity of industrial production. This capacity, in turn, rests on sectorial alliances between government and core indus-

tries, allowing these industries to profit with minimal interference. In spite of industry's strategic position with regard
to the country's international status, there are periodic hints
of these alliances faltering. This might occur through forming
new alliances, or permitting foreign trade and competition to
jeopardize older alliances. In British experience, Glyn and
Sutcliffe (1972) trace a decline in labor's share of surplus to
intensified international competition. Were this to occur in
the United States, the dual labor market of the future might
be more fragile than in the past. Costs could less readily be
passed on to consumers, and labor militance might well increase in a growing deadlock between wages and profits.

Given the strategic importance of industry to trade and
international affairs, it is doubtful that the government de-
liberately (or through neglect) would dismantle the oligopolistic control of core industries. Export data provide reasonably
good clues of the government's interests in this regard. At the
moment, the principal items in the export portfolio are food-
stuffs and machinery. In light of the profile of American industry, key exports are largely where they might be anticipated: principally in transportation, with the lion's share in
aircraft, aircraft parts, cars, and a variety of nonelectrical
machines (U. S. Bureau of the Census 1975b:818–19). As for
information processing, which Bell correctly identifies as the
technological thrust of the service economy, it plays a comparatively small (though not unimportant) role in exports.
There is no recent indication of the government forming sectorial alliances with information processing concerns. Indeed,
in the past several years, scientific programs in this area have
been undersupported; also the Department of Justice has pe-
riodically threatened antitrust action against information
processing corporations.

While few new sectorial alliances of government and business are on the horizon, there are periodic suggestions that
the government may not consistently protect older alliances
with core industrial firms. These suggestions are frequently
frantic cries from industry of insufficient protection from for-

eign competition. But lack of protectionism—if that is indeed the case—is not simply a move by the government to stimulate foreign competition. America's largest markets, with Canada and the European Economic Community, are based on reciprocity agreements—that entry into these markets is contingent on similar entry into the United States. It would be economically and politically difficult to deny foreign competition access to domestic markets. Even with Japan, where the balance of trade runs 80 percent in their favor, entry into American markets is consistently used to ease Japanese tariffs—albeit not always successfully. Furthermore, a strong import picture, at least in recent years, is a major weapon to redress balances of payment hurt in part by petroleum, and shore up the dollar to respectable rates of currency exchange.

An open trade policy is not abandonment of sectorial alliances. Its purpose is to maintain interests identified as vital to American growth and development. Recent decisions in the steel industry provide some indication of what these interests are. Steel production, given its traditional use as a reflection of industrial might, is an important area of concern. The value of metal imports, particularly steel, has increased approximately tenfold over the last fifteen years (U. S. Bureau of the Census 1975b:821). Much of this has been low-cost steel from highly efficient Japanese and West German mills. The usual hue and cry raised by domestic industries in the face of foreign competition calls for the imposition of quotas. In 1978, the Carter administration responded with an interesting economic move: a reference price system. The reference price system stipulates minimum prices for domestic sales. The minimum prices specified are intended to be somewhat higher than the usual prices for imported steel but not so high as to stifle foreign competition. Unlike quotas, reference prices are not intended to guarantee sales. They permit competition if the domestic steel industry can meet it. Importantly, in an era of widespread inflation, they require a tightening of profits and (labor) costs.

If the system is effective, it might be interesting to see

what the steel industry demands in the way of contained profits and wages. This would be even more curious given the
industry-labor pact of a moratorium on strikes. Yet the workings of the reference price system clearly reveal where the
government's interests lie. In mid-1979 most analysts agreed
that reference prices were about where the steel industry
wanted them—that the Carter program, in brief, was little
more than a symbolic gesture for public consumption. While
the steel industry is indeed in trouble, largely as a result of
antiquated production machinery, the odds at this point suggest government acquiescence to steel's demands, in tax and
depreciation concessions (*Business Week* 1979). Even were
these demands met, there is no guarantee that the industry
will follow through—and invest in modernized plants and
increased production. U.S. Steel's recent activities to acquire
Marathon Oil clearly illustrate their duplicity: At once pres-
suring the government on tax issues so as to increase capital
available for modernizing facilities and at the same time using
this capital to enlarge profits in a manner unrelated to domestic steel production.

The above illustrations suggest at the least that priority
in any government program will probably tip toward industrial corporations. This reflects not merely the interests of
government but the interests and power of business itself, in
spite of the ballyhoo about invasion of American markets by
foreign competition. While the traditional image is of an
America invaded by Datsuns and Toyotas, it also must be
noted that American automotive interests are not exactly suffering from foreign trade. Fully half of Ford Motor Company's
recent profits, for example, were ascribed to nondomestic ventures (*Minneapolis Tribune* 1979). If American strength is
based on industrial dominance, then government-industry
alliances are unlikely to be abandoned. What is more likely
is greater government intervention in wage-price controls,
subsidized industrial development, quotas if necessary—and
other policies to balance economic interests.

The consequences of a policy tipped toward strengthening

the industrial enterprise puts labor in the role of keeping up with rising consumer prices as the profit picture permits. Labor conflict is a key mechanism for affecting the wage-profit ratio. If the dual labor market persists, then conflict will persist as well. Even if changes in society were radical—calling for nationalized industries to deal with flagging productivity and foreign competition—it is unlikely that labor conflict would be reduced. For even under socialist governments, labor conflict remains (Hibbs 1976; Gifford 1974). Capitalism and socialism are similar in channeling capital not into profits but into economic expansion and development. When economic factors are bright, labor strikes to force its demand for higher wages.

There is little reason, then, to expect the contours of the core industrial labor market to waver: the respective parties involved—business, labor, government—are each interested in reducing risk against an uncertain future. This is accomplished by nurturing the symbiotic relations tying their self-interests together. If it continues, then American industry and its labor force will remain much the same in the emerging service society as in the past: structured for the benefit of particular groups with minimal commitment to altering the traditional distribution of economic wealth.

The Service Sector:
Labor Force Characteristics

In most theories of stratification, wages are a function of the prestige of work activities. The more important the work, the higher the esteem, the greater the wage. While numerous exceptions exist, white collar work is generally seen as important and prestigeful. One might conclude, therefore, that as services proliferate and white collar workers predominate, wages ought to rise. Furthermore, if current trends persist, and the labor force becomes more homogeneous in white collar

work, economic inequality should decline. But these anticipations are in error. Service workers generally are not more
highly paid than industrial workers, and growth in the service
sector may, if anything, increase inequality rather than reduce it.

The errors in these anticipations are in interpreting white
collar growth as an upgrading of the labor force. It is more
appropriate to see this predominance as furthering social and
economic differentiation. By differentiation I refer to the proliferation of statuses. My contention is that white collar workers are more differentiated than blue collar workers: as in
skill levels between a clerk and an atomic physicist, or as in
wage levels between a corporate executive and a secretary.
Differentiation is important in creating economic disparities.
Status differences provide, for employers and employees alike,
leeway to lower wages in some cases and raise wages in
others—but with the overall consequence of potentially increasing economic inequality.

Since white collar work is the most obvious and distinctive characteristic of the labor force in service economies, I
turn to this in the present section. To illustrate the range of
possible sources of differentiation, I selected three issues: (1)
skill levels, (2) sex differentiation, and (3) career commitment.
Although the focus in each of these issues is on differentiation
and inequality, the discussion extends my previous argument:
unplanned changes bear no specific consequences for inequality. At times, unplanned change may reduce inequality;
at times it may increase inequality. My contention is that
increases are in the cards as the service economy unfolds.

Skills and Wages. Past understandings of the relationship
between inequality and occupational skill are largely based
on experience with blue collar workers. Two factors are important in this connection: (1) industrialization and the mechanization of agriculture, which reduced the proportion of unskilled workers, the lowest paid group in the economy; (2)

unionization, which benefited most substantially poorly paid industrial workers. Both factors unquestionably attenuated differences within the blue collar stratum and between blue collar and white collar workers—and lowered the general levels of income inequality throughout the society.

Similar trends, however, may not occur for the white collar labor force. Blau (1974), for example, notes that trends in income equality do not parallel growth in the skill and professionalization of white collar workers. He attributes this to the failure of employers to utilize talent and skill. An alternate explanation suggests that as skilled white collar workers increase, supply outweighs demand, forcing down the price of white collar labor (Boudon 1973; Reynolds 1964).

These arguments fail to capture the intricacies of growth in the white collar labor force. Both assume a rise in highly skilled white collar labor; this is true, but only partially so. What the arguments miss is precisely the issue of differentiation previously noted. As large organizations grow, the demand for professional skills may rise but so may the demand for greater communication, resulting in growth in the relatively unskilled clerical labor force. This growth is implied in Bell's (1973) comments on the importance of communication in the postindustrial era and in more general treatments of organizational size and communicative functions (Kasarda 1974).

Unlike trends among blue collar workers, semiskilled white collar workers have not decreased. Since these semiskilled workers are poorly paid, their persistence partially explains recent stabilities in inequality. From 1950 to 1979, for example, white collar workers in the labor force increased from 36 to 51 percent. For white collar workers specifically, professional workers increased from 24 to 31 percent and clerical workers from 33 to 36 percent. By comparison, for the same time period, unskilled workers decreased from 20 to 13 percent of the blue collar labor force (U. S. Bureau of the Census 1953:261–66, 1980a:419–20).

These arguments are further complicated by pay differentials. Blau (1974), for example, assumes that increments of professional skill have not had anticipated dividends for reducing inequality. This is attributed to the failure of employers to fully utilize and reward highly skilled white collar workers. The reverse of this, however, is likely the case. In chapter 2 I suggested a dimension to inequality likely to materialize in the near future: inequality not between poor and moderate incomes but between moderate and inordinately high incomes (Henle 1972). These incomes may, as I suggested, reflect premiums paid for sophisticated training and skills.

Such trends are difficult to trace in short timespans. Yet even over the last several decades, these trends are evident. Again comparisons with the blue collar labor force are useful. In 1950, skilled blue collar workers were paid 109 percent more than unskilled blue collar workers; in 1978 this advantage was reduced by 10 percent. By contrast, professional workers were paid 35 percent more than clerical workers in 1950 and 78 percent more in 1970. These statistics are for both men and women; while not in keeping with much traditional thought, they are nonetheless what the facts of the matter are about (U. S. Bureau of the Census 1953:279–82, 1980b:244–45).

This suggests that the historic trends accounting for previous reductions in inequality have simply not materialized for white collar workers: the ratio of unskilled to skilled labor has not declined, nor have pay rate disparities—the reverse indeed being the case. If these trends persist, there is no reason why growth in the white collar labor force should attenuate inequality.

The unknown in this projection is the long-range stability in skills and rewards for the clerical labor force. Most clerical work is highly routinized (Braverman 1975). Advances in computer technology have replaced countless jobs in billing, bookkeeping, and other routine actuarial functions. If technological advances extend into communicative functions—such as typing, transcription, and dictation—routine clerical jobs may well parallel the historic decline in unskilled jobs among blue collar workers. And if they do, pay rates for clerks may likewise advance, reflecting the increased sophistication needed to operate complex office equipment. Such change depends not only on advances in technology but also on the relative costs in substituting machines for people. These possibilities introduce the same decisions about capital and labor intensitivity faced by corporations in peripheral and core industries. And the consequences may also be the same: bifurcating the clerical labor force into an upper and lower tier of salaried personnel.

Sex Differentiation and the Dual Career Families. An additional source of inequality is the sexual composition and marital status of white collar service workers. While trend data are not readily available, there is probably a connection between growth in services and increased participation of women in the labor force. The facts surrounding the increased sexual differentiation of the labor force are sufficiently well known: the dramatic increase in the number of working women; the larger number of women employed in services rather than industry; the greatest increase in working women occurring in professional occupations (U. S. Bureau of the Census 1972c:1–16, 1975b:344–49; Kreps and Clark 1975; Hayghe 1976).

The distinction between individual and family income inequality clarifies the relevance of these trends to my argument. Since women continue to occupy low-paying jobs, greater participation in the labor force may increase income inequality among individuals. But another angle of vision is relevant. If marriage partners are likely to be of similar occupational status—spouses, for example, with professional jobs—long-term effects may evolve a new strata of privilege: the two-career, highly paid family. In that families, not individuals, are the key units in stratification analysis, with spouses pooling resources toward common ends, this issue cannot be ignored.

Since trends in women working are unfolding so rapidly,

current research is almost unable to keep pace with developments. The traditional assertion is that working wives have either decreased inequality (Miller 1966; Thompson 1968) or left it unaltered (Treas and Walther 1978). This assumes that working wives come primarily from lower status homes, with their income used mainly to supplement the husband's. From this view, wives' income decreases economic differences between lower and higher status families, thus lowering family income inequality (Henle 1972).

These studies, unfortunately, do not account for the opportunities available to working wives, particularly in the service sector. Economists suggest "employability" to be a major determinant of wives working—a determinant perhaps more important than the husband's relative income (Cain 1966; Mincer 1962). Employability is a function of: (1) the skill level of the wife and (2) the demand for these skills in the marketplace. Since the demand for high level skills among women is wholly connected to the service economy—almost 95 percent of the women in professional and managerial positions work in the service sector (U. S. Bureau of the Census 1972c:1–16)—then added family income might well increase inequality as the service sector becomes more pervasive.

A number of pieces of evidence are pertinent. First, trend data suggest that highly educated, highly skilled married women are more likely to be in the labor force today than in the past (Kreps and Clark 1975). Second, highly skilled, highly educated wives are likely married to similarly skilled and educated husbands. Hence their contribution to family income will ordinarily exaggerate income dispersion. This is consistent with the finding that an increase in the husband's income is generally matched by an increase in the wife's income (Sweet 1973). Third, wives generally share the same market advantages as their husbands. This means they (1) can more easily attain a job in markets demanding professional skills (Matilla and Thompson 1968; Murray 1969) and (2) within these markets will benefit from the same high salary and wages their husbands receive. If we put these factors together—increased labor force participation of skilled, married women, marriage among status equals, similarities in demand, and remuneration for highly skilled spouses—they suggest a bourgeoning number of high-income families concentrated in select areas of the country.

Career Commitments: Managerial Innovations in Low Wage Services. A third source of differentiation in service activities is the varying career commitments of employees. In select services, particularly retail trade, workers are hired from marginal labor pools—ranging from housewives seeking part-time employment to students looking for after school jobs. The use of these workers is facilitated by widespread dispersion in many service activities. Unlike manufacturing, agriculture, or mining which are highly concentrated in select areas, services are typically represented in all communities. Managers can thus draw from available pools of individuals with no real career commitment—individuals, such as housewives or students, readily found in every locality. Many of these jobs require little training or experience; wages, therefore, are traditionally low. These employment patterns are not fortuitous. They reflect managerial strategies to minimize labor costs.

These strategies are most frequent in services such as retail trade. Retail trade accounts for more than one-quarter of all employment in service activities; at the same time retail workers are among the lowest paid groups in the economy (U. S. Bureau of the Census 1972c:1–16; 1975b:366). While low wages in retail sales might be attributed to small firm size, this is decidedly not the case. On the average, large firms dominate retail trade in much the same way they dominate industry. The largest 50 retailers, for example, account for approximately 20 percent of total sales; this compares with the largest 100 manufacturing concerns which account for 38 percent of total sales (U. S. Bureau of the Census 1975b:500). More comparable estimates probably would indicate levels of market concentration and control in retailing similar to that in manufacturing.

In spite of size and market concentration, retailers effect

a low wage profile throughout this sector. This is accomplished through selective work schedules and hiring patterns. In many giant retailing firms, hours are carefully monitored to keep personnel on part-time schedules. Nearly 50 percent of the labor force is composed of women; many of these and other workers are part-time employees from inexperienced labor pools—seasonal workers, homemakers, young persons, and students working after school hours. By systematically drawing on these pools, retailers depress wages. First, by capitalizing on inexperience, they can pay low wages. Second, by hiring those without career interests, they avoid raises for seniority. Third, since part-time workers may not qualify for social security or other retirement and health insurance plans, retailers bypass state and national requirements for fringe benefits. Fourth, part-time employees are difficult to unionize—hence decreasing the probability of labor friction and collective wage demands.

These strategies are important for understanding both the service economy and wage policies generally. Theorists in the dual labor market tradition consider labor force characteristics—age, sex, race, and so forth—to be factors incidental to the structure of an industry (see however, Beck, Horan, and Tolbert 1978). Their analysis typically relates, for example, structural dimensions such as market concentration to wages, with labor force composition statistically taken into account. Yet labor force characteristics may themselves be manipulated to sustain low wages and minimal labor friction. The issue then is not necessarily why certain economic sectors pay low wages—all other things being equal—but rather why all things pertaining to the labor force are unequal across varying economic sectors. Industrial relocations to rural areas or to the South merely may reflect strategies to alter the composition of the labor force so as to reduce wages. The same is likely true with part-time help in retail trade. These managerial policies are alternatives for oligopolistic industries to reduce labor costs and perpetuate existing inequalities between business and labor. Considered together with the material on skill and sex differentiation, they suggest a simple point: the evolving service economy is no guarantee of equality in income.

The Service Sector:
Organizational Characteristics

There is little reason to believe most service organizations have different goals than industrial organizations. Thus the range of issues previously discussed—the symbiotic ties of business, labor, and governments; the role of conflict in the context of stability; the transfer of mounting costs to consumers—may be as applicable to services as industry. Sears-Roebuck or American Express surely have the same stake in profits and growth as General Motors or Westinghouse. In fact, the interdependence of the two sectors—forged by interlocking directorates and giant financial institutions—suggests the futility of distinguishing services from industrials in the quest for profits, growth, and financial security.

Yet there are several problems in simply transferring this model to service-type organizations. One problem is the role of profits in by far the largest employer of service workers—the government. The second is a more technical problem related to marketplace control and the demand for critical services. Before concluding, I will briefly discuss these two concerns.

Profits: A Brief Note on the Public Sector. Governments are obviously not profit-making institutions. This is the traditional point of departure in distinguishing the public from private sector. The understanding is that government is different from business, and the two cannot be analyzed from a common perspective. But as a general orientation to understanding inequality, the distinction of public and private sectors has dubious worth. Profits are not the only issue central to inequality. What is more generally central is the appropriation of surplus funds. And it is in the use of these funds to support critical institutional interests, at the cost of lower-paid employees and powerless constituencies, that business and governments are remarkably similar.

This similarity is apparent in a variety of economic situations. I previously noted that nationalized industries do not necessarily upgrade wages. Strikes are as prevalent in countries with extensive nationalization as elsewhere, suggesting that the national pursuit of economic dominance and well-being perennially drains surplus funds. In the United States, where nationalization is of less concern, government appropriations to business in subsidies, contracts, tax breaks, and so forth are merely the other side of the welfare state. Commerce and economic development, for example, is the single largest item in the federal subsidy program (U. S. Bureau of the Census 1975b:231). While corporations receive only 30 percent of these subsidies, nearly all subsidy items have a distinctively business orientation, whether the recipient is a corporation or an individual.

Nor is there reason to believe that surpluses are not similarly handled at the state and local level. Unquestionably, the value of the surplus allocated to various interests is contingent on the interplay of political forces. Other things equal, where corporations are dominant in an area, less money is redistributed to the poor than where labor is dominant (Hicks, Friedland, and Johnson 1978). Yet whatever the variation, cities and states are constantly on the move to attract industry, with a view to increasing the area's stature and commercial appeal (Molotch 1976). Public funds are expended both for economic development and other facilities (e.g., athletic fields, museums, symphonies, convention centers) to increase residential and civic desirability—and attractiveness to prospective employers. Other governmental funds directly facilitate industrial and commercial growth: highways, pipelines, pollution devices, and so forth. Furthermore, public appropriations are known to economic interest groups, and governments are used by business to facilitate commercial ends (Molotch 1976:312):

The scarcity of developmental resources means that the government becomes the arena in which land-use interest groups compete for public money . . . localities thus compete with one another to gain the preconditions of growth. Historically, U.S. cities were created and sustained largely through this process; it continues to be the significant dynamic of the local political economy and is critical to the allocation of public resources.

Funds for commercial and economic development, of course, alternately can be used to effect greater equality. As it stands, however, they flow to increase profits, in spite of the fact that they are reported to create jobs (which they do not—see Molotch 1976). These expenditures, furthermore, are compounded by the fiscal difficulties of many local municipalities, strapped as they are by a large percentage of their budget allocated to fixed costs. Hence funds for equalitarian aims are lacking (Fried 1976). The upshot is clear: governments may not be businesses, but in a vague quest for dominance in regional, national, or international arenas they are run like businesses.

Marketplace Control and the Demand for Critical Services. There is an additional difficulty in transferring the discussion of core and peripheral industries to service activities. Dual labor market theorists assume that core industries, by virtue of large firm size, control the market and thereby pass labor costs on to consumers. I previously discussed a difficulty with these assumptions. Among retailers, for example, labor costs may be minimized in spite of market concentration. In this section I briefly note a further complication, suggesting that more attention be given in service activities to demand and legal regulations of the market than to corporate size as such.

More specifically, I suggest that when demand for particular services is highly inflexible and marketplace competition is regulated by government, then salaries or wages may be high regardless of size. This is readily illustrated in the top tier of the service sector—in medical and legal services, and in certain financial services as well. Through state licensing procedures and self-imposed bans on advertising, competition among professionals is virtually eliminated in a sector dominated by individual practitioners. Even among banks, which are topheavy with large institutions in financial capitals, government regulations eliminate competition at the local, community level, where such competition is at least hypothetically feasible.

Monopolistic advantages are compounded by inflexible demands. With many services, particularly medical and legal services, purchases cannot always be deferred. This means, then, that professionals can command inordinate fees and thus ride (and even profit from) whatever trends exist in the economy. This financial advantage is further compounded by widespread availability of insurance, which provides public and private subsidies for the top tier of the service economy.

The same type of inflexible demand characterizes many governmental services—transportation, sanitation, police— but their implications are somewhat different. Again the organization may be small, as in rural municipalities. But again size is not the critical issue; governments are simply the sole suppliers for certain critical functions.

Several issues complicate discussions of public services, making this area as ripe for intensive conflict as any existing in industrial settings. Not merely is demand inflexible but it is also continuous. Many public services cannot be stockpiled. While U. S. Steel, for example, builds reserves when contract negotiations approach, the public cannot do the same with respect to sanitation or protection. Conflict consequently can intensify in days or less if services are withheld.

At the same time, complications arise from responsibilities of officials to publics. These responsibilities limit concessions to government employees for salary demands. In the private sector no public accountability is demanded, except from the handful of stockholders outside the control of large proxy holders. In the public sector, accountability is high. While publics may be politically apathetic and legislators highhanded in accounting for their actions, tax dollars are the perennial issue, contrary to these generalizations.

The rising costs of government services, in part determined by demands for higher wages from employees, devolve not on the bankruptcy of corporations but on the fiscal crises of cities and states (O'Connor 1973). The result is the entire panorama of contemporary events: cries from the cities of fiscal rape by the federal government, proposition 13 advanced by outraged taxpayers, stern demands by banks and other fiduciary institutions that municipalities meet outstanding notes. All this is complicated by the alleged inefficiency of governmental services which, if true, prevents rising costs from being easily absorbed by increased productivity.

The competition for government funds is not likely to go away. Indeed, taxpayers may generally prove to be more financially stern and conservative than corporate boards of directors. To the extent that rising government costs reflect employee wage demands, governments will more likely meet these demands not by cutting protective services but by cutting "fringe" costs pertaining to education, recreation, and welfare. If conflict erupts, therefore, among striking employees, the issues may continue to spill over into broader arenas, such as the proper role of governments and their obligations to constituencies.

Conclusion

My brief discussion suggests that the service economy foreshadows no major alterations in institutional inequities. While services are not replicas of industry, they provide an alternate and highly differentiated context for the workings and consequences of capitalism. Industry remains in force in the present and future as much as in the past. Service workers are not better off than industrial workers—and, in some cases, as among employees in retailing, are much worse off.

As long as inequality exists, conflict is likely to occur. And, as with workers in industry, its source is more likely to be those of moderate means rather than those of modest means—government workers, for example, rather than retail clerks. As I have pointed out, the characteristics of governmental organizations make intense conflict as ripe as in industry, with implications extending into the fiscal nature of cities and states. But there is no reason to believe that conflict will be limited to this sector. If inflationary trends continue, unionization will probably increase, if only as a means of reducing economic risk. Even white collar workers seen in previous eras as apathetic (Mills 1951) do not seem immune to this trend (Kochan 1979).

It is this element—the reduction of economic uncertainty—which will continue to be central in America of the twenty-first century. The advent of double-digit inflation is a mere reflection of this problem. The institutional balance between business' and labor's shares has escalated wages and prices to a point of major influence, with ramifications throughout the economy. Each interest hedges its bets against an uncertain future. Each raises the ante to minimize the chances of being caught short. But the actions of each contribute to the problem rather than resolve it.

Any number of events touched on in this book could precipitate crisis in the institutional balance of business and labor: urban riots, persistent and high inflation, a breakdown of monopoly capital under threat of foreign trade, labor strife in the private and public sectors. But change is conditioned not so much by the nature of the precipitating event as by the interpretation given to it and the accommodations provided by the institutional actors involved. On this score, the actors in American capitalism today are most adaptable to short-range expediencies. From my view, as long as conflict is engaged in for situational reasons—to minimize risk rather than to advance broad ideological principles—then the prospects for effecting changes in institutional inequality will be remote. Situational challenges generate situational responses; compromise rather than change redressing old imbalances is the more likely outcome. This situational approach reflects the deep-seated absence in America of ideological commitments to economic equality.

In brief, if current economic trends persist, there may be a good deal more maneuvering, more negotiation, more use of threat, sanction, and conflict to obtain temporary gains than the consensus position sees or than Marxists are willing to admit. What we are seeing in the last decades of twentieth-century America is a full realization of the potential of organized interest groups. In the search for advantage, conflict mechanisms are readily deployed when balances drop. Yet if conflict is addressed only to situational concerns, symbiotic solutions are sought—and conflict can proceed without much change. This has been pretty much the story of many economic groups in America's recent past. There are few indications that the future will be otherwise.

R E F E R E N C E S

Abramson, Paul. 1975. *Generational Change in American Politics.* Lexington, Mass.: D. C. Heath.

Ackerman, F., H. Birnbaum, J. Wetzler, and A. Zimbalist. 1971. "Income distribution in the United States." *Review of Radical Political Economics* 3:20–43.

Adelman, Irma, and Cynthia Morris. 1973. *Economic Growth and Social Equity in Developing Countries.* Stanford: Stanford University Press.

Aigner, D. J., and A. J. Heins. 1967. "On the determinants of income inequality." *American Econonic Review* 57:175–181.

Alford, Robert R. 1963. *Party and Society.* Chicago: Rand McNally.

Allardt, Erik. 1954. "A theory of solidarity and legitimacy conflicts." In E. Allardt and Y. Littunen, eds., *Cleavages, Ideologies and Party Systems,* pp. 78–96. Helsinki: Westermarck Society.

Allen, Michael. 1974. "The structure of interorganizational elite cooptation." *American Sociological Review* 39:393–406.

Almy, Timothy. 1973. "Residence location and electoral cohesion: The pattern of urban political conflict." *American Political Science Review* 67:914–23.

Al-Sammarie, Ahmad, and Herman Miller. 1967. "State differentials in income concentration." *American Economic Review* 57:59–72.

Anderson, W. H. Locke. 1964. "Trickling down: The relationship between economic growth and the extent of poverty among American families." *Quarterly Journal of Economics* 78:511–24.

Atkinson, A. B. 1975. *The Economics of Inequality*. London: Oxford University Press.

Averitt, Robert T. 1968. *The Dual Economy: The Dynamics of American Industry Structure*. New York: Norton.

Banfield, Edward. 1970. *The Unheavenly City: The Nature and Future of Our Urban Crisis*. Boston: Little, Brown.

Baran, Paul, and Paul Sweezy. 1977. *Monopoly Capital*. New York: Penguin Books.

Barnett, Richard, and Ronald Muller. 1974. *Global Reach*. New York: Simon and Schuster.

Batchelder, Alan. 1964. "Decline in the relative income of negro men." *Quarterly Journal of Economics* 78:525–48.

Bechofer, Frank, and Brian Elliott. 1968. "An approach to the study of small shopkeepers and the class structure." *European Journal of Sociology* 9:180–202.

Bechofer, Frank, Brian Elliott, and Monica Rushford. 1971. "The market situation of small shopkeepers." *Scottish Journal of Political Economy* 18:161–80.

Bechofer, Frank, Brian Elliott, Monica Rushford, and Richard Bland. 1974. "Small shopkeepers: Matters of money and meaning." *Sociological Review* 22:465–82.

Beck, E. M., Patrick Horan, and Charles Tolbert. 1978. "Stratification in a dual economy." *American Sociological Review* 43:704–20.

Bell, Daniel. 1973. *Coming of Post-Industrial Society: A Venture in Social Forecasting*. Scranton, Pa.: Basic Books.

Ben-David, Joseph. 1963–64. "Professions in the class system of present-day societies." *Current Sociology* 12:245–330.

Bendix, Reinhard. 1961. "The lower class and the democratic revolution." *Industrial Relations* 1:91–116.

—— 1974. "Inequality and social structure: A comparison of Marx and Weber." *American Sociological Review* 39:149–61.

Benjamin, R. W., and J. H. Kautsky. 1968. "Communism and economic development." *American Political Science Review* 62:110–23.

Berelson, Bernard R., Paul F. Lazarsfeld, and William N. McPhee. 1954. *Voting: A Study of Opinion Formation in a Presidential Campaign*. Chicago: University of Chicago Press.

Bernard, Jessie. 1956. "Class organization in an era of abundance: A new principle of class organization." *Transactions of the Third World Congress of Sociology* 3:26–31.

Bernstein, Eduard. 1965. *Evolutionary Socialism*. New York: Schocken Books.

Bibb, Robert, and William Form. 1977. "The effects of industrial, occupational, and sex stratification on wages in blue-collar markets." *Social Forces* 55:974–97.

Birnbaum, Norman. 1969. *The Crisis of Industrial Society*. New York: Oxford University Press.

Blau, Peter. 1974. "Parameters of social structure." *American Sociological Review* 39:615–35.

Blau, Peter, and Otis Duncan. 1967. *The American Occupational Structure*. New York: Wiley.

Blauner, Robert. 1966. "The social psychology of job and class: Work satisfaction and industrial trends in modern society." In Reinhard Bendix and Seymour Lipset, eds., *Class, Status and Power*, pp. 473–87. New York: Free Press.

—— 1969. "Internal colonization and ghetto revolt." *Social Problems* 16:393–408.

Bloombaum, Milton. 1968. "The conditions underlying race riots." *American Sociological Review* 33:76–91.

Bluestone, Barry. 1972. "Lower-income workers and marginal industries." In Louis Ferman, Joyce Kornbluh, and Alan Haber, eds., *Poverty in America*, pp. 273–302. Ann Arbor: University of Michigan Press.

Bonacich, Edna. 1976. "Advanced capitalism and black/white race relations in the United States: A split labor market interpretation." *American Sociological Review* 41:34–51.

Bonjean, Charles. 1966. "Mass, class and the industrial community." *American Journal of Sociology* 72:149–62.

Bottomore, Tom. 1970. "Conservative man." *New York Review of Books* 15(October 8):20–24.

Boudon, Raymond. 1973. *Education, Opportunity and Social Inequality*. New York: Wiley.

Boulding, Kenneth. 1963. *Conflict and Defense*. New York: Harper and Row.

Bowen, Don, and Elinor Bowen. 1968. "Deprivation, mobility and orientation toward protest of the urban poor," *American Behavioral Scientist* 11:20–27.

Braverman, Harry. 1975. *Labor and Monopoly Capital*. New York: Monthly Review Press.

Breton, Raymond. 1964. "Institutional completeness of ethnic communities and the personal relations of immigrants." *American Journal of Sociology* 70:193–205.

Britt, David, and Omer R. Galle. 1972. "Industrial conflict and unionization." *American Sociological Review* 37:46–57.

—— 1974. "Structural antecedents of the shape of strikes: A comparative analysis." *American Sociological Review* 39:642–51.

Broom, Leonard, and Norval Glenn. 1965. *The Transformation of the Negro American*. New York: Harper and Row.

Browning, Harley, and Joachim Singleman. 1978. "The Transformation of the U.S. Labor Force." *Politics and Society* 8:481–509.

Budd, Edward C. 1970. "Postwar changes in the size distribution of income in the U.S." Paper presented at the annual meeting of the American Economic Association, New York.

Bulmer, M. I. A. 1975. "Sociological models of mining communities." *Sociological Review* 23:61–92.

Business Week. 1979. "Big steels liquidation." (September) 17:78–96.

Bwy, Douglas P. 1971. "Political instability in Latin America: The cross-cultural test of a causal model." In John V. Gillespie and Betty A. Nesvold, eds., *Macro-Quantitative Analysis*, pp. 113–39. California: Sage.

Cain, Gerald. 1966. *Married Women in the Labor Force*. Chicago: University of Chicago Press.

Cantor, Robert D. 1975. *Voting Behavior and Presidential Elections*. Itasca, Ill.: F. E. Peacock.

Caplan, Norman, and Jeffery Paige. 1968. "A study of ghetto rioters." *Scientific American* 219:15–21.

Cartter, Allan M. 1955. "Income shares of upper income groups in Great Britain and the U.S." *American Economic Review* 44:875–83.

Chinoy, Ely. 1955. *Automobile Workers and the American Dream*. Garden City, N.Y.: Doubleday.

Clark, Colin. 1940. *The Conditions of Economic Progress*. London: Macmillan.

Cnudde, Charles, and Donald McCrone. 1966. "The linkage between constituency attitudes and congressional voting." *American Political Science Review* 60:66–72.

Cole, Stephen. 1969, "Teachers strike: A study of the conversion of predisposition into action." *American Journal of Sociology* 74:506–20.

Coleman, James S. 1957. *Community Conflict*. Glencoe, Ill.: Free Press.

Collins, Randall. 1971. "Functional and conflict theories of educational stratification." *American Sociological Review* 36:1002–19.

Coser, Lewis. 1964. "Durkheim's conservatism and its implications for his sociological theory." In Kurt Wolff, ed., *Essays on Sociology and Philosophy*, pp. 211–32. New York: Harper and Row.

Cotgrove, Stephen, and C. Vamplen. 1972. "Technology, class and politics: The case of process workers." *Sociology* 6:169–85.

Cox, Kevin. 1970. "Geography, social contexts, and voting behavior in Wales, 1861–1951." In Erik Allardt and Stein Rokkan, eds., *Mass Politics*, pp. 117–59. New York: Free Press.

Cutright, Phillips. 1965. "Political structure, economic development and national security programs ." *American Sociological Review* 70:537–50.

—— 1967. "Inequality: A cross-national analysis." *American Sociological Review* 32:562–78.

Dahl, Robert. 1967. *Pluralist Democracy in the United States: Conflict and Consensus*. Chicago: Rand McNally.

Dahrendorf, Ralf. 1958. "Toward a theory of social conflict." *Journal of Conflict Resolution* 2:170–83.

—— 1959. *Class and Class Conflict in Industrial Society.* Stanford: Stanford University Press.

—— 1967. *Conflict After Class.* London: Longmans.

Davies, James C. 1962. "Toward a theory of revolution." *American Sociological Review* 27:5–19.

Davis, James A. 1959. "A formal interpretation of the theory of relative deprivation." *Sociometry* 22:280–96.

Davis, Kingsley, and Wilbert Moore. 1945. "Some principles of stratification." *American Sociological Review* 10:242–49.

Dean, Dwight. 1961. "Alienation: Its meaning and measurement." *American Sociological Review* 26:753–58.

Demerath, N., and R. Peterson. 1967. *System, Change and Conflict.* New York: Free Press.

Denison, E. F. 1954. "Income types and the size distribution." *American Economic Review Proceedings* 44:254–69.

Doeringer, Peter, and Michael Piore. 1971. *Internal Labor Markets and Manpower Analysis.* Lexington, Mass.: D. C. Heath.

Dogan, Mattei. 1960. "Le vote ouvrier en Europe occidentale," *Revue Française de Sociologie* 1:25–44.

Domhoff, William. 1967. *Who Rules America?* Englewood Cliffs, N.J.: Prentice-Hall.

Downs, Bryan. 1968. "The social characteristics of riot cities." *Social Science Quarterly* 49:504–20.

Dubin, Robert. 1965. "Industrial conflict: The power of prediction." *Industrial and Labor Relations Review* 18:352–63.

Dun and Bradstreet. 1976. *The Business Failure Record 1975.* New York: Dun and Bradstreet.

Duncan, Otis D. 1969. "Inheritance of poverty or inheritance of race." In Daniel Moynihan, ed., *On Understanding Poverty,* pp. 85–110. New York: Basic Books.

Duncan, Otis D., and Leo F. Schnore. 1959. "Cultural, behavioral and ecological perspectives in the study of social organizations." *American Journal of Sociology* 65:132–46.

Durkheim, Emile. 1960. *The Division of Labor.* Glencoe, Ill.: Free Press.

—— 1966. *Suicide.* Glencoe, Ill.: Free Press.

Dye, Thomas. 1969. "Inequality and civil rights policy in the states." *Journal of Politics* 31:1080–1101.

Edelman, Murray. 1967. *Symbolic Uses of Politics.* Urbana: University of Illinois Press.

Edelstein, J. David, and Malcolm Warner. 1977. *Comparative Union Democracy.* New York: Halstead Press.

Eisenger, Peter. 1973. "The conditions of protest behavior in America." *American Political Science Review* 67:11–28.

—— 1974. "Racial differences in protest participation." *American Political Science Review* 68:592–606.

Ennis, Philip. 1962. "The contextual dimension in voting." In William McPhee and William Glaser, eds., *Public Office and Congressional Elections*, pp. 180–211. Glencoe, Ill.: Free Press.

Erbe, William. 1964. "Social involvement and political activity: A replication and elaboration." *American Sociological Review* 29:198–215.

Farley, Reynolds. 1977. "Trends in racial inequalities: Have the gains of the 1960's disappeared in the 1970's?" *American Sociological Review* 42:189–208.

Feierabend, Ivok, and Rosalind L. Feierabend. 1971. "Aggressive behaviors within politics, 1948–62: A cross-national study." In John V. Gillespie and Betty A. Nesvold, eds., *Macro-Quantitative Analysis,* pp. 141–66. California: Sage.

Feldstein, M. S. 1973. *Lowering the Permanent Rate of Unemployment.* Washington, D. C.: U. S. Government Printing Office.

Fink, Clinton. 1968. "Some conceptual difficulties in the theory of social conflict." *Journal of Conflict Resolution* 12:412–60.

Fleisher, Belton. 1970. *Labor Economics: Theory and Evidence.* Englewood Cliffs, N.J.: Prentice-Hall.

Fogel, Walter. 1970. *The Negro in the Meat Industry.* Philadelphia: University of Pennsylvania Press.

Fogelson, Robert M. 1969. "Violence as protest." In Robert Connery, ed, *Urban Riots,* pp. 26–44. New York: Vintage Books.

Form, William, and Joan Huber. 1971. "Income, race and the ideology of political efficacy." *Journal of Politics* 33:659–88.

Form, William, and Joan Rytina. 1969. "Ideological beliefs on the distribution of power in the United States." *American Sociological Review* 34:19–31.

Fortune, Editors of. 1960. *America in the Sixties.* New York: Harper and Row.

Freeman, Richard B. 1980. "Unionism and the dispersion of wages." *Industrial and Labor Relations Review* 34:3–23.

Fried, Robert. 1976. "Party and policy in West German cities." *American Political Science Review* 70:11–24.

Frisbie, Parker. 1975. "Measuring the degree of bureaucratization at the societal level." *Social Forces* 53:306–16.

Fuchs, Victor. 1968. *The Service Economy.* New York: National Bureau of Economic Research.

—— 1969. "Comments on measuring the size of the low-income population." In Lee Soltow, ed., *Six Papers on the Size Distribution of Wealth and Income,* pp. 198–202. New York: National Bureau of Economic Research.

Galbraith, John. 1958. *Affluent Society*. Boston: Houghton Mifflin.
—— 1967. *The New Industrial State*. Boston: Houghton Mifflin.
—— 1977. *Economics and the Public Purpose*. New York: Penguin Books.
Gallman, Robert E. 1969. "Trends in the size distribution of wealth in the nineteenth century: some speculations." In Lee Soltow, ed., *Six Papers on the Size Distribution of Wealth and Income*, pp. 1–30. New York: National Bureau of Economic Research.
Gamson, William. 1961. "The fluoridation dialogue." *Public Opinion Quarterly* 35:526–37.
—— 1975. *The Strategy of Collective Protest*. Homewood, Ill.: Dorsey Press.
Giddens, Anthony. 1976a. *The Class Structure of the Advanced Societies*. London: Hutchinson.
—— 1976b. "Classical social theory and modern sociology." *American Journal of Sociology* 81:703–29.
Gifford, Adam. 1974. "The impact of socialism on work stoppages." *Industrial Relations* 13:208–12.
Glenn, Norval D. 1967. "Massification versus differentiation: Some trend data from national surveys." *Social Forces* 46:172–80.
Glyn, H., and B. Sutcliffe. 1972. *British Capitalism, Workers and the Profits Squeeze*. London: Penguin Books.
Gold, David, Clarence Lo, and Erik Wright. 1975a. "Recent developments in Marxist theories of the capitalist state, Part 1." *Monthly Review* 27:29–43.
—— 1975b. "Recent developments in Marxist theories of the capitalist state, Part 2." *Monthly Review* 27:36–51.
Goldberg, Albert. 1974. "The local community and teacher strike solidarity." *Industrial Relations* 13:290–98.
Goldman, Paul, and Donald Van Houten. 1977. "Managerial strategies and the worker." *Sociological Quarterly* 18:108–25.
Goldsmith, Selma F. 1957. "Changes in the size of distribution of income." *American Economic Review* 47:504–18.
Goldthorpe, John H., et al. 1968. *Affluent Worker: Political Attitudes*. New York: Cambridge University Press.
—— 1969. "Social stratification in industrial society." In Celia S. Heller, ed., *Structured Social Inequality*, pp. 452–65. New York: Macmillan.
Gordon, David. 1972. *Theories of Poverty and Under-employment*. Lexington, Mass.: D. C. Heath.
Gorz, Andre. 1971. *Strategy for Labor*. Boston: Beacon Press.
Gramont, Sanche de. 1970. *The French*. New York: Bantam Books.
Grant, Arthur. 1963. "Issues in distributive theory: The measurement of labour's relative share. 1899–1929." *Review of Economics and Statistics* 45:273–79.
Green, Alan. 1969. "Regional inequality, structural change and economic growth in Canada." *Economic Development and Cultural Change* 4:567–83.

Greer, Scott, and Peter Orleans. 1962. "The mass society and the parapolitical structure." *American Sociological Review* 27:634–46.

Grofman, Bernard, and Edward Muller. 1973. "The strange case of relative gratification and potential for political violence: The U-curve hypothesis." *American Political Science Review* 67:514–39.

Guest, Avery. 1974. "Class consciousness and American politics." *Social Forces* 52:496–510.

Gurr, Ted Robert. 1971. "A causal model of civil strife: A comparative analysis using new indices." In John V. Gillespie and Betty A. Nesvold, eds., *Macro-Quantitative Analysis,* pp 217–49. California: Sage.

Gusfield, Joseph R. 1962. "Mass society and extremist politics" *American Sociological Review* 27:19–30.

—— 1967. "Tradition and modernity: Misplaced polarities in the study of social change." *American Journal of Sociology* 72:351–62.

Hamilton, Richard F. 1967. *Affluence and the French Worker in the Fourth Republic.* Princeton, N.J.: Princeton University Press.

—— 1972. *Class and Politics in the United States.* New York: Wiley.

—— 1975. *Restraining Myths.* New York: Sage.

Harrington, Michael. 1968. *The Other America.* Baltimore: Penguin Books.

—— 1972. *Towards a Democratic Left.* Baltimore: Penguin Books.

Hauser, Robert, and David Featherman. 1974. "Socioeconomic achievements of U.S. men, 1962–1972." *Science* 185:325–31.

Haworth, Charles, and Carol Reuther. 1978. "Industrial concentration and interindustry wage determination." *Review of Economics and Statistics* 60:85–95.

Hayhge, Howard. 1976. "Families and the rise of working wives—An overview." *Monthly Labor Review* 95:16–27.

Herberle, Rudolf. 1945. *From Democracy to Nazism.* Baton Rouge: Louisiana State University Press.

Hechter, Michael. 1971. "Towards a theory of ethnic change." *Politics and Society* 2:21–45.

—— 1973. "Regionalism in the British Isles." *American Journal of Sociology* 79:319–42.

—— 1974. "The political economics of ethnic change." *American Journal of Sociology* 79:1151–78.

Heilbroner, Robert. 1976. *Business Civilization in Decline.* New York: Penguin Books.

Hempel, Carl. 1959. "The logic of functional analysis." In Llewellyn Gross, ed., *Symposium on Sociological Theory,* pp. 271–307. New York: Harper and Row.

Henle, Peter. 1972. "Exploring the distribution of earned income." *Monthly Labor Review* 95:16–27.

Henle, Peter, and Paul Ryscavage. 1980. "The distribution of earned income among women and men, 1958–77." *Monthly Labor Review* 103:3–10.

Herriott, R. A., and H. P. Miller. 1971. "The taxes we pay." *The Conference Board Record* 8:31–40.

Hibbs, Douglas. 1976. "Industrial conflict in advanced industrial societies." *American Political Science Review* 70:1033–58.

Hicks, Alexander, Roger Friedland, and Edwin Johnson. 1978. "Class power and state policy." *American Sociological Review* 43:302–15.

Higgins, Benjamin. 1977. "Economic development and cultural change: Seamless web or patchwork quilt?" *Economic Development and Cultural Change* 25:99–122.

Hill, Richard. 1974. "Unionization and racial income inequality in the metropolis." *American Sociological Review* 39:507–22.

Hoffmann, Stanley. 1956. *Le Mouvement Poujade*. Paris: Librairie Armand Colin.

Hong, Byung Yoo. 1978. "Inflation Under Cost Pass-Along Management." Ph.D. dissertation, Columbia University.

Horton, John, and Wayne Thompson. 1962. "Powerlessness and political negativism: A study of defeated local referendums." *American Journal of Sociology* 67:485–93.

Howells, J. M., and R. P. Alexander. 1968. "A strike in the meat freezing industry: Background to discontent in New Zealand." *Industrial and Labor Relations Review* 21:418–26.

Hughes, Rufus B. 1961. "Interregional income differences: Self-perpetuation." *Southern Economics Journal* 28:41–45.

Hurst, Charles E. 1972. "Class, race, and consciousness." *American Sociological Review* 37:658–70.

Ingham, Geoffrey. 1970. *Size of Industrial Organization and Worker Behavior*. New York: Cambridge University Press.

Institute for Social Research. 1975. *Racial Trends, 1964–1974*. Ann Arbor: University of Michigan Press.

International Herald Tribune. 1977a. "Corporate boards get a facelift." (September)16:9.

—— 1977b. "Chavez's farm union opens new battle—against machines." (September)21:4.

—— 1977c. "Italian economic reforms difficult to carry out." (October)17:2.

—— 1978a. "21 big investors hold major voting power in U.S. firms, panel says." (January)20:1, 7.

—— 1978b. "Califano cites growing slice of U.S. budget spent on aged." (January)24:3.

—— 1978c. "U.S. Treasury finds rich get most breaks." (February)14:3.

—— 1978d. "At stake in upcoming French elections: The basic quality of economic controls." (February)27:7.

—— 1978e. "Swedes, Swiss top U.S. per capita wages." (May)12:3.

Jackman, Mary, and Robert Jackman. 1973. "An interpretation of the relation between objective and subjective social status." *American Sociological Review* 38:569–82.

Jackman, Robert W. 1974. "Political democracy and social equality: A comparative analysis." *American Sociological Review* 39:29–45.

Jacobs, Paul, and Saul Landau. 1966. *The New Radicals.* New York: Vintage Books.

Janowitz, Morris, and David Segal. 1967. "Social cleavage and party affiliation: Germany, Great Britain, and the United States." *American Journal of Sociology* 72:601–18.

Jeffries, Vincent, Ralph H. Turner, and Richard T. Morris. 1971. "The public perception of the Watts riot as social protest." *American Sociological Review* 36:443–51.

Jencks, Christopher, et al. 1972. *Inequality.* New York: Basic Books.

Jenkins, Craig, and Charles Perrow. 1977. "Insurgency of the powerless: Farm worker movements (1946–1972)." *American Sociological Review* 42:249–68.

Jibou, Robert, and Harvey Marshall. 1971. "Urban structure and the differentiation between blacks and whites." *American Sociological Review* 36:638–49.

Kasarda, John. 1974. "The structural implications of social system size: A three level analysis." *American Sociological Review* 39:19–28.

Kemper, Theodore. 1976. "Marxist and functionalist theories in the study of stratification: Common elements that lead to a test." *Social Forces* 54:559–79.

Kerr, Clark and Abraham Siegel. 1954. "The interindustry propensity to strike—an international comparison." In Arthur Kornhauser, R. Dubin, and A. Ross, eds., *Industrial Conflict,* pp. 189–212. New York: McGraw-Hill.

Kerr, Clark, John Dunlop, Frederick Harbison, and Charles Myers. 1960. *Industrialism and Industrial Man.* Cambridge, Mass.: Harvard University Press.

Killian, Lewis M., and Charles Griggs. 1964. *Racial Crisis in America: Leadership in Conflict.* Englewood Cliffs, N.J.: Prentice-Hall.

Kingdom, John. 1967. "Politicians' beliefs about voters." *American Political Science Review* 61:137–45.

Knoke, David, and Richard B. Felson. 1974. "Ethnic stratification and political cleavage in the United States, 1952–68." *American Journal of Sociology* 80:630–42.

Knowles, K. 1954. "Strike proneness and its determinants." *American Journal of Sociology* 60:213–29.

Kochan, Thomas. 1979. "How American workers view labor unions," *Monthly Labor Review* 102:23–31.

Kornhauser, William. 1959. *Politics of Mass Society.* New York: Free Press.

—— 1966. "'Power elite' or 'Veto groups'?" In Reinhard Bendix and Seymour

Lipset, eds., *Class, Status and Power*, pp. 210–18. New York: Free Press.

Korpi, Walter. 1971. "Working class communism in western Europe: Rational or nonrational." *American Sociological Review* 36:971–84.

Kravis, Irving. 1959. "Relative income shares in fact and theory." *American Economic Review* 49:917–49.

—— 1973. "A world of unequal incomes." *The Annals* 409:61–80.

Kreps, Juanita, and Robert Clark. 1975. *Sex, Age and Work*. Baltimore: Johns Hopkins University Press.

Kuznets, Simon. 1958. "Quantitative aspects of the economic growth of nations. III. Industrial distribution of income and labor force by states, United States, 1919–1921 to 1955." *Economic Development and Cultural Change* vol. 6, no. 4, part 2.

—— 1963. "Quantitative aspects of the economic growth of nations, VIII. Distribution of income by size." *Economic Development and Cultural Change,* vol. 2, no. 2, part 2.

Lampman, Robert J. 1962. *The Share of Top Wealth-holders in National Wealth, 1922–1956*. Princeton, N.J.: Princeton University Press.

—— 1966. "How much does the American system of tranfers benefit the poor?" In Leonard Goodman, ed., *Economic Progress and Social Welfare*, pp. 125–57. New York: Columbia University Press for the National Conference on Social Welfare.

—— 1970. "Transfer approaches to distribution policy." *American Economic Review*, Papers and Proceedings, 60:270–79.

—— 1974. "What does it do for the poor?—A new test for national policy." *The Public Interest* 34:66–82.

Laumann, Edward O. 1966. *Prestige and Association in an Urban Community*. Indianapolis: Bobbs-Merrill.

Leggett, John C. 1968. *Class, Race and Labor: Working Class Consciousness in Detroit*. New York: Oxford University Press.

Lenin, Vladmir I. 1929. *What Is to Be Done?* New York: International Publishers.

Lenski, Gerhard. 1966. *Power and Privilege*. New York: McGraw-Hill.

Lewis, H. Gregg. 1963. *Unionism and Relative Wages in the United States*. Chicago: University of Chicago Press.

Lieberson, Stanley. 1963. *Ethnic Patterns in American Cities*. New York: Free Press.

—— 1970. "Stratification and ethnic groups." *Sociological Inquiry* 40:172–81.

—— 1971. "An empirical study of military-industrial linkages." *American Journal of Sociology* 76:562–84.

Lieberson, Stanley, and Arnold Silverman. 1965. "The precipitants and underlying conditions of race riots." *American Sociological Review* 30:887–98.

Lincoln, James. 1978. "Community structure and industrial conflict: An analysis of strike activity in SMSA's." *American Sociological Review* 43:199–220.

Linz, Juan J. 1959. "The Social Bases of West German Politics." Ph.D. dissertation, Columbia University.

—— 1969. "Ecological analysis and survey research." In Mattei Dogan and Stein Rokkan, eds., *Social Ecology*, pp. 91–131. Cambridge: MIT Press.

Lipset, Seymour. 1959a. *Political Man*. New York: Doubleday.

—— 1959b. "Social stratification and right wing extremism." *British Journal of Sociology* 10:346–82.

—— 1963. *The First New Nation*. New York: Basic Books.

—— 1964. "Three decades of the radical right: Coughlinites, McCarthyites, and Birchers." In Daniel Bell, ed., *The Radical Right*, pp. 373–446. New York: Anchor Books.

—— 1968. *Revolution and Counter-revolution*. New York: Basic Books.

Lipset, Seymour M., and Reinhard Bendix. 1952. "Social mobility and occupational career patterns." *American Journal of Sociology* 57:366–74.

—— 1959. *Social Mobility in Industrial Society*. Berkeley: University of California Press.

Lipset, Seymour, and Stein Rokkan. 1967. *Party Systems and Voter Alignments*. New York: Free Press.

Lockwood, David. 1968. "Sources of variation in working class images of society." In Joseph A. Kahl, ed., *Comparative Perspectives on Stratification—Mexico, Great Britain, Japan*, pp. 98–114. Boston: Little, Brown.

Long, James, David Rasmussen, and Charles Haworth. 1977. "Income inequality and city size." *Review of Economics and Statistics* 59:244–46.

Loomis, Charles and J. Allen Beegle. 1946. "The spread of German Nazism in rural areas." *American Sociological Review* 11:724–34.

Lupsha, Peter. 1971. "Explanation of political violence: Some psychological theories versus indignation." *Politics and Society* 2:89–104.

Lydall, Harold. 1959. "The long-term trend in the size distribution of income." *Journal of the Royal Statistical Society* 122:1–37.

—— 1968. *Structure of Earnings*. Oxford: Oxford University Press.

McDill, Edward, and Jeanne Ridley. 1962. "Status, anomie, political alienation and political participation." *American Journal of Sociology* 68:205–17.

MacDonald, J. S., and L. D. MacDonald. 1962. "Urbanization, ethnic groups, and social segmentation." *Social Research* 29:437–48.

McKinney, John C., and Linda Bourque. 1971. "The changing South." *American Sociological Review* 36:399–412.

Mack, Raymond, and Richard Snyder. 1957. "The analysis of social conflict: Towards an overview synthesis." *Journal of Conflict Resolution* 1:212–48.

Mann, Michael. 1970. "The social cohesion of liberal democracy." *American Sociological Review* 35:423–39.

Marcuse, Herbert. 1964. *One-Dimensional Man*. Boston: Beacon Press.

Marsh, Robert M., and William L. Parish. 1965. "Modernization and communism: A re-test of Lipset's hypotheses." *American Sociological Review* 30:934–42.

Marshall, T. H. 1965. *Class, Citzenship and Social Development*. Garden City, N.Y.: Doubleday.

Martson, Wilfred G. 1968. "Social class as a factor in ethnic and racial segregation." *International Journal of Comparative Sociology* 9:145–53.

Marx, Gary T. 1967. *Protest and Prejudice: A Study of Belief in the Black Community*. New York: Harper and Row.

Marx, Karl. 1936. *Capital*. New York: Modern Library.

—— 1938. *Critique of the Gotha Programme*. New York: International Publishers.

—— 1972. "Wage labor and capital." In Richard Tucker, ed., *The Marx-Engels Reader*, pp. 167–90. New York: Norton.

Matilla, John, and Wilbur Thompson. 1968. "Towards an econometric model of urban economic development." In Harvey Perloff and Lowdon Wingo, eds., *Issues in Urban Economics*, pp. 63–80. Baltimore: Johns Hopkins Press.

Matthews, Donald, and James Protho. 1966. *Negroes and the New Southern Politics*. New York: Harcourt, Brace, and World.

Mayer, Kurt. 1947. "Small business as a social institution." *Social Research* 14:332–49.

—— 1954. "The theory of social classes." *Transactions of the Second World Congress of Sociology* 2:321–35.

—— 1955. *Class and Society*. New York: Random House.

Mayer, Kurt B., and Sidney Goldstein. 1961. *The First Two Years: Problems of Small Firm Growth and Survival*. Washington, D.C.: Small Business Administration.

Miller, Herman P. 1966. *Income Distribution in the United States (1960 Census Monograph)*. Washington D. C.: U. S. Government Printing Office.

—— 1971. *Rich Man, Poor Man*. New York: Apollo Editions.

Miller, Seymour, and Pamela Roby. 1970. *The Future of Inequality*. New York: Basic Books.

Miller, Warren, and Donald Stokes. 1963. "Constituency influence in Congress." *American Political Science Review* 57:45–50.

Mills, C. Wright. 1951. *White Collar*. New York: Oxford University Press.

—— 1956. *Power Elite*. New York: Oxford University Press.

—— 1962. *The Marxists*. New York: Dell.

Mincer, J. 1958. "Investment in human capital and the personal distribution of income." *Journal of Political Economy* 66:281–302.

—— 1962. "Labor force participation of married women." In National Bureau of Economic Research, *Aspects of Labor Economics*, pp. 63–93. Princeton: Princeton University Press.

Minneapolis Tribune. 1976. "Increase reported in number on welfare." (May)20:2a.

——— 1977. "Schlesinger terms oil profits ample." (August)22:1.

——— 1979. "Ford's earnings drop 5.2%" (July)25:11a.

Mishan, E. J. 1967. *The Costs of Economic Growth.* Middlesex, Eng.: Penguin Books.

Mizruchi, Ephraim H. 1964. *Success and Opportunity: A Study of Anomie.* New York: Free Press of Glencoe.

Molotch. Harvey. 1976. "The city as a growth machine: Toward a political economy of place." *American Journal of Sociology* 82:309–32.

Moore, Wilbert E. 1963. *Social Change.* Englewood Cliffs, N.J.: Prentice-Hall.

Morgan, James, Martin David, William Cohen, and Harvey Brazer. 1962. *Income and Welfare in the United States.* New York: McGraw-Hill.

Morgan, William, and Terry N. Clark. 1973. "The causes of racial disorders: A grievance-level explanation." *American Sociological Review* 38:611–24.

Murray, Barbara. 1969. "Metropolitan interpersonal income inequality." *Land Economics* 45:121–25.

Myrdal, Gunnar. 1957. *Rich Lands and Poor.* New York: Harper and Brothers.

——— 1963. *Challenge to Affluence.* New York: Vintage Books.

Nelson, Joel. 1968a. "Participation and integration: The case of the small businessman." *American Sociological Review* 33:427–38.

——— 1968b. "Anomie: Comparisons between the old and new middle class." *American Journal of Sociology* 74:184–92.

——— 1978. "Income inequality: The American states." Paper presented at the annual meeting of the American Sociological Association, San Francisco.

Nelson, Joel, and Robert Grams. 1978. "Union militancy and occupational communities." *Industrial Relations* 17:342–46.

New York Times. 1976. "People and business." (November)16:69.

——— 1977. "Inflation sharpens division of top and bottom lines." (January)26:D1, D5.

——— 1978a. "An economic plan business ought to like." (January)28:28.

——— 1978b. "Washington and business: A study on blacks' jobs and pay." (March)10:79.

Nicolaus, Martin. 1968. "The unknown Marx." *New Left Review* 48:41–61.

Nisbet, Robert A. 1953. *The Quest for Community.* Oxford: Oxford University Press.

——— 1959. "The decline and fall of social class." *Pacific Sociological Review* 2:11–17.

Nolan, Richard, and Rodney E. Schneck. 1969. "Small businessmen, branch managers and their relative susceptibility to right wing extremism: An empirical test." *Canadian Journal of Political Science* 2:89–102.

Nordlinger, Eric. 1967. *The Working Class Tories*. Berkeley: University of California Press.

Oberschall, Anthony. 1973. *Social Conflict and Social Movements*. Englewood Cliffs, N.J.: Prentice-Hall.

O'Brien, Donal Cruise. 1972. "Modernization, order, and the erosion of a democratic ideal: American political science, 1960–70." *Journal of Developmental Studies* 8:351–78.

O'Brien, F. S. 1965. "Industrial conflict and business fluctuations: A comment." *Journal of Political Economics* 73:650–54.

O'Connor, James. 1973. *Fiscal Crisis of the State*. New York: St. Martin's Press.

Okner, Benjamin. 1974. "Individual taxes and the distribution of income." In James Smith, ed., *Personal Distributions of Income and Wealth,* pp. 45–73. New York: National Bureau of Economic Research.

Okun, Arthur. 1975. *Equality and Efficiency: The Big Trade-off*. Washington, D. C.: Brookings Institution.

Olsen, Marvin. 1970. "Social and political participation of blacks." *American Sociological Review* 35:682–97.

Orum, Anthony. 1966. "A reappraisal of the social and political participation of Negroes." *American Journal of Sociology* 72:32–46.

Ossowski, Stanislaw. 1963. *Class Structure in the Social Consciousness*. New York: Free Press.

Oxenfeldt, Alfred, and Gertrude Oxenfeldt. 1951. "Determinants of success in a small Western city." *Social Forces* 30:223–31.

Parsley, C. J. 1980. "Labor union effects on wage gains: A survey of recent literature." *Journal of Economic Literature* 18:1–31.

Parsons, Talcott. 1964. *The Social System*. New York: Free Press.

Paukert, Felix. 1968. "Social security and income distribution: A comparative study." *International Labour Review* 98:425–50.

—— 1973. "Income distribution of different levels of development: A survey of the evidence." *International Labour Review* 108:97–125.

Pechman, Joseph A., Henry J. Aaron, and Michael K. Taussig. 1968. *Social Security: Perspectives for Reform*. Washington D. C.: Brookings Institution.

Pechman, Joseph A., and Benjamin A. Okner. 1974. *Who Bears the Tax Burden?* Washington D. C.: Brookings Institution.

Peters, B. Guy. 1973. "Equality in Sweden and the United Kingdom: A longitudinal analysis." *Acta Sociologica* 16:108–20.

Petras, J., and M. Zeitlin. 1967. "Miners and agrarian radicalism." *American Sociological Review* 32:578–86.

Pettigrew, Thomas. 1964. *A Profile of Negro Americans*. Princeton: Van Nostrand.

Phelps Brown, E. H. 1968. *Pay and Profits*. Manchester: Manchester University Press.

Phillips, Joseph O. 1958. *Little Business in the American Economy*. Urbana: University of Illinois Press.

—— 1960. "Labors share and wage parity." *Review of Economics and Statistics* 42:164–74.

Pilisuk, Marc, and Thomas Hayden. 1965. "Is there a military industrial complex which prevents peace?" *Journal of Social Issues* 7:67–114.

Pinard, Maurice. 1967. "Poverty and political movements." *Social Problems* 15:250–63.

—— 1968. "Mass society and political movements." *American Journal of Sociology* 73:682–90.

Polsby, Nelson W. 1960. "Toward an explanation of McCarthyism." *Political Studies* 8:250–71.

Poulantzas, Nicos. 1973. *Political Power and Social Class*. London: Sheed and Ward.

Pratt, Samuel. 1948. "The Social Basis of Nazism and Communism in Urban Germany." M.A. thesis, Department of Sociology, Michigan State University.

Projector, Dorothy, and Gertrude Weiss. 1966. *Survey of Financial Characteristics of Consumers*. Washington D. C.: Board of Governors of the Federal Reserve.

Rainwater, Lee. 1974. *What Money Buys: Inequality and the Social Meanings of Income*. New York: Basic Books.

Ransford, H. Edward. 1968. "Isolation, powerlessness, and violence: A study of isolation and participation in the Watts riot." *American Journal of Sociology* 73:581–91.

Rees, Albert. 1952. "Industrial conflict and business fluctuations." *Journal of Political Economics* 60:371–82.

—— 1973. *The Economics of Work and Pay*. New York: Harper and Row.

Reich, Michael. 1971. "The economics of racism." In David Gordon, ed., *Problems in Political Economy*, pp. 107–13. Lexington, Mass.: D. C. Heath.

Reynolds, Lloyd. 1964. *Labor Economics and Labor Relations*. Englewood Cliffs, N.J.: Prentice-Hall.

Reynolds, Morgan, and Eugene Smolensky. 1977. *Public Expenditures, Taxes and the Distribution of Income*. New York: Academic Press.

Roberts, Markley. 1975. "The concentration of economic power." *American Federationist* 82:8–13.

Robinson, Joan. 1949. *An Essay on Marxian Economics*. London: Macmillan.

Rogers, D., and I. E. Berg. 1961. "Occupation and ideology: The case of the small businessman." *Human Organization* 20:103–11.

Rogin, Michael Paul. 1967. *The Intellectuals and McCarthy: The Radical Spectre*. Cambridge, Mass.: MIT Press.

Rokkan, Stein, and Angus Campbell. 1960. "Citizen participation in political life: Norway and the U.S.A." *International Social Science Journal* 12:69–99.

Rose, Arnold M. 1958. "The concept of class and American sociology." *Social Research* 25:53–69.

—— 1962. "Alienation and participation: A comparison of group leaders and the 'mass'." *American Sociological Review* 27:834–38.

—— 1967. *Power Structure: Political Process in American Society*. New York: Oxford University Press.

Rose, Richard, and Derek Unwin. 1969. "Social cohesion, political parties and strains in regimes." *Comparative Political Studies* 2:7–67.

Rosenbluth, Gideon. 1959. "The trend in concentration and its implication for small business." *Law and Contemporary Problems* 24:192–207.

Rosenborough, Howard, and Raymond Breton. 1968. "Perceptions of the relative economic and political advantages of ethnic groups in Canada." In Bernard Blishen, Frank Jones, Kaspar Naegele, and John Porter, eds., *Canadian Society*, pp. 604–28. Toronto: Macmillan.

Ross, Arthur. 1961. "The prospects for industrial conflict." *Industrial Relations* 1:57–74.

Ross, Arthur, and Paul Hartman. 1960. *Changing Patterns of Industrial Conflict*. New York: Wiley.

Rubinson, Richard. 1976. "The world economy and the distribution of incomes within states: A cross national study." *American Sociological Review* 41:638–59.

Runciman, W. G. 1966. *Relative Deprivation and Social Justice: A Study of Attitudes to Social Inequality in 20th Century England*. Berkeley: University of California Press.

Sackley, Arthur, and Thomas Gavett. 1971. "Blue collar and white collar pay trends: Analysis of occupational wage differences." *Monthly Labor Review* 94:5–12.

Scheuch, Erwin K. 1969. "Social context and individual behavior." In Mattei Dogan and Stein Rokkan, eds., *Social Ecology*, pp. 133–55. Cambridge, Mass.: MIT Press.

Schultz, T. Paul. 1971. "Long term change in personal income distribution: Theoretical approaches, evidence and explanations," Unpublished paper, Department of Economics, University of Minnesota.

Schumpeter, Joseph. 1962. *Capitalism, Socialism and Democracy*. New York: Harper and Row.

Schwartz, Mildred. 1974. *Politics and Territory*. Montreal: McGill–Queens University Press.

Sears, David O., and T. M. Tomlinson. 1968. "Riot ideology in Los Angeles: A study of negro attitudes." *Social Science Quarterly* 49:485–503.

Seeman, Melvin. 1959. "On the meaning of alienation." *American Sociological Review* 24:783–91.

Segal, David, and Thomas Smith. 1970. "Congressional responsibility and the organization of constituency attitudes." *Social Science Quarterly* 51:743–49.

Segal, David, and Stephen Wildstrom. 1970. "Community effects on political attitude: Partisanship and efficiency." *Sociological Quarterly* 11:67–86.

Seider, Maynard. 1974. "American big business ideology." *American Sociological Review* 39:802–15.

Selznick, Philip. 1952. *The Organizational Weapon.* New York: McGraw-Hill.

Shorter, Edward, and Charles Tilly. 1971. "The shape of strikes in France, 1830–1960." *Comparative Studies in Society and History* 13:60–81.

—— 1974. *Strikes in France, 1830–1968.* London: Cambridge University Press.

Siegel, Paul M. 1970. "On the cost of being a Negro." In Edward O. Laumann, Paul Siegel, and Robert Hodge, eds., *The Logic of Social Hierarchies*, pp. 727–43. Chicago: Markham.

Simon, Herbert. 1955. "The compensation of executives." *Sociometry* 20:32–35.

Skolnick, Alfred M., and Sophie R. Dales. 1972. "Social welfare expenditures, 1971–72." *Social Security Bulletin* (December):3–17.

Smith, Anthony. 1973. *The Concept of Social Change.* Boston: Routledge and Kegan Paul.

Smith, James, and Stephen Franklin. 1974. "The concentration of personal wealth, 1922–1969." *American Economic Review* 64:162–67.

Snyder, David. 1975. "Institutional setting and industrial conflict: Comparative analyses of France, Italy and the United States." *American Sociological Review* 40:259–78.

Snyder, David, and Charles Tilly. 1972. "Hardship and collective violence in France, 1830 to 1960." *American Sociological Review* 37:520–32.

Solow, Robert. 1960. "Income inequality since the war." In Ralph Freeman, ed., *Postwar Economic Trends in the United States*, pp. 94–138. New York: Harper.

Soltow, Lee. 1965. *Toward Income Equality in Norway.* Madison: University of Wisconsin Press.

—— 1968. "Long-run changes in British income inequality." *Economic History Review* 21:17–29.

—— 1971. *Patterns of Wealthholding in Wisconsin Since 1850.* Madison: University of Wisconsin Press.

Sombart, Werner. 1906. *Warum Gibst es in Den Vereingten Staaten Keinen Sozialismus?* Tubingen: J. C. B. Mohr.

Spilerman, Seymour. 1970. "The causes of racial disturbances: A comparison of alternative explanations." *American Sociological Review* 35:627–49.

—— 1971. "The causes of racial disturbances: Tests of an explanation." *American Sociological Review* 36:427–42.

Srole, Leo. 1956. "Social integration and certain corrollaries: An exploratory study." *American Sociological Review* 21:709–16.

Stein, Robert, and Janice Hedges. 1971. "Earnings and family income." *Monthly Labor Review* 94:13–24.

Steiner, Gilbert Y. 1974. "Reform follows reality: The growth of welfare." *The Public Interest* 34:47–65.

Stern, James. 1964. "Declining utility of the strike." *Industrial and Labor Relations Review* 18:60–77.

Sternlieb, Steven, and Alvin Bauman. 1972. "Employment characteristics of low-wage workers." *Monthly Labor Review* 95:9–14.

Stoetzel, Jean, and Pierre Hassner. 1957. "Resultats d'un sondage dans le premier secteur de la Seine." In Maurice Duverger, François Gognel, and Jean Touchard, eds., *Les Elections du 2 Janvier 1956*, pp. 199–248. Paris: Librarie Armond Colin.

Stolzenberg, Ross. 1975. "Occupations, labor markets and the process of wage attainment." *American Sociological Review* 40:645–65.

Stolzman, James, and Herbert Gamberg. 1973. "Marxist class analysis versus stratification analysis as general approaches to social inequality." *Berkeley Journal of Sociology* 18:105–25.

Street, David, and John Leggett. 1961. "Economic deprivation and extremism: A study of unemployed negroes." *American Journal of Sociology* 67:53–57.

Sullivan, John L. 1972. "A note on redistributive politics." *American Political Science Review* 66:1301–5.

Sweet, James. 1973. *Women in the Labor Force*. New York: Seminar Press.

Sweezy, Paul. 1964. *The Theory of Capitalist Development*. New York: Monthly Review Press.

Taeuber, Karl. 1968. "The problem of residential segregation." In Robert Connery, ed., *Urban Riots*, pp. 105–14. New York: Vintage Books.

Taeuber, Karl E., and Alma Taeuber. 1969. *Negroes in Cities: Residential Segregation and Neighborhood Change*. New York: Atheneum.

Tannenbaum, Arnold, and Robert Kahn. 1958. *Participation in Union Locals*. Evanston, Ill.: Row, Peterson.

Thompson, Wayne, and John Horton. 1960. "Political alienation as a force in political action." *Social Forces* 38:190–95.

Thompson, Wilbur. 1968. "Internal and external factors in the development of urban economics." In Harvey Perloff and Lowdon Wingo, eds., *Issues in Urban Economics*, pp. 43–80. Baltimore: Johns Hopkins Press.

Thurow, Lester. 1981. "The widening income gap." *Newsweek* (October 5):70.

Tilly, Charles. 1961. "Occupational rank and grade of residence." *American Journal of Sociology* 67:323–30.

—— 1973. "The chaos of the living city." In Herbert Hirsch and David Perry, eds., *Violence as Politics*, pp. 98–124. New York: Harper and Row.

Tilton, Timothy. 1974. "The social origins of liberal democracy: The Swedish case." *American Political Science Review* 68:561–71.

Tiryakian, Edward. 1975. "Neither Marx nor Durkheim . . . perhaps Weber." *American Journal of Sociology* 81:1–33.

Titmuss, Richard M. 1969. *Essays on "The Welfare State."* Boston: Beacon Press.

Townsend, Peter. 1974. "Poverty as relative deprivation." In Dorothy Wedderburn, ed., *Poverty, Inequality and Class Structure*, pp. 15–41. London: Cambridge University Press.

Treas, Judith, and Robin Walther. 1978. "Family structure and the distribution of family income." *Social Forces* 56:866–80.

Trieman, Donald J. 1970. "Industrialization and social stratification." *Sociological Inquiry* 40:226–27.

Trow, Martin. 1958. "Small businessmen, political tolerance, and support for McCarthy." *American Journal of Sociology* 64:270–81.

U. S. Bureau of the Census. 1953. *Detailed Characteristics: U. S. Summary.* Washington, D. C.: U. S. Government Printing Office.

—— 1963. *Trends in the Income of Families and Persons in the United States, 1947–1960.* Technical paper no. 8. Washington, D. C.: U. S. Government Printing Office.

—— 1970. *Historical Statistics of the United States.* Washington, D. C.: U. S. Government Printing Office.

—— 1971. *Statistical Abstracts.* Washington, D. C.: U.S. Government Printing Office.

—— 1972a. *Census of Population: 1970 General Social and Economic Characteristics, Final Reports. United States Summary.* Washington, D. C.: U. S. Government Printing Office.

—— 1972b. "Money income in 1971 of families and persons in the United States." *Current Population Reports*, ser. P-60, no. 85. Washington, D. C.: U. S. Government Printing Office.

—— 1972c. *Occupation by Industry.* Washington D. C.: U. S. Government Printing Office.

—— 1973. *Census of the Population: Detailed Characteristics, United States Summary.* Washington, D. C.: U. S. Government Printing Office.

—— 1975a. "The Social and Economic Status of the Black Population in the United States, 1974." *Current Population Reports, Special Studies,* ser. P-23, no. 54. Washington, D. C.: U. S. Government Printing Office.

—— 1975b. *Statistical Abstract of the United States.* Washington, D. C.: U. S. Government Printing Office.

—— 1975c. *Historical Statistics of the U.S.* Washington, D. C.: U. S. Government Printing Office.

—— 1976. *Statistical Abstracts*. Washington, D. C.: U. S. Government Printing Office.

—— 1977. *Statistical Abstracts*. Washington, D. C.: U. S. Government Printing Office.

—— 1978. "Money Income in 1976 of Families and Persons in the United States." *Current Population Reports*, ser. P-60, no. 114. Washington, D. C.: U. S. Government Printing Office.

—— 1980a. *Statistical Abstract of the United States*. Washington D. C.: U. S. Government Printing Office.

—— 1980b. "Money Income of Families and Persons in the United States, 1978." *Current Population Reports*, ser. P-60, no. 123. Washington D. C.: U. S. Government Printing Office.

—— 1981a. *1977 Census of Manufacturers, Vol. 111, General Area Statistics, (Part 1)*. Washington, D. C.: U. S. Government Printing Office.

—— 1981b. *1977 Census of Manufacturers, Concentration Ratios in Manufacturing*. Washington, D. C.: U. S. Government Printing Office.

U. S. Bureau of Labor. 1966. *Wages and Related Benefits*. Washington, D. C.: U. S. Government Printing Office.

U. S. Congress. 1972. House of Representatives. Committee on Ways and Means. *Estimates of Federal Tax Expenditures*. Washington, D. C.: U. S. Government Printing Office.

U. S. Department of Commerce. 1976. *Franchising in the Economy, 1974–1976*. Washington, D. C.: U. S. Government Printing Office.

—— 1979. "The Social and Economic Status of the Black Population," *Current Population Reports*, ser. P-23, no. 80. Washington D. C.: U. S. Government Printing Office.

U. S. Department of Labor. 1970. *Manpower Report of the President*. Washington, D. C.: U. S. Government Printing Office.

U. S. Department of the Treasury. 1979. *Individual Income Tax Returns*. Washington, D. C.: U. S. Government Printing Office.

Van den Berghe, Pierre. 1963. "Dialectic and functionalism: Toward a theoretical synthesis." *American Sociological Review* 28:695–705.

Von Eschen, Donald, Jerome Kirk, and Maurice Pinard. 1971. "The organizational substructure of disorderly politics." *Social Forces* 49:529–44.

Wachtel, Howard, and Peter Adelsheim. 1977. "How recession feeds inflation: Price markups in a concentrated economy." *Challenge* 20:6–13.

Wachtel, Howard, and Charles Betsey. 1972. "Employment at low wages." *Review of Economics and Statistics* 54:121–29.

Wallerstein, Immanuel. 1974. *The Modern World System*. New York: Academic Press.

Wall Street Journal. 1979. "Uneasy alliances." (January 2):1, 9.

Walsh, William. 1975. "Economic conditions and strike activity in Canada." *Industrial Relations* 14:45–54.

Wanderer, Jules J. 1969. "An index of riot severity and some correlates." *American Journal of Sociology* 74:500–5.

Ward, Michael. 1978. *The Political Economy of Distribution*. New York: Elsevier.

Weber, Max. 1958. "Class, status and Party." In H. H. Gerth and C. Wright Mills, eds., *From Max Weber: Essays in Sociology*, pp. 180–95. New York: Oxford University Press.

Wedderburn, Dorothy, and Rosemary Crompton. 1972. *Workers Attitudes and Technology*. Cambridge: Cambridge University Press.

Weingart, Peter. 1969. "Beyond Parsons? A critique of Ralf Dahrendorf's conflict theory." *Social Forces* 48:151–65.

Weintraub, A. R. 1966. "Prosperity vs. strikes: An empirical approach." *Industrial and Labor Relations Review* 19:231–38.

Weintraub, Sidney. 1958. *A General Theory of the Price Level, Income Distribution and Economic Growth*. Philadelphia: Chilton.

Weiss, Leonard. 1966. "Concentration and labor earnings." *American Economic Review* 58:96–117.

Westergaard, John, and Henrietta Resler. 1977. *Class in a Capitalist Society*. Middlesex, Eng.: Penguin Books.

Wilensky, Harold L. 1961. "Orderly careers and social participation." *American Sociological Review* 26:521–39.

—— 1964. "Mass society and mass culture: Interdependence or independence?" *American Sociological Review* 29:173–97.

Wilensky, Harold, and Hugh Edwards. 1959. "The skidder: Ideological adjustments of downward mobile workers." *American Sociological Review* 24:215–31.

Wiley, Norbert. 1967. "America's unique class politics: The interplay of the labor, credit, and commodity markets." *American Sociological Review* 32:529–41.

Williams, J. Allen, Jr., Nicholas Babchuck, and David R. Johnson. 1973. "Voluntary associations and minority status: A comparative analysis of Anglo, Black, and Mexican Americans." *American Sociological Review* 38:637–46.

Williamson, Jeffery. 1965. "Regional inequality and the process of national development." *Economic Development and Cultural Change* 13:3–84.

Wilson, William J. 1978. *The Declining Significance of Race*. Chicago: University of Chicago Press.

Young, Ruth, and Jose Moreno. 1965. "Economic development and social rigidity." *Economic Development and Cultural Change* 13:439–52.

Zeitlin, Maurice. 1974. "Corporate ownership and control: The large corporation and the capitalist class." *American Journal of Sociology* 79:1073–1119.

INDEX